Pragmatic Federalism

75

Pragmatic Federalism

An Intergovernmental View of American Government

Parris N. Glendening
Mavis Mann Reeves

University of Maryland, College Park

Palisades Publishers
Pacific Palisades, California

56337

For our fathers,
Raymond G. Glendening
and
Fletcher Wills Mann
because they believed in us.

Library of Congress Catalog Card Number: 76-29891

International Standard Book Numbers:
0-913530-09-3 (paper)
0-913530-10-7 (cloth)

Palisades Publishers
P.O. Box 744, Pacific Palisades, California 90272

Book design and cover art
by Larry Belliston and Kurt Hanks

Printed in the United States of America

Contents

56337

Preface

American government no longer can be understood from the singular perspective of the national, state, or local level—if it ever could. Its operations are too intertwined, engaging more than one level in almost all operations. Whether the function is as universally essential as sewage disposal or as esoteric as support for a symphony orchestra, more than one government is likely to be involved. Understanding requires consideration of all governments and their interactions. Furthermore, the relationships themselves have consequences for the adoption and implementation of public policy.

Over the years we have been disturbed by the one-level view of American government that often is presented. Experience on all levels, in party politics, and in teaching and research, convinced us that knowledge of how governments relate is necessary to a comprehension of governmental systems. One or the other of us, and sometimes both, has been a city council member, a county council member, a police commissioner, an associate chairperson of a state party executive committee, and a congressional fellow with the occasion to work with the Congress and on the White House staff. These opportunities to look at government and politics from inside, from various strata, and from different directions have sharpened our awareness of and our understanding of the interactions among governments. No level of government in the United States operates in a vacuum. Each depends to some degree upon the others. The formulation and implementation of public policy usually concern all three and, often, several on one plane.

This book is written in the hope of contributing to the filling of a gap in the study of American government. Although much has been published in recent years on federalism and intergovernmental relations, there have been few attempts to provide an overall analysis that includes interstate, state-local, and interlocal interactions along with the federal relations between the national government and the states. Nor has much attention been directed to the human element in these interactions or to people's points of view. A comprehensive approach is undertaken here. The information and analysis presented are partially the result of original research and personal experience; the remainder draws heavily on the efforts of our academic and professional colleagues in many localities, to whom we are indebted.

We write from a point of view—the view that American federalism is pragmatic. We believe that the intergovernmental relations within the system are constantly evolving, problem-solving attempts to work out solutions to major problems on an issue-by-issue basis, efforts that produce modifications of the federal and intergovernmental system. The government receiving the most pressure from citizen demands or possessing the greatest resources undertakes to solve the problem. A shift may later be made to another level, or one or more levels may share in the undertaking. As each shift of level or modification of program occurs, adjustments are made to accommodate to it, thereby creating more change. The elasticity of the arrangements help to maintain the viability of the American system. In other words, it is pragmatic.

Works such as this bring on many debts and, while we are unable to acknowledge them all, some deserve special mention. We thank those who have reviewed the manuscript in its many stages and through their detailed and insightful suggestions—most of which were happily accepted—helped to improve the final product. Special thanks go to reviewers John Bollens, Victor Jones, E. Lester Levine, David B. Walker, Deil S. Wright, and Joseph F. Zimmerman. Our departmental colleagues, Conley H. Dillon, Earlean McCarrick, and Thomas P. Murphy, also were helpful. A special note of appreciation goes to Pat Bowley for bibliographic assistance, to Frances Anne Hughes, Fern Piret, Andree E. Reeves, and Ben F. Reeves for their editorial help, to Patrick Chase for administrative assistance, and to Mary Keener and Jean Sproull for typing the manuscript.

Lastly, we are indebted to all those scholars who through

their insights and hard work have contributed to our understanding of federalism and intergovernmental relations, and to
those authors who, through their kindness, permitted liberal
quoting and citing of their works. We have not always agreed with
them and we are certain that our interpretations will not be
universally accepted. Nevertheless, we hope for their indulgence
in our efforts to present an overall view of intergovernmental
relations. We cannot, alas, pass to them the blame for any errors
or weaknesses in this work. Glendening accepts the basic
responsibility for chapters 5, 9, and 10, the dual federalism
section of chapter 4, and the regionalism section in chapter 6,
leaving Reeves to answer for chapters 1-4 and 6-8. Like
American intergovernmental relations, however, the work is
really indivisible with each author contributing ideas, criticism,
information, and sometimes writing to other parts. Therefore, we
happily blame each other.

P.N.G.
M.M.R.

1

Dynamics of Intergovernmental Accommodation

Dear Congressman:

I want you to help me. I am having all kinds of trouble getting my kids to school. I live here at the mouth of Piney Creek close to Foreman. The school board won't send the bus any closer than two miles because the road is so bad. Theres mud puddles in it deep enough to fish in and the school bus driver says he aint going to drive over it. I called the county and they claimed it wasn't their responsibility and for me to see the state highway department. I wrote them and they come and throwed a load of gravel on it and said it wasn't no use to fix it until the creek was dredged because the floods would ruin it again. I dont know who has to dredge the creek. Some said it was the core of engineers. Can you get something done? It's bad weather for little children to walk two miles to school. I'd be grateful.

Ans. Soon.

Henry Wooton

This letter illustrates an impact of intergovernmental relations on the citizen, an impact of which the citizen is not always conscious. He blames his frustrations on red tape, bureaucratic maze, or public officials who are not doing their jobs or who do not care. He is unaware that his frustrations frequently result from his position in a welter of governmental jurisdictions, all ministering to his needs and all requiring his support. At tax time he is more conscious of numerous governments, but even this may not always be so because tax bills are often combined, with one government doing the collecting for several. Coupled with the separation of powers of government among the legislative, executive, and judicial branches, this multiplicity of public units complicates the citizen's task of getting a problem solved. Such complications are the price Americans pay for the diversity within the governmental system, a diversity which allows variations in public policies so that one state may have less stringent laws on abortion, alcohol, and marijuana than another, for example. The individual who disagrees strongly with one way of doing things has the option of moving elsewhere.

The frustrated citizen trying to get a road built or a sewer repaired probably is not conscious of how many units of government there are in the United States—78,269 according to the most recent Census of Governments.[1] Most of these are local governments, including 3,044 counties, 18,517 municipalities, 16,991 townships (including New England towns), 15,781 school districts, and 23,885 other special districts. The total number of units has declined since the census of governments in 1942, despite a substantial increase in the number of municipalities and an almost fourfold rise in special districts. Almost all the decrease results from a reduction in the number of school districts, a product of the school consolidation movement. The number of townships is also somewhat smaller. Nevertheless, the thousands of local units still existing fragment the delivery of public services and increase the frustrations of citizens such as Henry Wooton who are trying to penetrate the maze of governments.

Governmental units are not spread uniformly throughout the United States. Nine states have nearly half of them (46 percent). Illinois has more than 6,000, Pennsylvania almost 5,000, and California, Kansas, Minnesota, Nebraska, New York, Ohio, and Texas more than 3,000 each. The average number for a state is 1,565, but looking at averages can distort one's view since Illinois has 6,386 while Hawaii has only 20. This means that one level of government is performing more functions in Hawaii or that its citizens are getting only a small fraction of the services provided for the citizens of Illinois. It also means that each citizen in Illinois is likely to live under the jurisdiction of more units of government than his counterpart in Hawaii.

Not only must a citizen find his way through a maze of governments, but also when he wishes to vent his frustration on an elected official, he must try to locate the responsible culprit from his portion of the more than 500,000 elected officeholders in the nation. No wonder, then, that frustration over the complexity of the system is often followed by exasperation over difficulties in pinpointing responsibility. Who, for example, does Henry Wooton, the writer of our opening letter, blame for his situation? The school board that refused to send the school bus further? The county commissioners who said it "wasn't their responsibility"? The governor who did not get the state highway department to act? The President, responsible for the Corps of Engineers? Or the congressman who has ended up with the problem? Understandably, Wooton is confused.

Citizens in some countries do not face as difficult a task of determining which government handles which function. It is a problem peculiar to federal governments, and perhaps even more to the United States than to other federal systems because of substantial state power based in constitutional provisions, uncentralized political parties, and the support state and local governments enjoy in public opinion.

Americans express preferences as to which level of government should undertake a given function. Table 1-1 indicates that both the general public and leaders in the United States think that consumer protests against high prices are best handled by the national government. Other activities, such as education and police protection, are viewed as functions which should be performed on a state or local level. Both citizens and leaders see other activities—housing, prevention of drug abuse, pollution control, welfare, handling racial demonstrations, racial integration in education, and getting rid of corrupt politicians— as ones to be shared. The table demonstrates that citizens recognize the existence of various levels of government and have preferences among them for the performance of activities. This does not mean, of course, that functions will necessarily be allocated entirely according to preferences. Other factors besides public opinion affect public policy.

Each of the 78,269 governmental units engages in one or more activities affecting citizens of the United States. The communication and interaction among these governments are the focus of this book. When so many governments exist, understanding the relations among them is essential to compre- hending how the American system works. One who looks only at the national government or state government or local govern- ment, sees only part of the picture, understands only part of the workings of the system.

In the following pages, the authors discuss the people involved in intergovernmental relations—because intergovern-

TABLE 1-1
LEVEL OF GOVERNMENT THAT BEST HANDLES SPECIFIC PROBLEMS

Question: Which level of government do you feel best handles the following problems?

	Public				
	National government	State government	Local government	None (vol.)	Not sure
	%	%	%	%	%
Achieving peace in world	93	4	4	2	2
Inflation	89	8	4	1	4
Income taxes	86	24	6	1	2
Making taxes fair to everyone	77	33	20	1	5
Consumer protests against high prices	64	20	16	3	9
Providing low cost housing #	57	35	14	2	5
Getting rid of corrupt politicians #	55	32	30	9	14
Drug abuse #	55	43	38	1	3
Controlling air and water pollution	54	41	24	1	5
Gun control	53	28	17	7	6
Providing adequate health services	52	38	18	3	6
Racial integration in education #	39	36	32	3	8
Taking care of people on welfare #	39	48	26	3	4
Racial integration in housing	38	35	31	4	8
Racial demonstrations #	37	34	36	3	10
Middle income housing #	35	45	20	4	9
Improving colleges	29	67	8	2	7
Building better highways	22	85	6	*	2
Improving public schools	14	50	51	1	3
Big rock concerts	9	32	53	4	11
Zoning for housing	8	25	68	1	6
Traffic congestion	5	37	69	1	3
Accidents on highways	4	82	18	1	1
Providing police protection	3	15	91	*	1
Uncollected garbage	*	3	95	1	1
Keeping the streets clean	*	5	95	*	*
Crime in the streets	*	*	*	*	*

#Functions for which there is a consensus that they should be shared.
*Not asked/not applicable/no response. Total percentages often exceed 100 because more than one choice was made.
SOURCE: Adapted from U.S. Senate, Committee on Government Operations, Subcom-

TABLE 1-1 (Continued)
LEVEL OF GOVERNMENT THAT BEST HANDLES SPECIFIC PROBLEMS

	Leaders				
	National government	**State government**	**Local government**	**None (vol.)**	**Not sure**
	%	%	%	%	%
Achieving peace in world	*	*	*	*	*
Inflation	*	*	*	*	*
Income taxes	87	49	16	*	3
Making taxes fair to everyone	72	62	48	2	3
Consumer protests against high prices	71	18	13	11	5
Providing low cost housing #	62	30	32	2	4
Getting rid of corrupt politicians #	59	53	54	9	8
Drug abuse #	49	58	66	*	2
Controlling air and water pollution	61	62	30		*
Gun control	58	30	25	12	3
Providing adequate health services	*	*	*	*	*
Racial integration in education #	41	42	56	4	2
Taking care of people on welfare #	51	56	35	1	1
Racial integration in housing	*	*	*	*	*
Racial demonstrations #	29	28	71	2	4
Middle income housing #	48	34	31	12	6
Improving colleges	*	*	*	*	*
Building better highways	50	86	15	1	*
Improving public schools	21	69	58	*	*
Big rock concerts	5	31	78	3	5
Zoning for housing	*	*	*	*	*
Traffic congestion	15	46	85	*	*
Accidents on highways	11	77	46	*	1
Providing police protection	7	23	94	*	1
Uncollected garbage	*	*	*	*	*
Keeping the streets clean	*	*	*	*	*
Crime in the streets	35	43	87	*	1

mittee on Intergovernmental Relations, **Confidence and Concern: Citizens View American Government. A Survey of Public Attitudes** (Washington, D.C.: Government Printing Office, 1973), II. 238-240. Survey conducted by Louis Harris and Associates.

mental relations are interactions among people in their roles as legislators, executives, judges, and bureaucrats—and emphasize the legal, historical, organizational, attitudinal, and behavioral framework in which these associations develop and what pattern emerges. It is our thesis that these relationships are dynamic; that is, they are in a constant state of change. As each problem involving more than a single governmental jurisdiction arises, it is dealt with in a pragmatic fashion; an individual solution is devised for it without reference to any general theory of intergovernmental relations. This may require a national-state interaction in one instance, a state-local one in another, or an interlocal one in a third or, indeed, it may involve interface among people in all these governments at the same time. It could include financial assistance, advice, or the creation of a new district, among other things. A similar problem arising else-where in the country, or five years later, may be handled in another way. Intergovernmental relations constantly change and adjust. They are at once cooperative, competitive, conflicting. Above all they are pragmatic and dynamic, tailored to and changing with the need and the times.

INTERGOVERNMENTAL RELATIONS AND FEDERALISM

Intergovernmental relations involve the whole range of interactions among all types and levels of governments. They are therefore different from federalism which is concerned with the relation of the central government to the constituent units. In the United States, for example, federalism pertains to the relation-ship of the national government to the states, with some attention to interstate and national-local relations. The term intergovernmental relations is a much more inclusive term that applies to both federal and nonfederal systems and often centers on people of various jurisdictions interacting in the governmental process.

DEFINITIONS OF FEDERALISM

No single definition of federalism is generally accepted: different authorities emphasize various aspects of it. Some experts have emphasized its contractual and legal status, while others have characterized it by its pragmatic and procedural nature. William H. Riker regards it as a bargain between prospective national leaders for the purpose of aggregating territory and raising taxes and armies. He regards a constitution as federal if: (1) two levels of government rule the same land and people, (2) each level has at least one area of action in which it is autonomous, and (3) there is some guarantee (even though merely a statement in the constitution) of the autonomy of each government in its own sphere.[2] Daniel J. Elazar also sees it as contractual. Separate polities are able to maintain their political integrity within an overarching political system by "contractually distributing power among general and constituent governments in a manner designed to protect the existence and authority of all."[3]

Richard H. Leach views federalism as a process and disagrees with those who regard it as a system of power distribution. He writes:

> It is a misconception to view American federalism as a power system. Despite common usage, power is not exercised systematically in the United States. Indeed, it is probably wrong to use the suffix "ism" for federalism, for the danger is always present that it will be read to mean adherence to a system rather than a process, which is all its use should imply. "System" suggests a regularly interacting group of power units, a power network, which performs its functions in a steady flow. That simply is not descriptive of federalism. Units there are aplenty, and interactions in great quantity, but there is nothing regularized about it, nor is there a steady flow of output. Power in the federal system moves irregularly, in spurts even as water overcomes obstacles and flows on again until it meets another. It is characterized by disorder and seldom moves twice in precisely the same way to accomplish its objectives.[4]

Michael D. Reagan distinguishes between old-style federalism which is "a legal concept, emphasizing a constitutional division of authority and functions between a national government and state governments, with both levels having received their powers independently of each other from a third source—the people," and a new-style federalism which he defines as "a political and pragmatic concept, stressing the actual interdependence and sharing of functions between Washington and the states, and focusing on the mutual leverage that each level is able to exert on the other."[5]

We incorporate both pragmatic and contractual dimensions, regarding federalism in the United States as an arrangement whereby: (1) the same territory and people are governed by two levels of government, both of which derive their authority from the people and both of which share some functions and exercise other functions autonomously of each other; (2) the existence of each level is protected from the other; and (3) each may exert leverage on the other. Basic to this arrangement are the spirit of self-restraint in interfering with the powers of the other and concern for maintaining the arrangement. The relations under this basic pattern are flexible, fluid, and pragmatic, ever changing and adjusting with shifts in power loci and public attitudes. By pragmatic federalism we mean a constantly adjusting arrangement fashioned to current needs with an emphasis on problem-solving and a minimal adherence to rigid doctrine. A problem solved in one manner at a given time and place may be solved differently in another period and setting. As each change occurs, the entire system adjusts, even if ever so slightly. For clarity, and to distinguish the federal arrangement, the term "national government" will be used for the most part in this book to designate the central government.

CHARACTERISTICS OF
INTERGOVERNMENTAL RELATIONS

Intergovernmental relations were traditionally thought of in terms of federalism; however, the term now has a broader meaning. A pioneer in the study of intergovernmental relations, William Anderson, perceived it "to designate an important body of activities or interactions occurring between governmental units of all types and levels within the federal system."[6] It could certainly be applied to relationships within nonfederal systems and to polities other than the United States,[7] but at present its usage is generally applied to the American system.

Both Anderson and Deil S. Wright, who also has worked at defining the term, emphasize that the concept of intergovernmental relations has to be understood in terms of human behavior. Wright says, " . . . strictly speaking, then, there are no intergovernmental relations, there are only relations among the officials in different governing units." He further characterizes intergovernmental relations as "continuous, day-to-day patterns of contact, knowledge, and evaluations of the officials who govern."[8] Informal as well as formal interactions are involved. The scope of intergovernmental relations extends to all public officials—administrators as well as elected executive, legislative, and judicial officers—and it encompasses political, economic, and administrative interactions as well as legal ones. To this the present authors would add that intergovernmental relations include the attitudes of public officials, an idea implicit in the definitions of Anderson and Wright. These attitudes, behavior, and interactions of the people involved must be seen in the light of the environment in which public officials operate, including all the constraints and stimuli within that environment as well as those imposed from the outside.

Then, for the purposes of this book, *intergovernmental relations are the interactions, attitudes, and behavior of elected officials and bureaucrats of two or more units of government functioning in their public capacities. They reflect their environment—their historical, cultural, legal, organizational, financial, political, and geographical settings. They may occur on both horizontal and vertical planes. That is, not only are the federal relationships of the national government and the states included, but so are the interstate, state-local, interlocal, and national-local relations.* They must be understood in the context of American federalism.

HORIZONTAL AND VERTICAL RELATIONS

Intergovernmental relations may be divided into two categories, horizontal and vertical. Horizontal relations occur among equals, such as state with state, county with county, and township with township. In these relationships there is ordinarily no legal compulsion for officials to interact, although encouragement for them to do so may come from the state or national government in the form of requirements for grants-in-aid or other provisions. Proximity is often a major factor in these interactions because officials in jurisdictions bordering each other frequently find it necessary to cooperate to solve a problem affecting both. Officials of other units may have no relationships at all, except, perhaps, as they convene at national meetings. For the most part, personnel in units operating horizontally expect noninterference from each other and they hope, at least, for cooperation in solving mutual problems.

Vertical relationships are more complex and diverse. They occur between officials of larger or more central governments and geographically smaller constituent units. The federal relationship between the national government and the states was mentioned above. In contrast to that is the unitary relationship between the states and their local units, an arrangement whereby the larger jurisdiction determines the powers of the smaller ones unilaterally with state officials often exercising some administrative supervision over local personnel. While the absolute legal control of the state is somewhat modified by political and other resources of the localities, determination of what local officials legally may do rests with the state.

Relations between counties and the municipalities are a different matter. The county officials normally have no authority over municipalities, and, in many instances, their relationships resemble horizontal ones. At other times, however, counties are quite strong and county officials often are able to control the incorporation of new municipalities, determine boundary changes, and affect other facets of municipal activity. Generalizations are difficult because of the differences in state laws and practices applying to city-county relationships. In some states, enactment of special local legislation affecting only one situation further diversifies the arrangements.

Infinite variation occurs in relationships between counties and other local units. Generally, townships are likely to be subject to some county authority since they are county subdivisions. Relations with school districts, as well as with other special districts, reflect a similar variety. Some states have no independent school districts, leaving management of education to the state, county, city, or township. In other states, districts devoted exclusively to school operation exist. They have their own taxing power and are run by independently elected officials.

In their relations with larger jurisdictions, officials of smaller units seek autonomy, financial assistance, and policies with which they agree.[9] Those in central jurisdictions look to the constituent units for administrative assistance in program implementation, and for responsibility for certain functions, such as law enforcement, which can be better undertaken in a smaller geographic area.

FACTORS STIMULATING INTERGOVERNMENTAL RELATIONS

It is a truism to state that no government operates in a vacuum, but obviously some government officials are involved in intergovernmental relations to a greater degree than others. What stimulates intergovernmental intercourse? Contributing factors vary with the government and activity concerned. A list of major ones would include (1) proximity; (2) legal requirements; and (3) financial assistance of one jurisdiction to another, but a host of other stimuli operate.[10]

Proximity plays a major role, especially on a horizontal basis. It stands to reason that New York and California will not likely be engaged in boundary disputes or controversies over air pollution with one another. Texas and Louisiana may need to reach accommodation, however, on many matters and certainly Kansas City, Kansas, and Kansas City, Missouri, have mutual problems to resolve simply because they are neighbors. It would be interesting to know how proximity affects national-state and national-local relations. Research suggests that states or localities near Washington, D.C., may interact with the national government more than do those further away.[11] Part of this may be a factor of personal acquaintance. Bureaucrats from surrounding jurisdictions may be personally acquainted with national officials, and this personal contact promotes official interactions. Location of national facilities doubtlessly promotes interface also.

Legal requirements contained in constitutions, statutes, and court decisions, and the executive orders or administrative regulations and guidelines promulgated to effectuate them, often require government officials to interact. Provision for rendition of a fugitive from one state to another requires intergovernmental contact between law enforcement personnel of the state desiring the return of the fugitive and those of the state to which he fled. State election laws mandate certain actions by local officials in the conduct of elections. Court decisions may require national agency approval of local school desegregation plans. National statutes or guidelines provoke joint activities among officials within a region.

Financial assistance from one level of government to another, particularly from the national government to the states, often has been given primacy as a stimulant for intergovernmental relations. All national grants-in-aid require some intergovernmental action by the receiving government be it the filing of a grant application, the submission of reports on the use of the money, or one of a myriad of other actions. It would be a mistake, however, to regard financial aid as the catalyst in all intergovernmental relations or necessarily as the most important factor. A case study of low-income housing in Montgomery County, Maryland, for example, found that the county waited twenty-seven years after grant availability to take advantage of federal housing money. Thus, neither the legal provision nor the availability of funds stimulated intergovernmental interaction in housing in this instance. More important were environmental factors such as population growth, rising housing costs, and shifts in public attitude concerning the provision of housing. These developments produced demands on the county government which responded by creating a local housing authority and moving into the provision of low-income housing.[12]

The same variables that determine the existence of intergovernmental relations are important in its tone. Once established, relations among the people involved may be harmonious or abrasive, competitive or complimentary, frequent or occasional. These elements are difficult to quantify, but seemingly relations are smoothest when the individuals involved have compatible goals, are personally acquainted, and when both have a knowledge of the particular area and problems. There is often a mild distrust of the other jurisdiction and, although goals are the same, differences develop over how to administer a program. Each jurisdiction is concerned with maintaining its own viability. Each has a separate political culture and environment in which it operates. Each has a different constituency to please.

FACTORS CONTRIBUTING TO CHANGE

Regardless of the sources of their stimulation, intergovernmental relations undergo constant change and adjustment. New demands place new stresses on the political system. Numerous factors, including catastrophic events, demographic changes, and technological developments, alter the political arrangements. Cataclysmic events, such as war or depression, often require shifts of government functions from one level to another, usually from a smaller to a larger level, in order to provide swift and comprehensive action. The Depression of the thirties, for example, saw a welfare system which had formerly relied almost entirely on private support, with local units furnishing county poor farms and orphanages and occasional emergency relief, shifted to the states with a strong input of national public assistance. In some states, additional functions, such as schools and roads, also became state activities while in other instances states joined localities in their support. Interactions among levels of government increased as governments undertook more programs or shared existing ones.

GROWING AND MIGRATING POPULATION

Population changes have had a major impact in altering relationships. Since 1920 when the number of urban dwellers tipped the balance and the United States first became an urban nation, three continuing movements of population have substantially altered the demographic makeup of the country. First was the massive movement from the farms to the cities, a migration that changed the nation from predominantly rural to overwhelmingly urban in less than three decades, with more than three-fourths of the population now residing in urban areas. This urbanization was followed by accelerated suburbanization in the 1950s and 1960s. The impact of these changes has been a great increase in the representation of urban areas at all levels of government, particularly after the judicial spur of fair apportionment. As suburbanization separated the poorer, non-white, and ethnic citizens of the central city (except in the South and Southwest) from the wealthier, overwhelmingly white suburbs, both parochialism and conflict increased. New municipalities were formed, adding to the separateness of various groups and making problem solving for metropolitan areas more difficult.[13] Although the central cities are at the height of their political power, their relative decline in population as compared with the suburbs forecasts a diminution of their strength in the political arena.

Nevertheless, the growth of urban power has meant more effective urban demands on the national government—demands that have resulted in increased national-local interactions and have stimulated direct national-local interface, bypassing the states which traditionally were the circuits through which national-local communication moved. States, too, have felt the pressures of urban growth, reacting with more home rule and increased financial assistance to localities.

The third trend was the less noticed movement of the highly mobile American people from the interior of the nation to the peripheral states, especially those of the "sunshine belt." This peripheralization is demonstrated by table 1-2. Note, as an example, that while the percentage of population increase for the interior West North Central region is consistently far below that of the nation as a whole the peripheral Pacific region's increase is consistently far above the national average. The selected states in the table further demonstrate the outward migration pattern. It is important to understand the magnitude of the population

TABLE 1-2

POPULATION CHANGE BY SELECTED REGIONS AND SELECTED STATES, 1920-1970

	1920-30	1930-40	1940-50	1950-60	1960-70
United States Total	16.2%	7.3%	14.5%	18.5%	13.3%
West North Central Region*	6.0	1.7	4.0	9.5	6.0
Pacific Region #	46.7	18.7	47.8	40.2	25.1
Major population losers, selected states					
North Dakota	5.3	−5.7	−3.5	2.1	−2.3
South Dakota	8.8	−7.2	1.5	4.3	−2.1
West Virginia	18.1	10.0	5.4	−7.2	−6.2
Major population gainers, selected states					
California	65.7	21.7	53.3	48.5	27.0
Florida	51.6	39.2	46.1	78.7	37.1
Texas	24.9	10.1	20.2	24.2	16.9

*Minnesota, Iowa, Missouri, North Dakota, South Dakota, Nebraska, and Kansas.
#Alaska, California, Hawaii, Oregon, and Washington.

SOURCE: **Adapted from the Statistical Abstract of the United States, 1975** (Washington, D.C.: Bureau of the Census, 1975).

shifts behind the percentages of change. California, for instance, increased from less than three and one half million people in 1920 to twenty million in 1970, adding five million new residents in each of the last two decades.

Peripheralization brought with it shifts in political power and problems for both the states losing and those gaining population. There have been consequent intergovernmental ramifications. With the diminishing proportion of population in the interior states came a slower growth in financial support both from local revenues and in the proportionate share of intergovernmental aid. At the same time the income of the people of the area often diminished. Outside help was sometimes required. Peripheral areas experienced growth in demands for services which outstripped revenues to pay for them. The lag between the time a service or facility is needed and the time it can be provided creates stresses on the system. If a new subdivision is constructed and families with 500 children move there, those children require school buildings and teachers immediately and cannot wait for construction and training to take place. The inability of one level of government to meet such demands is likely to result in the city or county officials of the area involved making demands on state or national officials for assistance.

The transient nature of the population in itself has consequences for intergovernmental relations because it increases the interdependence of all governmental jurisdictions horizontally. For example, untrained laborers do not always stay in the areas where training is poor but move to other jurisdictions and raise the unemployment rate there. Or the better-supported welfare programs in one state may attract the indigent of others, thus stimulating officials of the receiving jurisdiction to agitate for a national welfare program. Further, this constant movement may increase the orientation of citizens to the national government because this is the only public unit in which they consistently reside as they wander nomadically from state to state.

TECHNOLOGICAL DEVELOPMENT

Technological developments alter the balance in society, thus creating stresses in the social system which produce demands on government. For example, mass production of the automobile permitted the affluent to move away from downtown areas of cities, thus avoiding a share of the problems existing there. At the same time, the automobile increased the range of criminal activity so that apprehending fleeing criminals might require the cooperation of several governments. Television exerts tremendous impact on all levels of government and on their relationships. Not only does it provide a homogenizing influence on the nation, but a divisive one as well as it exhibits for all to see the disparities in American society. This creates pressures for remedial measures by whatever government has the resources— usually the national government. Television, furthermore, along with newspapers and radio, educates the public in pressure group techniques and provides a forum for citizen action that brings forth demands on the political system.

FACTORS IMPEDING CHANGE

Drastic change in governmental systems rarely occurs except as a result of crisis. Most change is incremental and the system has time to accommodate to it without severe stress. This is true of intergovernmental relations as well. Modifications in the general pattern have occurred, but they have been largely adopted piecemeal and adjustment to them could be managed a little at a time. The exceptions occurred with the replacement of the Articles of Confederation by the present Constitution, altering substantially the balance between the central government and the states, and during the Depression of the 1930s when the economic situation necessitated an upward shift of functions to larger governmental jurisdictions.

Numerous factors operate to impede change. Existing legal provisions in constitutions and statutes serve to keep things the same. So do court decisions for the most part although they have occasionally catalyzed intergovernmental shifts. Law is a conservative force in most situations. Bureaucratic resistance based on fear of loss of status in a new situation, habit, or simply the inertia of large organizations supports the status quo. Pressures of entrenched interest groups reenforce the existing arrangements because those with access to government are reluctant to have to establish it anew. Existing boundary lines also impede change since they are difficult to alter, state boundaries especially. Those who advocate the abolition of states are not cognizant of the reservoir of power there, not to mention the deep-seated loyalties states engender from their citizens. Local boundaries inspire similar loyalties in some instances and provide protection from higher taxes, different service levels, and social problems existing in other areas. All these things, along with general conservatism toward change and the demands for on-going public services, erect obstacles that slow the change process.

HOW CHANGE OCCURS

Incremental though it may be, change over a period of time can produce substantial modifications in intergovernmental arrangements. It emanates from accumulated pressures produced by events as well as demographic, economic, and other inputs into the environment, and by individuals, usually organized into groups. Adapting their techniques to the prevailing value system and public opinion, interest groups exert pressures on the legislatures, executives, bureaucracies, and through judicial branches of all levels of government to achieve their goals. Many have federal-type organizations corresponding to the American governmental system. They apply their pressure where they have the most leverage, a condition varying with the issue or with the group. Elected officials also respond to the verdicts of the citizens at election time and to their opinions reported in the polls or expressed by letter, telephone, or telegraph or in person. They themselves pressure each other; and the bureaucrats, because of their expertise and continued presence, exert a powerful influence.

The aggregation of sufficient pressures, from whatever source, forces public officials to act. Incremental action deflates the pressure and may actually deter major reform. A problem has to approach crisis proportions to compel fundamental change. The civil rights struggle and the efforts to control environmental pollution are pertinent examples in this connection. Certainly blacks had suffered from discrimination since the Colonial period, but sustained pressure for reform produced fundamental changes only twice, at the time of the Civil War and in the middle of the current century. Environmental pollution existed for a long time before conditions got bad enough that sufficient sentiment for change surfaced, and then the energy shortage mitigated its force.[14]

It should be understood that not all the action, or the pressure to act, relates to the adoption of legislation. Changes in administrative regulations, personnel, or organization can substantially alter public policy, and knowledgeable interests operate with that in mind. Note, for instance, the effect of the Nixon Administration's impoundment of funds for certain programs previously enacted by Congress—an action accomplished by executive fiat and not by legislation. Another illustration is a decision by the national Office of Management and Budget that Prince George's and Montgomery counties, Maryland, should have the activities of their planning boards (parts of a bi-county agency) included in determining their revenue-sharing allotments, resulting in an increase of several million dollars for each of them. Such a decision afforded these counties the pleasant job of adjusting to more revenue while local units elsewhere faced the sad duty of adjusting to less.

Judges also contribute to the shifting relations among

governments. They always have been the arbiters of intergovernmental change, sometimes through the settlement of disputes between the states, and often through cases not raising intergovernmental questions directly but whose impact stimulates alterations in intergovernmental arrangements. Probably no better example of the latter exists than *Brown* v. *Board of Education of Topeka*[15] which, in requiring desegregation of schools, also set off a chain of events and decisions that gave the national government a powerful club (withholding of funds) over local school districts.

ACCOMMODATION

Change in the governmental system, whatever its cause, requires a corresponding adjustment. This is true of the relations among governments as well as of other aspects of the system. And it is true of minor shifts in routine as well as of major shifts. A study of intergovernmental relations in housing found, for example, that changing a form so that a checkmark could be substituted for a comment altered the route of intergovernmental communications. More important changes, such as a national requirement for review of certain local projects by a regional agency, precipitated the creation of new governmental agencies (i.e., councils of government or regional councils) to perform this function and produced an entirely new pattern of interactions.[16] New inputs into the system modify the existing arrangements with consequent adjustment all along the line.

EMERGING PATTERNS

Even the casual observer of American government can hardly fail to perceive its growth. On all levels governments are expanding into additional fields, taking on new functions. Space exploration and atomic energy development immediately come to mind, but more mundane although important functions such as consumer protection provide good examples. Not only is there a national agency of consumer affairs, created in 1971, but all fifty states also have such organizations, mostly established in the late 1960s or early 1970s and some large cities and counties even have separate counterparts. Government's concern for the consumer comes recently to the American scene, *caveat emptor*—let the buyer beware—was the motto of both the vendor and of government, for the most part, for generations.

Some expansion of public functions on the state and local levels has resulted from national legislation, particularly grants-in-aid. The grant programs either stimulated or required the offering of new or enlarged services, the creation of new agencies, and the hiring of more personnel. Other programs pursued by the states and localities were designed to meet demands of their own citizens. Innovative ones, such as consumer protection, were later adopted and promoted by the national government.

The growth of governmental activities, coupled with improved communication and burgeoning problems requiring multi-government action for solution, brought on an accelerating number of governmental interactions. They are not subject to a precise count because of the endless number of routes through which they could occur. However, the increase in the number of grants-in-aid, the growth of intergovernmental organizations and agencies such as the Advisory Commission on Intergovernmental Relations (ACIR)—a national agency in which all levels of government and the public are represented—and the more frequently scheduled meetings of public officials from more than one jurisdiction testify to their expansion.

Accompanying the more frequent interactions is greater intergovernmental cooperation. This is evident in many ways. Some are the more frequent adoption of interstate compacts and other cooperative agreements, development of new regional organizations on an interstate, substate, and metropolitan-area basis, and national legislation such as the Intergovernmental Cooperation Act and the Intergovernmental Personnel Act. Others are the proliferation of state agencies to provide assistance for local governments, consolidation of functions on an interlocal basis, increase in national financial and other assistance to state and local governments, and more state financial aid to localities.

Increased cooperation, along with problems not confinable to existing jurisdictional boundaries, beget governmental units which cover larger geographic areas. This may be seen in the development of regional organizations such as the Appalachian Regional Commission, in the patterns of statewide substate district systems developing rapidly, and in the sporadic but persistent efforts at metropolitan governmental reorganization. The emphasis is on cooperative and coordinated development rather than on governments with coercive capabilities.

In the fiscal field, intergovernmental financial aid from

nation to states and localities, and from states to localities has expanded in amount and in purpose. National fiscal assistance has multiplied manyfold, its emphasis has shifted, the methods of delivery have been diversified, and attempts are underway to improve its administration. Not only have the number and total dollar amount of grants-in-aid multiplied, but also the proportion of state and local revenues received from the national government has increased. The addition of revenue sharing makes the smaller units even more dependent on the national bounty. Some observers argue that revenue sharing with its relatively unrestricted provision of funds for states and localities will establish a tripartite federal system by upgrading localities and decreasing their dependence on the states through giving them revenue sources the states cannot control. If revenue sharing continues and increases until it reaches, say, 10 percent of local revenues, the localities would be placed in such a position of dependence on the national government that a threat of withdrawal of funds could be used as a club to force conformity. The effect of revenue sharing depends to a substantial degree on national largesse and on congressional restraint in attaching conditions to its receipt.

Emphasis in the national grant program fluctuates. The earlier trend of assisting states and localities with their priorities gave way during the 1960s to an emphasis on national choice. With this change the national government made use of the states and local governments to advance some national programs, so that to some extent the states and localities became "handmaidens" of the central government, to use Roscoe C. Martin's term. With the advent of the new manpower programs and other efforts to develop block grants and to devolve authority in the period since 1966, a more mixed pattern has emerged.

Developing side by side with improved cooperation is stronger competition between states and their local units and between cities and counties. Localities, fortified by some direct federal grants-in-aid and by revenue sharing, are competing against the states in the national political arena. For example, their representatives now appear before congressional committees urging that the states be bypassed in the financing and administration of certain national programs. Also, representatives of their public-interest groups are consulted on national regulations and guidelines for administering grant-in-aid programs. The city-county conflict develops in some states as each of these units tries to occupy the dominant local government position. In New England, especially in Connecticut where counties were abolished, it has been a losing battle for the counties while in other states, such as Maryland, the paramount position of counties has been reenforced by restrictions on the incorporation of new municipalities.

As a result of continuing urbanization and the spread of metropolitan areas outward from the central city, for a hundred miles in some instances, new types of local governments are developing that also have consequences for intergovernmental relations. The rise of new suburban municipalities with limited functions and the increase in the number of urban counties, which resemble cities in organization and function, require adjustment of other jurisdictions such as central cities who have to deal with them. They block boundary extensions of existing municipalities and compete for revenue-sharing funds and other financial assistance, as well as demand representation on intergovernmental agencies.

After a long period of continual despair, there is evidence of the resurgence of states as strong partners in the federal system. The pattern is uneven, however, and it is not true for some states or for some activities. The criticisms of states growing out of the "urban crisis" and the threat posed to them by the rising power of the cities, as well as the states' own mounting problems, prodded some to organize for dealing with these matters by constitutional revision, executive reorganization, and legislative reform. Their viability is increasing and they may develop as the only jurisdictions sufficiently large to administer metropolitan areas, although obviously even they are not large enough to encompass some metropolitan areas that transcend state boundaries.

The most dominant pattern emerging from intergovernmental change is that of pragmatic intergovernmental relations within the federal system—a constantly evolving, problem-solving attempt to work out solutions to major problems on an issue-by-issue basis, resulting in modifications of the federal and intergovernmental systems. The government receiving the most pressure from citizen demands or possessing the greatest resources undertakes the function. Later a shift may be made to another level, or one or more levels may share in the undertaking. As each shift of level or modification of program occurs, adjustments are made to accommodate to it, creating more change. The very elasticity of the arrangement helps to maintain the viability of the American system. Both federalism, in its more limited definition, and the broader concept of intergovernmental relations, then, must be understood in terms of their pragmatic nature.

NOTES

1. U.S. Bureau of the Census, *1972 Census of Governments: Governmental Organization* (Washington, D.C.: 1973), Vol. I, p. 23.
2. William H. Riker, *Federalism: Origin, Operation, Significance* (Boston: Little, Brown and Company, 1964), p. 11.
3. Daniel J. Elazar, *The Principles and Practices of Federalism: A Comparative Historical Approach* (Philadelphia: Center for the Study of Federalism, Temple University, n.d.), p. 3. See his *American Federalism: A View From the States*, 2nd edition (New York: Thomas Y. Crowell Company, 1972), chap. 3, on the American federal system as a partnership.
4. Richard H. Leach, *American Federalism* (New York: W. W. Norton and Company, 1970), pp. 58-59. See also his "Federalism: A Battery of Questions," in *The Federal Policy*, edited by Daniel J. Elazar, a special edition of *Publius: The Journal of Federalism*, Vol. 3, No. 2 (Fall, 1973), pp. 11-47.
5. Michael D. Reagan, *The New Federalism* (New York: Oxford University Press, 1972), p. 3. Several authors discuss federalism in *The Federal Polity*. See also K. C. Where, *Federal Government* (Fourth edition: New York: Oxford University Press, 1964).
6. William Anderson, *Intergovernmental Relations in Review* (Minneapolis: University of Minnesota Press, 1960), p.3. This is the tenth in an important series directed by Anderson and Edward W. Weidner on intergovernmental relations in Minnesota. Another pioneer was W. Brooke Graves whose *American Intergovernmental Relations* (New York: Charles Scribner's Sons, 1964) is a standard reference in the field, although somewhat dated.
7. Jesse Burkhead, "Federalism in a Unitary State: Regional Economic Planning in England." *Publius*, Vol. 4, No. 2 (Summer, 1974), pp. 39-61.
8. Deil S. Wright, "Intergovernmental Relations: An Analytical Overview," *The Annals*, Vol. 416 (November, 1974), p. 2. See also his "Intergovernmental Relations in Large Council-Manager Cities," *American Politics Quarterly*, Vol. 1, No. 2 (April, 1972), pp. 151-153, and his "Intergovernmental Relations and Policy Choice," *Publius: The Journal of Federalism*, Vol. 5, No. 4 (Fall, 1975), pp. 1-6.
9. See Suzanne Farkas, *Urban Lobbying: Mayors in the Federal Arena* (New York: New York University Press, 1971), chap. VIII.
10. Some other significant stimulating factors are: (1) structural organi-

zation of governmental units; (2) voluntary agreements; (3) compatibility of goals; (4) issues; (5) environment, including the density and spread of population and the attitudes and perceptions of public officials; (6) tenure of personnel; (7) personalities of public officials and bureaucrats; (8) personal acquaintance of governmental figures; (9) political realities including support in public opinion for interactions; (10) interest group activity which may both draw together officials from various jurisdictions and pressure individual governments to interact; and, (11) the development stage of a program or project. See Mavis Mann Reeves, "Change and Fluidity: Intergovernmental Relations in Housing in Montgomery County, Maryland," *Publius: The Journal of Federalism*, Vol. 4, No. 1 (Winter, 1974), pp. 5-44.
11. *Ibid.*
12. *Ibid.*
13. For discussions of suburbanization and its effects, see, among others: Earl M. Baker, editor, *The Suburban Reshaping of American Politics*, Vol. 5, No. 1 of *Publius: The Journal of Federalism* (Winter, 1975). Note especially Baker's introductory essay, "The Suburban Transformation of American Politics: The Convergence of Reality and Research," pp. 1-14; and, Thomas P. Murphy and John Rehfuss, *Urban Politics in the Suburban Era* (Homewood, Illinois: The Dorsey Press, 1976).
14. See Parris N. Glendening and Mavis M. Reeves, "The Future of State and Local Government and American Federalism," in Reeves and Glendening, *Controversies of State and Local Political Systems* (Boston: Allyn and Bacon, Inc., 1972), pp. 471-483.
15. 374 U.S. 483 (1954).
16. Parris N. Glendening, "The Federal Role in Regional Planning Councils," *The Review of Regional Studies*, Vol. 1, No. 3 (Spring, 1971-72).

2

The Human Factor: People In Intergovernmental Relations

Intergovernmental relations are often viewed as a mechanical series of interactions among institutions; but, in reality, they are carried out by human beings in organizations. In considering federalism, revenue sharing, and interstate compacts, for instance, it is easy to forget that interactions among governments are not sterile mechanisms operated somewhere "out there." They involve, in fact, people-to-people interactions.

People, acting both as individuals and in groups and both inside and outside governmental institutions, determine what intergovernmental relations will be. As they campaign, vote, elect, pressure, adjudicate, negotiate, administer, and engage in other activities, they are impressing upon the American system their values as to which level of government should do what. For the most part, these people are probably attempting to achieve some other aim, such as improving schools or roads, or economic conditions. It is doubtful if they consider the ramifications for the intergovernmental system. But the sum total to all the actions they take on a piecemeal basis is the resulting intergovernmental system.

THE CITIZENS

The Henry Wootons of this country help to determine intergovernmental relations in the United States. As voters, they can influence governmental policy directly through initiative and referenda—although this is more frequent in some places than in others—or indirectly through their representatives, or they can reject a program or an administration on election day.

Individuals vote for candidates on all levels of government, and the people they select determine the relationships among these governments. A majority of congressmen, for example, since the 1930s, have taken a liberal view of the national role in providing public services although the location of program management still reflects their local orientation. Election of a more conservative majority might diminish the national participation. President Nixon's "New Federalism" was among his campaign themes. Whether it swayed many voters is doubtful; but upon election, he made a conscious effort to strengthen the position of the states and localities in the federal system.

By his vote, as well as in other ways, the voter has a direct influence on his party—what it is, what it does, whether it wins or loses. He participates, directly in many states and indirectly in others, in the election of delegates to the national presidential nominating conventions and to state and local conventions and committees. His approval or disapproval thus is reflected indirectly in the position political parties take on such issues as expanding the national role in the federal system. More Americans regard themselves as Democrats than Republicans, and consequently could be said to support the expanded national role; however, about one-third of the adult population considers itself as Independent. Other issues could be regarded more important in a given election, thus making considerations about intergovernmental relations or the nature of federalism of minor concern to a voter deciding how to cast his ballot.

DIRECT INFLUENCE

Occasionally voters have the opportunity to influence intergovernmental relations directly through the use of the initiative or referendum. In the eighteen states permitting the initiative, voters by petition may originate legislation affecting intergovernmental relations (such as local home rule). Many cities allow its use. The opportunities for voting on intergovernmental legislation in referenda are more numerous. Fourteen states and many localities permit citizens to petition already enacted legislation to referendum for decision by the voters. Such a case occurred in Wheeling, West Virginia, when an ordinance establishing an urban renewal agency was petitioned to referendum and repealed fifteen years later to prevent a blighted downtown area from being converted to a mall. This public action effectively eliminated the operation of the national program for urban renewal in that locality, at least for the time being.[1] About half the states permit the legislature to submit controversial proposals to local option, as might happen when the sale of alcoholic beverages is permitted in all those local jurisdictions where citizens vote favorably on the question. Certain proposals might be required by the state constitution to be submitted to popular vote. California cities must submit public housing proposals to referenda, and many states require changes in local boundaries or functions to be placed on the ballot. As an illustration, in Ohio proposals to transfer municipal functions to the county must be approved by majority votes in both the city and the county.[2]

Also, state constitutional amendments usually are voted upon by the public. Intergovernmental factors would be involved, for example, in the submission of an amendment issuing bonds and levying a tax to repay them for the purpose of matching federal funds for highways. Because some state constitutions prohibit state debt, the incurring of it requires an amendment. It is doubtful if voters regard such a vote as a judgment on intergovernmental relations. They are more inclined to be concerned with whether the roads are built, where they will be constructed, and the amount of taxes required to pay the state's share. Adoption of new constitutions changing state-local or interlocal arrangements, or a referendum on an amendment to the same effect (such as home rule for counties) raises the intergovernmental question directly. With the recent surge in the adoption of home-rule amendments, the electorate appears to be knowingly approving some changes in the intergovernmental structure.

Referenda voting fluctuates strikingly, depending on its emotional appeal and how well the voters understand the issues involved. Most voters seem to be less interested in issues than in candidates, and the participation rate for those voting on constitutional amendments and other proposals submitted to referenda is substantially below that for candidates even when the issues are on the same ballot. The influence of voters on intergovernmental relations should not be underestimated, nonetheless. By their votes for representatives in Congress, the state legislatures, and state ratifying conventions for federal amendments, and through election of delegates to a national constitutional convention, if one is ever held, the voters can play the final trump card that determines whether the federal system will continue to exist, and, if so, in what form.

INTERGOVERNMENTAL PERCEPTIONS

Citizens' perceptions of intergovernmental relations and their knowledge and understanding of the people and problems at each level may determine their participation in elections. Other attempts to influence public officials may be affected, too. Survey data indicate that the politically attentive portion of the American public distinguishes among the levels of government and follows national and local affairs more closely than those of the states.[3] Yet a poll on the question of understanding local as opposed to national issues indicated that substantially more people understood local issues than national ones.[4] As for citizen knowledge of officials on each level, a survey for the U.S. Senate Committee on Government Operations showed that 91 percent of those questioned thought they knew who their governor was and 98 percent of this percentage actually did know. Knowledge of U.S. senators and congressmen was substantially less. Sixty-four percent thought they knew their senator and 93 percent of them did. Only 53 percent thought they knew their congressman and 88 percent of them were correct. As far as utilizing this knowledge for political purposes was concerned, a total of 33 percent had written to a congressman, 19 percent to a local official, and 27 percent had participated in a school board decision.[5]

POLITICAL PARTIES

As American government has grown in recent years so has the complexity of its interrelated parts. Citizen Henry Wooton viewing the multiplicity of governmental units often feels frustrated in his attempts to weave through the maze of jurisdictions and gain access to those who can solve his problem if, in fact, he can figure out who they are. His access is conditioned by both the federal system and the separation of powers. To accomplish a given result, he cannot look only to officials at one level of government; he may have to influence all of them. Nor may he be sure of the outcome if he directs his activity toward legislators; in a particular situation, the executive, a bureaucrat, or a judge may be more important, and more than one of them may be necessary for the desired result.

Accordingly, the citizen tends to work through organizations skilled at influencing government—especially political parties and interest groups—which serve as links between him and his government. A few individuals may be so personally influential that they can achieve a favorable result on their own initiative or in collaboration with friends, but for most people organized activity is more fruitful.

Many individuals are organized into political parties with an avowed purpose of affecting government through the electoral process. In contrast to the unified, disciplined parties existing in many parts of the world, American parties may be characterized as noncentralized, undisciplined, non-ideological, and with diverse and open membership. There are only two parties of any importance most of the time. This duality is preserved by an electoral system characterized by (1) a single-member district system for electing members of Congress, in which the candidate with a plurality of the popular vote wins, and (2) the selection of the President and Vice President by the Electoral College. A two-party tradition and the reluctance of voters to risk wasting a vote on a third-party candidate have aided in retaining two-party dominance.

People often talk in terms of THE Democratic Party or THE Republican Party, but this is fiction. The two major parties are very loose federations of state parties coming together every four years for the nomination and election of the President and Vice President. In the intervals they are not very active despite the maintenance of national headquarters. In particular, the defeated party is likely to be fractionated because of lack of clear leadership. Sometimes it is helpful to think of the parties as fifty-one Democratic and fifty-one Republican parties (including the District of Columbia) with widely divergent ideas and interests among the parties in each category. The Alabama Democratic party, for example, may be more like the Alabama Republican party than like the Democratic party in Massachusetts. The parties lack unity on a national level with respect to both leadership and ideas. Strength rests in the state and local parties, which control most nominations for Congress and for state and local offices, rather than at the national level. This gives state and local party groups an input into national decision-making.

Despite the hierarchical appearance of party structure, the national committees of both parties have no control over their state and local counterparts; in fact, the latter two may be stronger. Confederations of the state and local units often control the nomination for President and Vice President. This noncentralization of power in the political parties is supported by the federal arrangement in American government; and pluralistic power centers in the parties help maintain the federal bargain. The result is the inability of the national government to control state decision-making.

Lack of discipline in the parties helps to augment local strength. The national party cannot control the actions of public officials elected under its banner. The President may try to persuade members of his party in the Congress to go along with his programs. He has some rewards to disperse, but he has no effective means of disciplining recalcitrant members whose first responsibility is to local constituencies. The problems of the President are multiplied if he is dealing with a governor or a mayor. Congressional party leaders can be somewhat more effective than the President in dealing with fellow partisans because they have more influence over the developing power of the member, being able to control committee assignments and other internal matters. But their actions are tempered by the knowledge that sanctions that diminish constituent strength at home may eventually weaken the party position in the House or the Senate. Neither members of Congress nor state and local officials rely on the national organization for nomination and election to office. As a consequence, this local orientation is felt by federal administrative agencies as congressmen exercise influence on them in behalf of local constituents, whether they are individuals, groups, or governments.

The Democratic and Republican parties are broad, umbrella organizations. Anyone eligible to vote may register as a Republican or a Democrat and each party includes people from every spectrum of life. Republicans are rich, poor, old, young, black, white, well educated, unlettered, native American, and foreign born. So are Democrats. Both parties include farmers, bankers, doctors, lawyers, teachers, technicians, machinists, unskilled laborers, students, unemployed—in fact, people from every walk of American life, a mixture quite unlike their European counterparts. Generally non-ideological, both American parties contain liberals, conservatives, reactionaries, radicals, racists, and all shades of political thinkers. However, both tend to be centrists—that is, take a position in the political center—in advocating programs. Not all of these groups appear in equal proportion in each party nor are they spread equally on a geographic basis.

Party choice is influenced by many factors including party identification of parents, geographical location, occupation, income level, ethnic and religious heritage, and catastrophic events such as the Depression of the 1930s or the Civil War. Parental party identification is likely to be the most determinative.

Parties divide on their concept of the role of the national government. William Buchanan emphasizes that Republican voters are more opposed to national administration than Democratic voters. The proportion who object to it increases as one goes up the hierarchy from rank and file Republicans to local party workers, to state and national leaders. Apparently pronouncements of party leaders have an effect on voter attitudes; the proportion of Republicans in favor of federal aid to education decreased from 62 percent in 1956 to 54 percent in 1958, to 40 percent in 1960 when party leaders spoke out on the issue.[6] Deil S. Wright found in studying the 86th and 87th Congresses that party members in those bodies divided on the issue of a greater or lesser role for the national government in federal grants-in-aid, with the Democrats overwhelmingly more favorable to federal grants than Republicans. A 1974 survey of congressional attitudes toward revenue sharing found Republicans much more favorable than Democrats to state discretion in the use of these funds. Of those responding, 54 percent of the Democrats favored nationally-established priorities for state spending while only 19 percent of the Republicans supported these restrictions.[7]

Party organization differs from state to state and sometimes between parties in a state, often presenting a confusing array of apparatus. Furthermore, political power does not always rest within the organization; it may be in the hands of an individual or a group outside the formal structure. It could be built around a local elective official such as sheriff or mayor or other prime sources of patronage such as probate judges in New York or superintendents of schools in some Appalachian counties.[8] Nevertheless, political power is frequently exercised through party organization. It is identified with those able to determine the party nominees or to set the qualifications for them. The exercise of this power fluctuates; often members of the same party work against each other and cooperate with members of the opposition party. A governor out of favor with the faction of his party that controls the state legislature may build a coalition with the opposition party to get his program enacted.

PARTIES AND FEDERALISM

The close relationship between federalism and the political party system has been emphasized repeatedly in the literature on American federalism.[9] Morton Grodzins posits the thesis that localization or noncentralization of government in the United States is a consequence of the character of the American party system. He writes:

> American political parties operate to maintain a division of strength between the central government and the geographical (and other) peripheries. This division of strength has many values; not the least of them are the widespread generation of energies and allocation of responsibilities, and the defenses erected against authoritarian rule. The defects of the system include, most importantly, the nation's occasional slowness in responding to national leadership in a period of crisis.... Tightening party control at the top decreases strength at the base.[10]

Grodzins argues that if highly disciplined and programmatic parties were achieved, legislation taking into account the desires of state and local governments and other highly decentralized power groups would be less likely to be adopted. Concurrently, national legislators would be deterred from pushing nonnational interests in their dealings with the national administration. Furthermore, centralized parties would deprive administrative officers of strengths now used to foster state and local powers and would "dampen the process by which individuals and groups, including state and local leaders, take multiple cracks at the national government" in order to promote legislative and administrative actions amenable to them.

William H. Riker places particular emphasis on the structure of the party system as a primary factor in sustaining the federal arrangement. He writes:

> Whatever the general social conditions, if any, that sustain the federal bargain, there is one institutional condition that controls the nature of the bargain in all the instances here examined and in all others with which I am familiar. This is the structure of the party system, which may be regarded as the main variable intervening between the background social conditions and the specific nature of the federal bargain.[11]

If Grodzins and Riker are correct in their assessment of the importance of uncentralized parties to the maintenance of the federal system, recent reforms in methods of selecting delegates to the national presidential nominating conventions may weaken the federal arrangement. Adopted by the Democratic party (and the Republicans to a lesser degree) in 1972, but modified later, they have the effect of strengthening the control of the national organization over state parties to insure the representation of minorities, young people, and women in national conventions. If there is a continued adherence to the reforms, the locus of power in the party would then shift upward, and all along the line individual and organizational accommodation would be required. Local power bases would be eroded. More centralized parties could develop. In 1975, in *Cousins et al. v. Wigoda et al.* the Supreme Court held by an eight-to-one vote that national political party rules prevail over state laws on seating of delegates to national party nominating conventions, thereby giving impetus to this trend. Similar upward shifts of power have been suggested as likely results of changes in the Electoral College system, for example, direct election of the President.

Francis E. Rourke contends that political parties make it difficult to maintain boundaries between national and local affairs because the strategies of political actors and actions on both levels are "indissolubly linked." He points out that success in local politics holds out promise of success nationally and that national reputations can be advantageous in local politics, for both individuals and organizations. Failure also has intergovernmental consequences. Furthermore, action on one level may have intergovernmental ramifications. The example cited by Rourke of a Kennedy appointment indicates this type of interplay.

> President Kennedy's appointment in 1962 of Cleveland Mayor Anthony J. Celebreeze as Secretary of Health, Education, and Welfare was widely interpreted as an adroit maneuver in the politics of federalism, designed to strengthen simultaneously (a) the Democratic Party in Ohio by the honor thus bestowed upon one of its principal leaders; (b) the Kennedy administration in Washington with voters of Italian extraction across the country who were alleged to be dissatisfied with the recognition thus far accorded to them by the administration; and (c) the candidacy of the President's younger brother, Edward Kennedy, in Massachusetts, locked in a primary duel for the Democratic nomination to the United States Senate and anxious to obtain the support of Italian voters in the state.[12]

An interesting intergovernmental consequence of attempts

to regulate party influence in government—the Hatch Act of 1939, prohibiting certain political activities by federal employees —receives scant attention except around the Washington, D.C., area. As a result of its restrictions on employees of the national government being candidates for partisan public office, many important local government and party positions in suburban Maryland and Virginia are opened to women who might otherwise have little chance of election because of sexual discrimination. Some are wives of husbands said to be "hatched" by the federal law.

The influence of parties can be found throughout American intergovernmental relations. They are part of the web binding together the various levels of the American system. They participate in determining the basic sharing of functions among levels of government. They link the values, attitudes, and desires of the numerous segments of society to the governmental system, reflecting them in all their variety and confusion, and help these groups to change or modify government activity. They fracture power, working against its concentration in one place and assuring its retention by many groups in numerous places. Because of their undisciplined condition, they contribute to what Morton Grodzins called the "multiple crack" in the federal system; that is, a situation where individuals and groups attempt to influence public policy at every step of the legislative-administrative process.[13] Sometimes they augment public action, greasing the intergovernmental machinery. At other times they inhibit it, but they almost always mirror prevailing American sentiments which are diverse enough to maintain the federal bargain.

INTEREST GROUPS

Not all the activities mentioned above are the exclusive domain of political parties; many are manifest in interest or "pressure" groups. To accept David Truman's definition, an interest group is "a shared-attitude group that makes certain claims upon other groups in society." When these claims are made upon any institutions of government, it is a political interest group.[14] Interest groups differ from political parties in their aims and in their methods. Their purpose is to influence specific polity rather than to gain control of government; in contrast to parties, they do not try to do this by electing their candidates to office. The interest groups may participate in almost every stage of the election process from selecting the nominee to financing the campaign and getting out the vote, but they do not run candidates in their own name.

Although protected by the First Amendment guarantee of freedom "to petition the Government for a redress of grievances," interest groups predated the Constitution. For example, James Madison, writing as "Publius" in Number Ten of *The Federalist*, a series of essays designed to provoke the ratification of the Constitution in New York State, enveighed against the "mischiefs of faction." By faction he meant a number of citizens united by some common interest adverse to the welfare of the general public. Another example involved others of our forefathers. The Federalists in Pennsylvania were so anxious to see the proposed constitution adopted that they brought before the state legislature the question of calling a ratification convention before the congress submitted the proposed document to the states. Outnumbered, the Anti-Federalists absented themselves from the legislative chamber to thwart the existence of a quorum. Undaunted, the Federalists roused the Anti-Federalists from their taverns, carried them into the chamber, and then sat upon the recalcitrant members until the call for the convention was approved. This is not the usual type of pressure employed, but it indicates a long history of legitimacy for such activities.

Interest groups are a characteristic and important aspect of American politics. They perform the very basic function of translating the values and interests of minority groups of all kinds into demands on the governmental system. That is, they supplement the geographic representation that prevails in American government with functional and minority representation. Doctors can be represented through the activities of the American Medical Association although they are so few in number that they would have little opportunity for representation *as doctors* on a geographic basis. Truck drivers, widely scattered throughout the country, can make their wishes known through the Teamsters Union. Interest groups such as these bring together those with similar interests and articulate their views. They make government aware of groups which might otherwise be overlooked. They may serve as liaison among the three levels of government and expedite transactions. They provide linkage with the political parties and government for many citizens. Interest groups also serve as two-way streets in providing information both to the government about constituent demands and to their own members about the activities of government. Accordingly they stimulate interest and participation in politics and, sometimes, by supplying data about candidates in the information they provide their membership they help them separate the "statesmen" from the "scoundrels" in the political fray. It is impossible to imagine American democracy operating without interest groups.

PRIVATE AND PUBLIC INTEREST GROUPS

For purposes of assessing their impact on intergovernmental relations and its impact on them, interest groups may be divided between those representing the interests of private citizens and those representing governments or government officials, usually referred to as Public Interest Groups (PIGs). The former exist in wide variety and profusion. There are literally thousands, ranging from the National Pin Manufacturers' Association to the National Association of Home Builders, with many organized on economic lines. They cover almost every gamut of human activity from conception (Planned Parenthood) to death (Funeral Directors' Association), from richer (The Mortgage Bankers' Association) to poorer (Welfare Mothers' Association), through sickness (American Hospital Association) and health (American Public Health Association). They may be established primarily for other purposes but engage in lobbying as a facet of their work, or they may make influencing government activity their prime concern. The AFL-CIO is chiefly concerned with labor-management relations, but its political arm exerts great force on public policy at the local, state, and national levels. The League of Women Voters of the United States, on the other hand, exists primarily to promote certain governmental policies and devotes almost all its time to educating and stimulating its members to do this. The programs it advocates are not especially for the benefit of its members but for what it regards as the public interest—such things as strengthening the United Nations, election law reform, and better public school financing —as are the goals of the more recently organized Common Cause. The latter organization and Ralph Nader's Center for Responsive Law serve as public advocates in taking cases to court.

Public interest groups exist in much smaller numbers, but some are of major importance, especially in their effect on intergovernmental relations. Included in this category are such organizations as the National League of Cities, the United States Conference of Mayors, the International City Management Association, the National Association of Counties, the Council of State Governments, the Governors' Conference, the National Association of Regional Councils, the National Conference of State Legislatures, and a large number of functionally-oriented organizations. Although set up as a statutory agency by Congress and not intended to be an interest group, the Advisory Commission on Intergovernmental Relations has a marked intergovernmental impact as it proposes and works for legislation. These groups are comprised for the most part of elected public officials, or their representatives, and when they act it is normally governments pressuring other governments.

Too much can be made, of course, of the public-private dichotomy: private organizations may represent local interests vis-a-vis the state and national governments in much the same way that public interest groups do. Local chambers of commerce, for example, take on an aura of being public rather than business organizations as they lobby for programs and policies that will benefit their local communities. Often public and private groups work hand in hand.

STRATEGIES

Both public and private interest groups employ a wide variety of strategies, too numerous to mention here, depending on the program or policy they are trying to influence. Their activities are prescribed by the prevailing public sentiment about the program or policy and the timing of their demands, the acceptance of the particular groups as a legitimate voice for the interests purportedly represented, their reputations and those of their lobbyists, and the resources they can command in terms of membership, finances, and contacts are also determinative of success. Important, too, are the coalitions they can develop with other organizations concerned with the same subject, as well as the opposition they encounter. To illustrate the points about prevailing public sentiment and timing, at one time legalized abortion had no noticeable organized support; today, it is readily available in some states. Its adoption in certain states and not in others indicates the differing social and political cultures existing among the states. Another example of cultural differences is the several reactions to the Supreme Court ruling on pornography among various communities, reactions that often cluster into regional patterns. The success of environmental groups in combating air and water pollution is evidence of timing as a factor in interest-group success. Certainly both types of pollution have been long with us, but only recently has a combination of events precipitated demands for action.

If each function of government were performed only by a single level of government, the strategies of interest groups would be much simpler. But such a sharing of functions exists in the American system that any one function is likely to involve all levels. Thus, an interest group attempting to insure adequate public support for elementary and secondary education, for example, would have to pressure both the legislative and the executive branches of the national government as well as the state, the local school district, and possibly some other local jurisdiction such as the city or county, responsible for levying taxes for schools. In doing this the group would perform the "honeybee function," that is, provide a channel for information from one level of government to another as well as make an input of information at each level. Conversely, the participation of all levels in an activity means that the interest organization has to be geared to operate on all levels. To obviate this, some groups work to concentrate a function at the national level (or the state level) because they can be more effective. Urban organizations, for example, function more adequately at the national level, while certain business groups as the National Association of Manufacturers or the United States Chamber of Commerce may be able to achieve better results with the states. The federal-type organization of some interest groups often helps their efforts at each level when functions are shared.

It should be emphasized that interest groups do not confine their activities to the executive branch or the legislative branch of government. The ever-increasing number of federal-aid programs adopted during the 1960s made even more urgent efforts to convert the responsible administrative agency to the proper point of view. Administration has become as important as program adoption and when a group cannot change a program, it tries to alter the way it is carried out. If the organization cannot get Congress to adopt a policy an effort is made to "maneuver it through the back door under the guise of interpretation of regulations."[15] Neither are the courts neglected. They have become principal focal points for civil rights and environmental groups and for those attempting to delay government actions.

GOVERNMENTS LOBBYING GOVERNMENTS

Pressure-group actions are usually thought of as efforts of private interests to influence the government, and most lobbying efforts occur in this context. But governments pressure governments; and parts of one level of government attempt to influence other parts of it. Public interest groups serve as important liaison here. This function has been institutionalized by the Bureau of the Budget (now Office of Management and Budget) circulars A-85 and A-90 in pursuance of an executive order. They require that executive agencies, assisted by the Advisory Commission on Intergovernmental Relations (ACIR), consult with the United States Conference of Mayors, the National League of Cities, the Council of State Governments, the National Association of Counties and the National Governors' Conference about all major administrative regulations affecting many national urban programs among the three levels of government. This procedure is not always followed and, often, when it is, it occurs only after the proposed regulations are in final form. Nevertheless, when adhered to, it provides opportunity for access to the decision-making process.

Government lobbying government has been further legitimized by the establishment of the ACIR, a congressionally-created agency in which all levels of government, along with the public, are represented. While the national interest is represented on the ACIR, the agency is an effective spokesman for the states and localities and has pushed hard for such policies as revenue sharing. It also has influence with state legislatures and local governments. Because this organization represents all facets of the federal system, it sometimes has difficulty speaking with one voice.

Additional organizations are equally important in "governments lobbying governments." The Council of State Governments and the Governors' Conference, for instance, advocate the interests of the states. Other important groups are organized on a *functional* rather than a *level* basis. Associations such as the American Public Health Association, the National Association of Superintendents of Schools, or the International Association of Chiefs of Police lobby for policies favorable to health, education, or law enforcement and may in these efforts exert pressures which counteract *level* group activities. That is, central policy body associations, such as the Council of State Governments and the National League of Cities, may find themselves undercut on efforts to coordinate policies of law enforcement, education, and health by the chiefs of police lobbying on law enforcement, by the educational pressures of the school superintendents, and by the health program demands of the public health association. Allied with national and state bureaucracies in their respective fields, these functionally-oriented bodies exert a fractionalizing impact on efforts to present a united front from the general government's viewpoint. The Office of Management and Budget circulars mentioned above provide additional input from the general government groups as opposed to the functional groups.

Also an individual public official such as a mayor, a county executive, or a governor may use the prestige of his office to push the interests of those he represents. It is not unusual to see a governor before a congressional committee supporting legislation that would help the state and, in fact, public interest groups use their members for this purpose.

Government on government lobbying is complicated by a variety of factors. Insofar as pressuring Congress is concerned, it is well to remember that congressional committees are organized along functional lines, state and local governments on geographic ones. There is simply no one place for a state or locality to go to pressure the national government. If the need is in the educational field, a state or locality may have to deal with the Office of Education in the Department of Health, Education, and Welfare, the Committee on Education and Labor in the House of Representatives, and the Committee on Labor and Public Welfare in the Senate, as well as with its own members of Congress. On fiscal matters, the appropriate subcommittees of the Committees on Appropriations also may be involved. The problem for urban interests is even more fractionated because there is no congressional committee possessing exclusive jurisdiction over urban affairs. Housing is handled by the House Committee on Banking and Currency and the Senate Committee on Banking, Housing, and Urban Affairs, highways by the Committees on Public Works in both houses, and health by the Committee on Interstate and Foreign Commerce in the House and the Senate Committee on Labor and Public Welfare. Furthermore, urban interests themselves are far from united, often split between large and small cities, northern and southern localities, and those with varying ideological and occupational predilections.

An interest group's behavior is affected when its membership consists of elected public officials. In the first place, the organization has easier access to those it wishes to see. Furthermore, its legitimacy as a representative of a public interest is assumed, and its activities are likely to have more effect. Policies and goals espoused are more carefully noted because they may be signals as to future political alignments of parties, people, and issues. At the same time, relations with other governments are much more complicated than those of an ordinary clientele group—they may exist at more points in the political system.[16] Furthermore, political rivalries may be highlighted, jealousies provoked, and groups prodded into action because of political competition.

The programs of only a few interest groups include direct positions on federalism. The most prominent of those which do are those designated as review organizations by the previously mentioned Office of Management and Budget (OMB) circulars; namely, the Council of State Governments (COSG), the United States Conference of Mayors (USCM), the National League of Cities (NLC), the National Governors' Conference (NGC), the National Association of Counties (NACO), and the Advisory Commission on Intergovernmental Relations (ACIR). A number of other groups concentrating on particular programs—such as labor, education, conservation, industrial safety, medical care, or welfare organizations—press for national power in their given areas of interest. Perhaps the most interesting division among groups is that between those local-oriented associations pressuring the national government for direct federal aid and those state related groups insisting on maintaining the traditional arrangement of the state as the gate through which federal-local communications, especially funds, pass. Among the groups desiring direct national-local interactions are the USCM, NLC, NARC, the National Housing Conference, the Urban Coalition, the National Association of Home Builders, and the National Association of Housing and Redevelopment Officials. State interests center around COSG, NGC, the National Association of Real Estate Boards, the National Association of Manufacturers, and some bankers' associations including the Mortgage Bankers of America. Some groups object to bypassing state governments, others to large-scale federal spending, and other oppose the banking activities of the national government.[17]

Often what is in the best interest of the governmental interest group conflicts with the advantage of their constituents. This was clearly demonstrated by the intense efforts of national and state legislators to overturn the Supreme Court's legislative apportionment decisions. Suzanne Farkas points up the possible divergence between the interest of the government and the interest of constituents in regard to representation of metropolitan areas. The urban lobbies which represent the elected officials, such as the mayors, work to gain legislative representation and access for municipalities as presently constituted. The question arises as to whether this fragmented individual city approach is consistent with the interest of the citizens of the metropolitan area. Farkas asks, "Is government acting on government limited in its capacity to consider the metropolitan area as an urban interest by virtue of the vested concerns of the intergovernmental lobby?"[18] This question deserves further research.

THE LEGISLATORS: MEMBERS OF CONGRESS, STATE LEGISLATORS, COUNCIL MEMBERS

An important way in which citizens influence government and change policies is through their representatives in local, state, and national legislatures and through their ability to elect public officials on all levels. In fact, local control of higher levels of government results from these elective and representative processes. Control here does not refer to absolute direction of government but to influence at many access points. Since in an overall sense the same citizens make inputs at all levels, they can, through their local representatives, make demands upon state and national governments. Furthermore, they can call upon state and national representatives to act in behalf of local interests. These latter officials are locally oriented by the nature of their constituencies. The local orientation of members of Congress, for example, produces legislation vesting important powers in state and local governments. Grants-in-aid are evidence of this. Rather than national construction of all hospitals, members of Congress provide for the sharing of this activity with states and localities through grants-in-aid. They also funnel local influence into national administration.

LEGISLATORS INTERRELATING

Representatives on all levels interrelate either as individuals or through the legislative bodies of which they are members.

Some of these interactions are formal, sometimes being required for the operation of the American governmental system; others are attempts on their part to respond to public demands. Contacts are often informal as legislators meet in political party, professional, business, or social settings, or through their participation in public interest groups, such as the National Conference of State Legislatures.

Legislators' partisan relations pervade the system as representatives endorse each other's candidacies, cooperate on slates in primary elections, join in campaigns, serve as members of party committees, and attend meetings, rallies, and conventions. State legislators from several states relate as Democrats (or Republicans) as they attend the national nominating conventions, for instance. National, state, and local representatives share the same platform in a campaign to elect party members. These are often the interactions which make the American system, with its federal structure and separation of powers, work. They contribute a unifying force.

Social, business, and professional contacts also provide grease for the governmental machinery. Individuals who are acquainted are likely to perceive each other as more trustworthy, and thus find it is easier to call or write them. The church, the veterans' organization, the chamber of commerce, and the bar association all stimulate interactions for legislators as for others in the intergovernmental system.

Legislators relate to one another in public organizations outside the legislature, such as regional councils, advisory commissions on intergovernmental relations, and multijurisdictional agencies such as metropolitan-area transit commissions. These relations are likely to be more extensive in heavily urbanized areas, but their frequency, tenor, and effect depend on a wide variety of factors influencing intergovernmental relations.

The more formal interactions often required for the operation of government usually involve legislators relating in their institutional settings and as legislators. In the instance of constitutional change, for example, Congress submits proposed amendments to state legislatures for ratification by three-fourths of them before the changes become part of the Constitution. All amendments except the Twenty-first were ratified in this way, which may say as much about America's thirst as about its propensity for a particular ratification process. A state legislature may petition Congress to call a national constitutional convention for consideration of constitutional amendments. Although this procedure has often been attempted, the required two-thirds number of the states has never been achieved. However, it was only one state short on the proposal for an amendment to overturn the Supreme Court's legislative apportionment decision. Congressional consent is needed for the adoption of interstate compacts, which state legislatures must also approve, and for the admission of new states into the Union and the division of existing ones.

Though not required, other formal interactions between legislative bodies take place. State legislatures may adopt resolutions calling on Congress to take a certain action such as ending the Vietnam War. The resolutions are then forwarded to Washington. Locally, the city council or county board makes requests of the state legislature. Resolutions of this type are aimed primarily at bringing public opinion to bear on higher authorities. The locality may operate through its legislative delegation in urging the adoption of special legislation to change a city charter or expand local taxing authority. In some jurisdictions, such as California, considerable antagonism at times exists between local officials and the legislative delegation, resulting in less than cooperative undertakings.

OTHER INTERGOVERNMENTAL INFLUENCES

Legislators affect intergovernmental relations in other ways than by passing laws or by directly influencing each other, and some of these may be very important. National and state lawmakers have an input into the selection of judges whose court decisions may be determinative in intergovernmental relations. The United States Senate approves the nomination of judges for the national judiciary and, in some states, state senators have a similar role. Hearings on these nominations sometimes bring out attitudes of prospective judges on intergovernmental relations. In five states—Connecticut, Rhode Island, South Carolina, Vermont, and Virginia—the legislature has an even more powerful input by selecting the judges.[19]

At all levels there are legislative pressures on the executive and the bureaucrats to take or refrain from taking certain actions that have intergovernmental consequences. Congress may be in a better position than legislatures on any other level to influence executive and bureaucratic actions—principally because of its staffing and its year-round operation—although the personal acquaintanceship factor operates most strongly at the local level.

The separation of powers concept is more jealously guarded at the national level than at any other; nevertheless, Congress is continuously involved in influencing the administration. In addition to the traditional activities of appropriating money to run the government, enacting legislation establishing agencies or programs, exercising oversight of agencies included in a committee's purview, holding hearings at which members of the executive branch testify, overriding presidential vetoes, and approving presidential appointments and treaties, Congress influences the administration in other ways. It conducts the dreaded investigations of administrative activity, such as Watergate, and has the ultimate power to impeach civil officers and to convict them on the charges. Individual members of Congress often intervene directly in the day-to-day operations of the administration as they serve as "ombudsmen" for their constituents. Kenneth E. Gray suggests that such interference "on the behalf of individuals, associations, and state and local governments is a key characteristic of American federalism and an effective mechanism of decentralization in national administration."[20]

INTERGOVERNMENTAL COMMITTEES

Congress recognized the importance of intergovernmental relations by the creation of subcommittees dealing with the subject in both houses. Pursuant to the Legislative Reorganization Act of 1946, both houses established Subcommittees on Intergovernmental Relations of their Committees on Government Operations. In addition to the compilation and dissemination of much research on intergovernmental relations, both subcommittees have sponsored legislation and have been leaders in the resolution of important intergovernmental problems. This does not mean, of course, that members of these committees have the most influence on intergovernmental affairs. Actions of other committees, especially the Ways and Means, Finance, and Appropriations committees, which handle the taxing and spending bills, markedly affect intergovernmental activities.

State legislatures are likely to have committees on local government, by some title or other, that deal with matters affecting the state's subdivisions. Members may also serve on commissions on interstate cooperation established to work for the solution of interstate problems. They promote uniform and reciprocal legislation, interstate compacts, and other arrangements affecting more than one state. In some states, legislative councils serve as commissions on interstate cooperation. It must be noted that state and local legislators are not the principal intergovernmental actors for their jurisdictions. That role belongs to the executive branch. Many legislators engage in very few intergovernmental actions. On the local level, council members rarely are prime movers,[21] although in metropolitan areas many participate in interlocal organizations and devote substantial amounts of time to intergovernmental problems.

EXECUTIVES

The President is the most conspicuous of the formal decision-makers of government and has the most power to affect the federal process. But in the words of W. Brooke Graves,

> ... the orderly development of intergovernmental relations has suffered because so few presidents have given any serious or sustained attention to them, and then usually only in periods of crisis. The rest of the time, vital decisions on many problems affecting intergovernmental relationships have been made with little or no consideration being given to their probable effects on the relations between the Nation and the States.[22]

Different presidents have had different views on relations in the federal system; some have been concerned with maintaining the federal balance, others simply with getting needed functions performed at whatever level. All have been constrained by public opinion, the Congress, and the courts and sometimes by state and local governments in their decision-making.

Crises have produced presidential leadership in intergovernmental matters. President Lincoln consulted with northern governors and kept them informed during the Civil War. President Theodore Roosevelt called together governors in 1908 to stress the need for more intelligent use of natural resources, thereby providing the stimulation for the establishment of the Governors' Conference. Many other presidents have had occasions to exercise national powers in cooperation or conflict with state officials in their role as chief enforcers of national law. President Cleveland sent federal troops into Illinois in 1894 over the protest of the governor when the Pullman strike threatened to interfere with the carrying of the mail. President Harding responded to the request of the governor of West Virginia for federal troops to preserve order during a coal strike in 1921.

More recently, presidential action has involved the protection of individual civil rights as the nation faced the turmoil of integrating schools, public accommodations, and housing. Presidents Eisenhower and Kennedy both had to use force to see that national constitutional provisions and court rulings were upheld. Perhaps the most interesting confrontation occurred in 1957 in Little Rock, Arkansas, when the local school board voted to integrate a high school in compliance with a court order subsequent to *Brown v. Board of Education of Topeka*. Governor Orval Faubus called up the Arkansas National Guard (which is under the control of the state unless called into national service) to prevent integration. President Eisenhower ordered the Army's 101st Airborne Division to Little Rock to enforce the court order and called up the Arkansas National Guard for national service. Guardsmen who one minute were ordered to prevent integration soon found themselves protecting the right of black children to attend a previously white school. President Kennedy resorted to the use of United States marshals to force admission of students to the University of Mississippi and to the University of Alabama. In the latter situation Governor George Wallace "stood in the school house door" to prevent their admission.

Presidential action may be directly focused on intergovernmental relations in non-crisis situations and recent presidents have exerted leadership in this field. President Eisenhower had strong confidence in the states. Three such actions during his administration stand out: (1) creation of the Commission on Intergovernmental Relations (usually referred to as the Kestnbaum commission) which made a two year study (1953-1955) of intergovernmental problems; (2) establishment of the Federal-State Joint Action Committee (1957-1959) composed of governors and top-level national officials whose report called for turning over certain functions to the states; and (3) the creation of the Advisory Commission on Intergovernmental Relations in 1959, the most enduring of these three actions.[23] President Johnson's actions seemed aimed more at cities, as in his administration significant strides were made in direct national-city relations. Also during Johnson's tenure an explosion of grants-in-aid and proposals for revenue sharing were pushed.

The Nixon administration had an almost continuous focus on intergovernmental relations with the "New Federalism" attempting to revitalize state and local governments in a number of moves. Included were the successful adoption of revenue sharing, whereby states and localities share in revenues from federal income taxes, and promotion of various proposals to consolidate former categorical grant programs into special revenue-sharing programs in such fields as law enforcement, education, and urban development. Furthermore, the Nixon administration reorganized and decentralized many national agencies to expedite state and local interactions with them, establishing regional offices for national departments in ten regions of the country.

Presidents probably have been most effective in influencing state and local policies by their personal contacts with governors and mayors. The President of the United States can be a powerful persuader when he seeks to encourage or discourage an action or asks for assistance. He operates from a position of strength—not strength in law, although he has that—but strength from having been elected by the nation as a whole and from the prestige of his office.

PRESIDENTIAL-GUBERNATORIAL RELATIONS

Contacts between the national and state executives are so varied and numerous that it would be impossible to list all of them. The effect they have covers a broad range. It is important to keep in mind that the influence is not a one-way street but travels in both directions. If presidential actions often influence states, so do actions of state governors have an effect on presidential maneuvering. The President seeks the support of governors of his party in furthering his ambition for a second term; and they may want his endorsement or assistance. Presidential cutting back of Health, Education, and Welfare requests for funds for social service grants may seriously hamper the efforts of a governor to balance his state's budget. On the other hand, failure of governors to put the strength of their moral suasion (and sometimes force) behind the effort to protect individual rights, especially those of women, blacks, Indians, and Chicanos, may place the President in a position of having to use national enforcement machinery.

GOVERNORS

Governors are highly political animals. Like others involved in political careers, they have ambitions to move to higher office, such as the presidency, a cabinet post, and the United States Senate, or to make a career of the office they have. The patterns of their political careers are guiding elements to their activities, according to Joseph Schlesinger, who argues that politicians respond to their office ambitions.[24] These ambitions affect not only the governor but those around him as well. They have an impact on the everyday operation of his office, his relations with the public and the press, and his role in intergovernmental affairs, in which he is a central figure. Were it not for the recognition it brings, which might be useful in some other context, what governor would want to devote the time to being chairman of the Governors' Conference, heading an interstate compact, or performing a thousand and one other duties that may not advance the fortunes of his state?

Increasing national financial assistance to states has strengthened the hand of the governor in some respects and weakened it in others. Grants-in-aid place large amounts of money at state disposal, albeit with restrictions; but in spending the money the governor can provide services for his state that are otherwise unavailable, even though they may not be the services the state most desires. A governor looks good cutting ribbons to open interstate highways, even if 90 percent of the money for them comes from national sources. And a plaque bearing his name on a college dormitory, paid for partly by national grants and student rentals, and by only a minimum amount of state funds, is a lasting testimonial to his administration. Revenue sharing enables him to operate with more freedom from the national government in determining state programs, but it also brings the handicap of public expectancy of more than can be delivered. It is also shifting more of the focus of interest groups to the state and local levels. The possibility exists, of course, that revenue sharing may weaken the governor in dealing with the state legislature, just as grants-in-aid weakens his administrative control over agencies receiving national funds and circumscribes his budgetary priorities. In his study of governors Coleman Ransone, Jr. concluded that their control over both policy and management of the agencies administering grants was weakened by grants-in-aid.[25]

Some students of intergovernmental relations point to the increasing importance of the governor as a "federal system official" as the result of a trend in national legislation to designate the governor as chief planning and administrative officer in the state for federal programs. The Omnibus Crime Control and Safe Streets Act, the Comprehensive Health Planning Act, the Economic Opportunity Acts, the Land and

Water Conservation Acts, and the regional development programs such as the Appalachian Regional Commission are examples of this trend.[26] This development has come about partially from the pressure exerted by governors and their organization aimed at strengthening the state's chief administrator and from the experience gained from other programs which undermined general local governments.

Whether or not one agrees that the governors have become "federal system officials," it is apparent that they are increasingly oriented toward Washington, D.C. Their decisions are often conditioned by decisions made at the national level, just as the reverse is true. Governors in their testimony before congressional committees, through personally initiated letters, telephone calls, and visits, and even by their public speeches, writings, and actions, influence the adoption of legislation by Congress. Conversely, they may be requested to comment on guidelines for federal programs, head presidential commissions, or give advice. Excellent indications of the pull toward the national capital are the creation of a staff for the Governors' Conference in Washington, D.C., and the growth of state "Washington Offices" which provide a continuous state presence in the capital.

Legally the governor is charged with certain formal activities affecting relations with other governments. He is a party to rendition of accused criminals from one state to another. He signs legislative enactments which adopt compacts with other states or establish uniform laws. He calls on the President for assistance in quelling domestic disorder when the legislature is not in session. He may appoint or remove some local officials and perform various other activities that are discussed throughout this book.

Most gubernatorial relationships with the individuals in other governmental jurisdictions are informal, however. Unfortunately, little systematic data exist about those actions; but it is apparent from observation that a governor visits with mayors and county officials in his own state, either by appointment, or because they are both present at the same dedication ceremony. He may be invited to attend a White House dinner or reception, to breakfast with his state's congressional delegation when he is in Washington, or he may entertain members of Congress at the governor's mansion when they come home. He meets other governors at interstate conferences and often follows through with personal meetings and telephone conversations. He joins with other governors in the National (and Regional) Governors'

Conference and participates in the Council of State Governments and other national and regional organizations. These and many other types of activities on a person-to-person basis help grease the wheels of the machinery of government.

Governors are divided in their attitudes toward national action, both from governor to governor and, paradoxically, within their own minds. More seem to favor further national activities if the resolutions of the National Governors' Conference are indicative. Deil S. Wright's study shows that there were overwhelmingly more calls for national action than resolutions adopted in opposition to it at such conferences between 1946 and 1969. The number of resolutions favoring state action about equaled those favoring national government activity. Interestingly, the support for more interstate action just about equaled the number opposed to national action.[27]

LOCAL EXECUTIVES

Local executives, like local governments, exist in great variety. The mayor comes most readily to mind, but there are managers, chairpersons of boards of county commissioners (or supervisors), county judges (who are administrative officers), and county executives, to name the most prominent. Their powers vary as widely as their titles and so do other features affecting their offices. It is well to keep in mind that all these officials are elected except the managers who, whether city or county, are chosen by the governing bodies of the units concerned. The elected mayors and county officials have two factors operating in their favor in their intergovernmental relations. First, those elected on a partisan ballot have added access through influence within their political parties. Second, all have the advantage of a popular mandate to represent their constituencies and proven local political support.

Managers also are important in intergovernmental relations. Sometimes they become almost full-time intergovernmental directors as they negotiate for and manage the services provided for their jurisdiction by another governmental unit. Under the "Lakewood Plan" as used in Los Angeles County, in particular, municipalities may contract for almost all their services with the county. The municipal executive then incurs more intergovernmental activities than he would normally have.[28] It is expected that in the future managers' roles as determiners of intergovernmental policies will increase because of: (1) their sustained exposure to problems; (2) their professional training; and (3) because their pivotal position in local administration gives them a generalist approach to local problems. Furthermore, their training and experience contrast favorably with those of elected executives and they experience more direct involvement than academic urban specialists.[29] In fact, managers have been in the forefront in the creation of new regional institutions as it becomes more evident that additional organizational tools are needed to solve problems in metropolitan areas.[30]

Whatever the type of executive that operates in a local jurisdiction, this person is important in intergovernmental relations. Because of size and multiplicity and their legal status in relation to the states, local units are constantly interacting with some other unit of government, either horizontally or vertically. The more urbanized the area, the more frequent this interaction. Although local executives are not the only operators of intergovernmental manipulations, they are the most likely local officials to be involved in any wide range of functions. They are the most visible local public officers and officially represent their jurisdictions in interlocal, state-local, regional, or national organizations. They may serve as representatives to a metropolitan council of governments, to a bicounty transit authority, or on a state advisory commission on intergovernmental relations, for example.

When anyone "speaks" for the locality in intergovernmental relations, it is the executive, by whatever title he may be called. Increasingly, as the states and the national government expand their activities, executives work on routine matters with state and congressional representatives and governors. An important part of the relations of local executives with individuals on other levels comes from the professional and public organizations in which they participate such as the International City Management Association, the National Association of Counties, the National League of Cities, and the United States Conference of Mayors. They also belong to other intergovernmental groups, such as state municipal associations, and are represented on the Advisory Commission on Intergovernmental Relations.

BUREAUCRATS

Sometimes the most unrecognized but undoubtedly the most active individuals in intergovernmental relations are the national, state, and local bureaucrats. Legislatures may adjourn, executives may take vacations, and the courts may stand in recess, but the administrative apparatus of government goes on every day and, often around the clock. Most governmental interactions occur among the people involved in day-by-day public operation—the bureaucrats. They interact in dozens of ways as programs are put into effect, regulations enforced, and the general business of government carried out. Both inside and outside the office, they relate constantly, whether it is through professional organizations such as the American Society for Public Administration (ASPA) or the International Personnel Management Association (IPMA), or because they are next door neighbors in Washington, Omaha, Kansas City, or Los Angeles. The very way bureaucrats get together has an impact on intergovernmental relations.[31] Some associations are weak, others strong. The cross-fertilization which occurs when administrators from various functional areas meet in sessions at an ASPA Conference, for instance, is missing in more specialized sessions of the IPMA. This narrows the input for stimulating intergovernmental action.

Literally millions of people work for the various levels of government, with most of the civilian force working for state and local governments. The Bureau of the Census reports that in 1974 the national government had 2,742,654 full-time equivalent civilian employees as compared to 9,881,000 for states and localities. Of the state and local total, 7,228,000 were local employees. Almost half of the state and local employees were involved in education.[32] These government workers communicate, not only with coworkers in their own offices, but with those in offices in other jurisdictions as well.

The bureaucrats are the people who take most of the actions involved in national-state, interstate, state-local, interlocal, and national-local relations. They inspect, advise, provide information, seek grants, set standards, and authorize actions. They also inspect results, audit accounts, approve or disapprove programs, appoint and remove officials, and perform a multitude of other functions. Consequently, they cooperate, conflict, criticize, applaud, or react in other human ways to what other human beings are doing. They have all the human virtues of honesty, diligence, dependability, and industry reflected in the general population, and they possess the same failings of selfishness, procrastination, deviousness, and pride as the rest of us do.

As a group, bureaucrats are likely to become creatures of habit and their conservatism serves to restrain change. Some research suggests that the attitudes of bureaucrats on intergovernmental relations may be malleable, but that the shifting nature of the variables producing attitude changes may make their identification so difficult that the variable may not be pinpointed until the time for change has passed.[33]

FUNCTIONAL FEDERALISM

National funds with their related conditions and restrictions fertilize the growth of vertical relations among national, state, and local bureaucrats. Professionals involved in health programs, for example, regardless of the governmental level, have a tendency to work together, in what may be regarded as largely self-governing professional guilds, to develop their concept of the role of public health activities. Sometimes this is done in a manner which makes it difficult for elective officials responsible to the public to control these activities. Considerable concern has been expressed over this "functional feudalism" which hampers coordination on any level of government as well as control by elected officials responsible to the public. According to a Senate Sub-Committee analysis, national government administrators are not concerned about the intergovernmental ramifications of the grant-in-aid programs but are more interested in protecting the integrity of the program.[34] Edward Weidner's Minnesota study revealed similar attitudes for state and local officials in that state.[35] Responses to several surveys demonstrate that national grants-in-aid are welcomed by state bureaucrats and that these grants also have lessened control of state administration by the governor and the legislature.[36] Harold Seidman, a long-time administrator in the national Office of Management and Budget, writes:

> Federal "professional" agencies and their State and local counterparts may have their differences, but they are as one when it comes to combating attempts by outsiders to encroach upon their fiefdoms. Outsiders include any lay administrators and competing professions, but the most feared are elected executives charged with representing the broader public interests—the President of the United States, governors, and mayors—and those such as budget officers who assist political executives in a general staff capacity.[37]

Seidman's assessment is confirmed by the survey of national

grant-in-aid administrators. Respondents indicated that elected policy makers were perceived to be obstructionists rather than collaborators in a multi-level program.[38]

INTERGOVERNMENTAL PERSONNEL INFLUENCES

Bureaucrats are influenced in many ways by other levels of government, one of the most important, as far as their own professionalism is concerned, being inputs of higher levels into the personnel practices of lower levels. The national government has made several attempts to upgrade and professionalize state personnel. A 1939 amendment to the Social Security Act required all departments of state government receiving funds under the act to establish merit systems for their employees. Covered employees were principally in public welfare, but other departments—such as health, employment security, and conservation—were later included. Originally supervised by the national agencies concerned with the programs, the limited merit systems eventually were transferred to the jurisdiction of the U.S. Civil Service Commission.

In 1940 Congress moved to curb the flagrant misuse of public jobs for partisan purposes with the enactment of amendments to the Hatch Act which prohibited a variety of partisan actions—such as running for public or party office, campaigning, and soliciting funds on government property—by state and local bureaucrats paid from national funds. The 1974 Federal Election Campaign Act eliminated many Hatch Act restrictions. State and local employees, who previously could not do so, may now serve as party officers, manage campaigns, solicit votes, act as poll watchers, and transport voters to the polls. They are still subject to important prohibitions regarding coercion of fellow employees, on-the-job financial solicitation, use of official authority to influence nominations and elections, and actual candidacy for partisan or elective political office. In certain instances the national government is using its power to set standards of political conduct for state and local employees thus neutralizing some of them politically. This removes them from the executive's control to some extent and makes them less amenable to his leadership.

The growth in national programs administered by the states and localities and the expansion of state and local activities to include functions previously performed privately or not at all (for example, environmental protection, consumer protection, and promotion of foreign trade) aggravate state and local personnel problems. National regulations require the performance of certain activities for which states and localities have experienced some difficulty in securing personnel. An illustration is the large number of national grant-in-aid programs stipulating comprehensive planning. Trained planners do not appear overnight, and many jurisdictions found locating them difficult. The same can be said for grant requirements in mental health, police administration, and other programs. Coupled with the lack of a positive personnel program, this situation produced a woeful shortage of trained personnel in some instances.

In response to state and local government and other pressures, Congress moved to meet the need by enacting the Intergovernmental Personnel Act of 1970 (IPA). This legislation authorized technical assistance to states and localities in training employees. It also attempted to broaden the understanding of intergovernmental problems by bureaucrats on all levels. The act permits, among other things, loan of personnel from one jurisdiction to another. Although the expectation was that most "borrowing" would be from the national bureaucracy by states and localities, and indeed that has been the early experience, considerable expertise exists in the lower levels which may be useful to national agencies as well as to other state and local jurisdictions. Despite the program's promise, it encountered difficulties in its initial stages. An analysis of Florida's IPA administration indicated that several factors operated to prevent the state from taking maximum advantage of the act. The low visability and newness of the program and the limited funding available resulted in few proposals for assistance, at least in the early years. Large metropolitan areas were loath to commit the time required to prepare applications when only small grants would result. Furthermore, the state personnel agency needed considerable financial support to carry out broad basic programs.[39]

State governments attempt to upgrade local personnel by requiring local merit systems in certain functional areas, such as police and fire protection. Some cooperate with their localities in holding joint examinations, exchanging information, and giving technical advice and assistance. IPA has provided some stimuli here as well as to interlocal cooperation.

Collective Employee Action. Bureaucrats, like employees of private enterprises, often join unions or organize into employee associations resembling unions—a development of astonishing increase in recent years. Consequently, they both exert pressure on their employing governments and frequently bargain with them, often with success. Not all bargaining is for wages; other public policies, such as treatment of minorities or the size of teachers' classes, are being influenced in this manner.

Many of these unions and associations are intergovernmental in nature. In these instances, they afford an opportunity for exchange of ideas and assistance as well as providing the potential for a success (or failure) "spillover." This means that if a group in one jurisdiction is successful in obtaining the desired results from its employer (such as higher wages for trash collectors or hospital employees), this success may trigger pressure on other governmental jurisdictions by their employees.

Other intergovernmental implications are important in employee relations. The national government may provide mediation services or conduct organizing elections for unions. And there have been efforts to enact national legislation permitting public employee bargaining on the state and local levels. The state government may be called on for assistance in the event of strike by essential employees such as police officers, firefighters, or hospital employees. All levels are concerned with the effect of policies of employee organizations on minority groups.

JUDGES

The significance of judges in the intergovernmental system is shown throughout this book. The important thing to remember here is that courts are composed of people. Space does not allow detailed consideration of all the factors affecting how these individuals act. However, their judicial decisions and, consequently American intergovernmental relations, are obviously affected by such things as social characteristics, career patterns, tenure considerations, and the appointment (or election) process. For example, social characteristics or ambition might affect a judge's rulings on school busing to achieve racial integration; or the fact that almost all judges have been (and are) men probably slowed women's efforts for equal rights under existing law. An appeal on either of these issues from a state supreme court to the United States Supreme Court may bring into play differing social characteristics as well as contrasting legal interpretations.

The judicial selection process often mobilizes all the different interest groups and political considerations discussed throughout this chapter. Note the very controversial Nixon nominations of Clement Haynesworth and Harold G. Carswell to the Supreme Court. Their earlier positions on integration, among other things, affected the Senate's refusal to consent to their appointments.

The federal system itself reflects some of the individual responses of judges. Contrast Chief Justice John Marshall's ideology of strong national power with that of Chief Justice Roger Taney which was much more state centered. A more contemporary example is the difference between the Court under Chief Justice Earl Warren and the Court under his successor, Chief Justice Warren Burger. The Warren court was much more activist as an intervener, the Burger court less so. In addition, the Burger court abandoned many of the strict "one man, one vote" requirements established by the Warren court for drawing representative legislative district lines and instead permitted variations (up to 16 percent) to meet state and local indigenous requirements.

Tenure on the courts for any length of time may build in a lag between the judges and public opinion as far as values are concerned,[40] a lag which may heighten the tensions of inter-governmental relations. The most notable example of lag occurred in the 1930s when the "nine old men," with an average birth date of 1864, declared unconstitutional significant portions of Franklin Roosevelt's New Deal program. Roosevelt responded with an attempt to "pack" the Court by increasing the number of justices. This failed, but the lag was eventually overcome as sitting judges were gradually replaced as over time they retired or died.

Because of the federal arrangement in the United States there may be a gap between the national judges and state political systems. The values of a majority of the justices in the Brown case on school desegration obviously did not correspond to the values of a majority of the elected southern state and local officials or judges who dominated public policies in that area. Furthermore, because of the operation of the party system, the political structure of Congress, and the method of electing the President, sometimes the judges are the only national decision-makers in a position to assume the initiative on controversial policy issues. Later actions by other agencies may then legitimize the judges' decisions as they did in the national policy of racial integration in education. Equally important in an intergovernmental analysis, is the restructuring of the state and national legislative systems as a result of *Baker* v. *Carr* and subsequent legislative reapportionment decisions. It must be emphasized, however, that the gap also may be in the other direction, as state court judges in some states, such as California, move ahead of national public opinion.

Judges collectively as members of courts have a tremendous impact on American intergovernmental relations: they resolve conflict, they legitimize national actions with which localities disagree, and they disallow local or state actions opposed by national majorities.[41] In their court functions, nonetheless, they rarely meet on an intergovernmental basis. There may be more continuous interaction when the courts perform duties of a more administrative nature. Personnel from the national administrative agencies responsible for administering certain national laws regarding naturalization and guardianship of veterans, for instance, have met with state and local officials in an advisory capacity concerning their duties under the laws. Interactions are present between national judges and local officials on the use of local jails for temporary housing of federal prisoners. State and municipal judges interact with local officials and bureaucrats on juvenile delinquency, mental patient commitments, and probation matters, among others.

As individuals, judges may be members of the American Judicature Society or the American Bar Association and its state and local affiliates, or they may belong to other organizations whose memberships cross jurisdictional boundaries. For the most part, however, the intergovernmental actions of the judiciary are limited to court activities, although some state and local judges may participate in the Judicial Conference of the United States, a national agency to propose rules for the national courts, by staffing study groups. They are doing this, however, as members of a professional organization, such as the American Bar Association, rather than as members of the courts of other jurisdictions.

INTERGOVERNMENTAL DEVELOPMENTS

Possibly the most significant recent development in intergovernmental judicial relations is the growth of cooperative efforts on the national-state levels. The creation of the Federal Judicial Center in 1967,[42] and its state counterpart, the National Center for State Courts Board, stimulated the establishment of state-federal judicial councils in most states where state and national judges in a state meet to work out problems.[43] This provides a formalized vehicle for interaction on a regular basis.

In addition, a number of conferences are held between national and state judges such as the State-Federal Judicial Appellate Conference. Funds from the Law Enforcement Assistance Administration of the national government are used for support in some instances. A whole subsystem of national-state judicial cooperation appears to be developing. It revolves around these organizations and the Judicial Conference of the United States, the Conference of Chief Justices, the American Bar Association, and the American Judicature Society and other groups including the U.S. Department of Justice. The Federal Judicial Center assists state courts by providing research material and advice and by participating in programs when requested. Its Office of Inter-Judicial Affairs maintains liaison with the American Bar Association, the Appellate Judges Conference, the National Conference of State Trial Judges, and the National College of State Trial Judges, among others. The trend is toward greater national-state interaction here.

PEOPLE IN ORGANIZATIONS

The legislators, executives, bureaucrats, and judges who interact in the intergovernmental system are not necessarily protagonists. They often work together to achieve a common goal, and they interrelate in as many ways as opportunity and institutional practice allow. They constantly mingle on an individual basis, and ideas from one level find their way to others.

It should be kept in mind, however, that in politics the people-to-people interactions are normally group processes. Each group has a unique role and function and operates within its own restraints and with its own options, and on all levels groups have similar patterns of activity. Their perceptions of each other are made from the viewpoint of their individual organizations, and these are really perceptions of how other people work.

This is not to say that individual personalities do not affect governmental relations. A particular official's penchant for initiating contacts, for following through on rapprochement by others, for presenting a cordial and inviting front, for assuming a "prima donna" role in relations with others, for furthering personal ambitions, or simply how he feels on a given day may spur or deter interchange of ideas and information. Nevertheless, because this individual is director of a local housing authority, for example, means that regardless of his personal desires, he may have to take initiative, respond cordially, or act firmly to get a job done—a job whose successful completion may determine his reputation or the success of his career. His actions are conditioned considerably by the organization of which he is a part.

It is people who bring about change in American government, who oil the "squeak points," who take the "cracks" out of the system. They do the bargaining and make the adjustments. They initiate, respond, legislate, implement, correct, argue, agree, and require. They also approve, review, sue, prevent, influence, and accommodate. They take these actions in the name of a government or an organization, but it is people doing them just the same.

NOTES

1. *New York Times*, September 1, 1972, p. 28.
2. *Constitution of the State of Ohio*, Art. X, Sec. 1. Joseph F. Zimmerman has an excellent discussion of provisions relating to transfers of functions in "Mutative Federalism: Functional Assignments in Transition," a paper presented at the Institute for Urban Studies, University of Maryland, College Park, March 25, 1976.
3. Kent Jennings and Harmon Zeigler, "The Salience of American State Politics," *American Political Science Review*, Vol. LXIV (June, 1970), p. 525. See particularly: Merle Black, David M. Kovenock, and William C. Reynolds, *Political Attitudes in the Nation and the States* (Chapel Hill: Institute for Social Science Research, University of North Carolina-Chapel Hill) for data from the 1968 Comparative Elections Project; Kent Jennings, "Pre-Adult Orientations to Multiple-Systems of Government," *Midwest Journal of Political Science*, Vol XL, No. 3 (August, 1967), p. 296; and National Assessment of Educational Progress, *Political Knowledge and Attitudes*, Report 03-55-01 (Denver: Education Commission of the States, 1973), pp. 25-26 for attitudes of juveniles; U.S. Senate Committee on Government Operations, Sub-committee on Intergovernmental Relations, *Confidence and Concern: Citizens View American Government* (Washington: Government Printing Office, 1973) for a 1973 Harris survey of citizen knowledge; and Mavis Mann Reeves and Parris N. Glendening, "Areal Federalism and Public Opinion," *Publius: The Journal of Federalism*, Vol. 6, No. 2 (Spring, 1976), pp. 135-167 for a survey of data on citizens' perceptions of government levels. The last named reference cites other more specialized studies relating to this subject.

4. Donald J. Devine, *The Political Culture of the United States* (Boston: Little, Brown and Company, 1972), p. 40.
5. U.S. Senate Committee on Government Operations, Part I, pp. 242, 244, and 256.
6. William Buchanan, "Politics and Federalism: Party or Anti-Party," *The Annals of the American Academy of Political and Social Science*, Vol. 359 (May, 1965), p. 108.
7. Deil S. Wright, *Federal Grants-in-Aid: Perspectives and Alternatives* (Washington: American Enterprise Institute for Public Policy Research, 1968), p. 75, and U.S. House of Representatives, Committee on Government Operations, Subcommittee on Intergovernmental Relations. *Replies by Members of Congress to a Questionnaire on General Revenue Sharing*, 93d Cong., 2d sess., 1974.
8. The superintendent of schools must be a political leader because his tenure of office depends on his ability to get supporters elected to the school board. Furthermore, in many poor counties of Kentucky, for example, the superintendent has the biggest payroll, public or private, in the county and thus has considerable patronage with which to work.
9. See, for instance, Buchanan, pp. 107-115; William H. Riker, *Federalism: Origin, Operation, Significance* (Boston: Little, Brown and Company, 1964); David B. Truman, "Federalism and the Party System," in *Federalism: Mature and Emergent* edited by Arthur W. MacMahon (New York: Russell and Russell, Inc., 1962), pp. 113-136; Morton Grodzins, "American Political System," *Western Political Quarterly*, Vol. 13 (December, 1960); and Richard H. Leach, *American Federalism* (New York: W. W. Norton and Company, 1970).
10. Morton Grodzins, *The American System: A New View of Government in the United States*, edited by Daniel J. Elazar (Chicago: Rand McNally and Company, 1966), p. 288.
11. Riker, p. 136.
12. Francis E. Rourke, "Urbanism and National Party Organizations," *Western Political Quarterly*, Vol. 18 (March, 1965), p. 150.
13. Grodzins, *The American System*, pp. 274-275.
14. David Truman, *The Governmental Process* (New York: Alfred A. Knopf, Inc., 1951), p. 37.
15. Suzanne Farkas, *Urban Lobbying: Mayors in the Federal Arena* (New York: New York University Press, 1971), p. 7.
16. *Ibid.*, pp. 133, 236-237. See also Donald H. Haider, *When Governments Come to Washington: Governors, Mayors, and Intergovernmental Lobbying* (New York: The Free Press, 1974) for a discussion of public-interest groups.
17. Farkas, p. 77n.

18. *Ibid.*, p. 27.
19. Council of State Governments, *State Court Systems* (Lexington, Ky.: The Council, 1970).
20. Kenneth E. Gray, "Congressional Interference in Administration," in *Cooperation and Conflict: Readings in American Federalism*, edited by Daniel J. Elazar, R. Bruce Carroll, E. Lester Levine, and Douglas St. Angelo (Itasca, Ill.: F. E. Peacock Publishers, Inc., 1969), p. 521.
21. Deil S. Wright, "Intergovernmental Relations in Large Council-Manager Cities," *American Politics Quarterly*, Vol. 1 (April, 1973), p. 163.
22. W. Brooke Graves, *American Intergovernmental Relations* (New York: Charles Scribner's Sons, 1964), p. 177.
23. *Ibid.*, p. 178n and chapter XXV.
24. Joseph A. Schlesinger, *Ambition and Politics: Political Careers in the United States* (Chicago: Rand McNally, 1966).
25. Coleman Ransone, Jr., *The Office of Governor in the United States* (University, Alabama: University of Alabama Press, 1956), p. 250.
26. Thad Beyle and J. Oliver Williams, *The American Governor in Behavioral Perspective* (New York: Harper and Row, Publishers, 1972), pp. 3-4, 185.
27. Deil S. Wright, "The States and Intergovernmental Relations," *Publius: The Journal of Federalism*, Vol. 1 (Winter, 1972), p. 43.
28. John C. Bollens and Henry J. Schmandt, *The Metropolis: Its People, Politics and Economic Life*, 3rd edition (New York: Harper and Row, Publishers, 1975), pp. 301-303.
29. Charles T. Henry, "Urban Manager Roles in the '70s," *Public Administration Review*, Vol. 31 (January/February, 1971), p. 22. This issue contains a symposium on the city manager. See also Wright, "Intergovernmental Relations in Large Council-Manager Cities," pp. 151-188.
30. Walter Scheiber, "Regionalism: Its Implications for the Urban Manager," *Public Administration Review*, Vol. 31 (January/February, 1971), p. 43.
31. E. Lester Levine, "Federal Grants-in-Aid: Administration and Politics," in Elazar, Carroll, Levine, and St. Angelo, *Cooperation and Conflict*, p. 180.
32. Bureau of the Census, *Public Employment in 1974* (Washington, D.C.: Government Printing Office, 1974), pp. 1, 7, and 9.
33. Deil S. Wright, "States and Intergovernmental Relations," *Publius*, Vol. 1 (Winter, 1972), p. 40.
34. *The Federal System as Seen by Federal Aid Officials.* A Study Prepared by the Sub-Committee on Intergovernmental Relations of the Committee on Government Operations, U. S. Senate, 89th Congress, December, 1965, p. 22. An earlier Sub-Committee survey,

The Federal System as Seen by State and Local Officials (Washington, D.C.: Government Printing Office, 1963) had such a low response rate as to be statistically unreliable.

35. Edward W. Weidner, Intergovernmental Relations as Seen by Public Officials (Minneapolis: University of Minnesota Press, 1960), pp. 29-30.

36. Wright, Federal Grants-in-Aid, p. 10.

37. Harold Seidman, Politics, Position, and Power (New York: Oxford University Press, 1970), p. 136.

38. The Federal System as Seen by Federal Aid Officials, p. 97.

39. Annie Mary Hartsfield, "Florida's IPA Program: First Two Years," Governmental Research Bulletin (Tallahassee: The Florida State University Institute for Social Research) Vol. X, No. 3, September, 1973. For assignments under the act, see table 4-2 in chap. 4 of this book.

40. See Glendon Schubert, Judicial Policy-Making (Glenview, Ill.: Scott Foresman and Company, 1965), pp. 66-67.

41. Ibid., p. 68. For a discussion of the intergovernmental impact of a dual court system, see John W. Winkel III, "Dimensions of Judicial Federalism," Annals of the American Academy of Political and Social Science, Vol. 416, No. 4 (November, 1974), pp. 67-76.

42. 81 Stat. 664; 28 U.S.C. 620.

43. Alice O'Donnell, Director, Inter-Judicial Affairs and Information Services, Federal Judicial Center, Washington, D. C., telephone conversation, September 14, 1973.

3

National-State Relations: Evolving Federalism

The states and the national government have maneuvered for position and power since the formation of the Union. At one time their relationships were so brittle that they could be shattered by the Civil War. At other times they have been marked by the smooth cohesion of a defense effort. But most of the time they have been somewhere in between. Currently they reflect the pragmatic give-and-take of governments adjusting to an increasingly urbanized and technological society.

Before the adoption of the Constitution, the states and localities performed most functions of government in the United States. The threat of cities as "third partners in the federal system" had not been voiced. One of the major trends since that time has been the increasing activities of the national government—many think at the expense of the states. Why might this be so?

In the first place, under the original allocation of power the colonies had all the power, except what the Continental Congress had assumed, and the states gave up very little authority with the adoption of the Articles of Confederation. There was no way for the national government to go but "up" in the acquisition of power. Second, changes in American society created demands for an increasing role for government on all levels. Population growth and migrations, coupled with general affluence and rising expectations, generated problems such as housing shortages, environmental pollution, civil unrest, colossal traffic jams, and energy shortages. Population mobility, abetted by massive national highway programs, magnified problems.

The constant crises in international affairs in recent decades necessitated the expansion of national activities to provide for the national defense. A consequent development of a goliath military-industrial complex intensified pressure for national action. Domestic crises, such as the great depression of the 1930s and the civil rights revolution of the 1960s, moved the national government into additional fields, some not previously occupied by any government.

The advances in technology and the creation of mammoth industrial systems necessitated more government and government by larger units. Problems such as education and law enforcement are no longer regarded as substantially local. The Sixteenth Amendment, which authorized Congress to levy a national income tax, enriched the national coffers to the extent that former state and local functions could be and are financed from the national treasury in what some regard as a purchase of power. The deluge of grants-in-aid in the 1930s and 1960s augmented a trend toward expansion of national activities that may not be stemmed by the "New Federalism" or the general-revenue sharing legislation of the 1970s.

The very visibility of the national government as contrasted to that of the states, focused demand for action on national agencies, just as increased visibility for the President often strengthened his hand with respect to Congress. National news flooded the television networks and press services, but in some sections of the country it was and is extremely difficult to find out about the activities of the states. Neither the newspapers nor radio or television reported their activities in depth.

States contributed to the deterioration of their public image by their unwillingness to modernize to meet twentieth-century problems, by archaic representation systems, and by the resistance of their citizens to increased taxes to meet public needs, especially of an urban nature. The desire for a scapegoat to bear the burdens of problems derived from massive population growth and shifts, desegregation, and the deterioration of the environment and quality of living found them a ready mark as middlemen between the national government and the cities.

The growth of national power is hardly open to argument; but the loss of state power is subject to debate. Although some commentators and politicians regard the expansion of the national role as being at the expense of the state, the fact is that the states, too, are doing more, spending more, and employing more people, and so are local governments. If the total functions of American government are viewed as fixed, an increase in the portion of one government automatically decreases the shares of the others. If, on the other hand, governmental functions are viewed as undergoing expansion at all levels, this may not necessarily be true. Figure 3-1 illustrates this point by use of the traditional pie.

In the first pie, one sees an *arbitrarily* assumed original division of powers. Pie 2 shows what happens under a concept where the amount of governmental power remains static. As N (national) increases, S (state) and L (local) get smaller. Pie 3 illustrates approximately the same division of powers as Pie 1, but with a bigger pie, which includes part of the area of total activities previously performed by neither the public nor private sector or carried out by the private sector. We believe this is what is happening in the United States: the powers of all governments are increasing. This does not mean that private activities are necessarily on the decrease, but it does mean that the sphere of government in general is larger. The compass or range of human activities has expanded within both the public and private sectors, albeit unevenly, and some functions have contracted. In an era of expansion of governmental activities, abandonment of a public function or activity often goes unnoticed; nevertheless, the contraction of government control, sometimes at judicial instigation, in the area of morals, such as divorce, birth control, and abortion, is impressive.

FIGURE 3-1

CONTRASTING VIEWS OF GROWTH IN GOVERNMENTAL POWERS

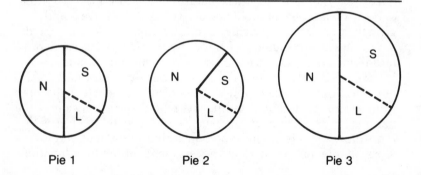

Pie 1   Pie 2   Pie 3

THE FORGING OF FEDERALISM

American political institutions did not spring full blown from the writing of the present United States Constitution, but owe much of their form and substance to the 167 years of the Colonial period. During this time Anglo-Saxon traditions of law were established, recognizing a government of laws and the rights of man, particularly the rights of Englishmen. It was then, too, that local governments were created of necessity, most bearing distinctive hallmarks of their British heritage; and many cities and counties existed before the states. The experiences of the Colonial period produced a host of ideas that shaped the subsequent development of American ideas of government—fear of the executive, trust of the legislature, and judicial supremacy. Basic governmental institutions and relationships have their roots in a time when the colonists not only disagreed with the British Crown, but also were jealous and distrustful of each other. Some wars of the period encouraged temporary cooperation, but at the time of the American Revolution, the colonies were held together by little more than a desire to be independent of British rule. Commenting on the "Forging of Federalism," Carl Swisher wrote:

> A common hate can bring temporary unity and co-operation, but it offers no guarantee of survival of togetherness. Our pattern of federal relations was a product of a forging process; it was to be forged not merely by the traumatic experience of the Revolution but also in the crucible of continuing struggle after the adoption of the Constitution, with the Supreme Court as one of the major instruments of the forging process.[1]

Several attempts at union were made in the period before independence. The New England Confederation (1643-1684) provided a valuable precedent, but eventually it came to naught because of the serious conflicts among its members. Benjamin Franklin presented a plan of union to the Albany Congress in 1754; nine of the colonies met in the Stamp Act Congress in New York in 1765 and declared that act unconstitutional and asked for its repeal. This cooperative effort served as a forerunner of the First Continental Congress which met in 1774. Two years earlier Samuel Adams originated his committees of correspondence among the colonies and within a year a complete network of committees existed. Numerous scholars have pointed out that these groups performed many of the functions of modern political parties. As basic organizers of the rebellion, the

committees exchanged information and ideas, elected the
Continental Congress, and provided an agency through which its
decisions were enforced. In addition, they constituted an
extra-legal system growing up alongside British institutions.

The Continental Congresses, the First in Philadelphia in
1774 and the Second in the same city in 1775, were looked upon
as temporary, having been created to function in emergency
situations. The First arranged to join in a non-importation, non-
exportation, and non-consumption agreement extending
throughout the colonies that was enforced by the committees of
correspondence. The Second assembled shortly after the battle of
Lexington and Concord. It was in itself a revolutionary body,
because the British Ministry had sent letters to the governors to
prevent election of members.

The Declaration of Independence, finally agreed upon in
1776, established a new nation, subject of course to the
successful conclusion of the war. It endowed the colonies with
sovereignty—both internally and externally—so that the future
actions of the Congress had the sanction of law. The Declaration
raised a question which has intergovernmental consequence to
this day. Was one nation created by this declaration, or were
thirteen of them thus established? If only one government were
created then it alone had the authority to declare war, send
ambassadors, and make treaties: if thirteen, then all could. The
wording of the document was ambiguous enough that states'
rights advocates could call attention to one group of selected
phrases and nationalists to others. W. Brooke Graves makes this
comparison:

States' Rights	Nationalists
Emphasized that these United Colonies are and of right ought to be free and independent states. . . . "They have full power to levy war, conclude peace, and contract alliances, establish commerce, and do all other acts and things which independent states may of right do."	Stressed statement that Declaration was made "in the name and by the authority of the good people of these colonies" by "the representatives of the United States of America, in general Congress assembled."[2]

During the time from the Declaration of Independence until
the adoption of the present Constitution in 1789 several significant
events bearing on the forging of federalism occurred: adoption
of the first state constitutions, adoption of the Articles of
Confederation with the expansion of central government

powers under them, attempts at revision of the Articles through the Annapolis Convention, and finally the Constitutional Convention of 1787 in Philadelphia.

RELATIONS UNDER THE ARTICLES OF CONFEDERATION

The United States had no constitution until 1781 when it adopted the Articles of Confederation. In the interim the Continental Congress continued to be the official organ of government. The Articles established a very loose confederation, not a national government at all, because "Each state retained its sovereignty, freedom, and independence, and every power, jurisdiction and right... not... expressly delegated" to the Congress. They made very little change in existing government structure, establishing a unicameral congress as the sole instrument of government. It was quite weak, being elected by the state legislatures annually. Each state sent from two to seven delegates whom it paid and could recall. Voting was by states with each state possessing one vote. Attendance of nine states was required for a quorum and sometimes was difficult to achieve. Congress was given many of the powers the British government exercised during the Colonial period and all of its powers were explicitly stated: none was implied. It could declare war, conclude peace, conduct foreign relations, requisition revenue and soldiers from the states, and build a navy. It could further borrow money, emit bills of credit, settle disputes among the states, establish a postal system, regulate weights and measures, create courts for limited purposes, and appoint committees and officials. Nine states had to concur for the exercise of these powers, except for the authority to amend the Articles, which required unanimous action. At a time such as the present, when government reaches into almost every aspect of daily life, it is difficult to imagine a government operating with such a frugality of institutions and paucity of powers unless one looks at the United Nations or regional councils of government, which in many respects markedly resemble the operation of the United States under the Articles. But at the time of adoption each state regarded itself as sovereign; conflicts and jealousies among the states and fear of a strong central government were such that it is amazing that any agreement was reached at all. Like the U.N. and regional councils, the Congress had no relations with individuals but dealt only with states. It was unable to enforce its requisitions for money. It could ask for anything, but had no way to compel compliance. But it did serve as a transition to a stronger form of government, one not politically acceptable at the time of the adoption of the Articles.

At the time of their inception, the Articles were the kind of arrangement desired by the people, but it became apparent almost immediately that they were not working well. Problems with the currency (resulting from the lack of a uniform medium of exchange with each state circulating its own money), inability of the Congress to enforce its requisitions on the states so it could pay its debts and deal with both British and state violations of the peace treaty, difficulties of negotiating trade agreements with other nations, and trade conflicts among the states all demonstrated the weakness of the central government and brought on demands for change. Eventually the Virginia legislature adopted a resolution calling on the states to send delegates to Annapolis to discuss uniform trade regulations.

The Annapolis Convention was significant for recommending that another convention be held in Philadelphia for the purpose of considering changes in the Articles. Attendance at Annapolis indicated the lack of enthusiasm with which the states regarded efforts to improve their relations. Delegates from five states attended, four other states appointed delegates who failed to appear, and the remaining four states, including Maryland, the host state, took no action.

THE PHILADELPHIA CONVENTION

Attendance was better in Philadelphia in 1787, although some delegates were a long time in arriving, and Rhode Island did not name any representatives. The Convention moved almost immediately from its narrow focus on revision of the Articles to a general consideration of a whole new governmental arrangement. Several plans for the central government were offered at the Convention. The Virginia Plan, presented by Edmund Randolph, expressed the views of large states, which wanted a strong central government and representation in the Congress based on population. It would have established three branches of government with the national legislature having the power "to negative" all state laws not in agreement with the Constitution and with the power to use force, if necessary, against any state failing to fulfill its duty under the document. The central government would have been authorized to admit new states and to guarantee a republican form of government to each state.

The New Jersey Plan, put forward by William Paterson, also would have strengthened the powers of the central government but not so drastically as the Virginia Plan. Supported by the smaller states, it proposed to limit the national government to a unicameral congress whose members were to be elected by state legislatures with each state being granted one representative. The executive under this proposal was to be an executive council chosen by the Congress. The council would select a supreme court which would serve during good behavior. The New Jersey Plan contained some provisions especially important for intergovernmental relations. All acts of Congress and all ratified treaties were to be the supreme law of the land, state laws conflicting with national laws would be forbidden, and the national government would have the power to use force against the states. Alexander Hamilton and Charles Pinckney also presented plans, but neither had much influence on the final outcome. Both would have strengthened the central government. After extensive debate and conflict that almost wrecked the possibility of any agreement, a compromise arrangement, known as the Connecticut Compromise, was adopted which set out the current structure and representation in the Congress and laid the foundation for the present federal system of American government.

The Congress in operation since acceptance of the Articles of Confederation received the proposed Constitution from the Convention in 1787 and soon forwarded copies to the state legislatures. Debates over the advisability of adopting it continued for two years before New York approved the document. The necessary nine states had ratified by June, 1788, but neither New York nor Virginia had acted and, without them, the new government had little chance of success. New York's location split the country, and Virginia was the most populous state. Finally, by November, 1789, both had agreed—the New York Convention by three votes—and the Constitution went into effect. North Carolina and Rhode Island ratified shortly thereafter.

The great debates that occurred over the ratification of the Constitution brought forth a substantial amount of literature, published in pamphlets and in the press. Richard Henry Lee's *Letters from the Federal Farmer to the Republican* were probably the best attack on the new document, the most telling point being its lack of a bill of rights. The defense came from Alexander Hamilton, James Madison, and John Jay using the name of *Publius*. Their *Federalist Papers*, published in New York newspapers, have been cited as classics in political science.[3] As impressive and influential as these papers and other documents were, they probably were not as influential as the support of both Washington and Franklin for ratification.

ENLARGING THE PARTNERSHIP

While the thirteen colonies became the charter members of the Union, the remainder of the states have entered in various ways, all depending on action by Congress, which has the constitutional authority to admit new states. Thirty were admitted from territorial status, the procedures differing slightly between the "incorporated" and "unincorporated" territories. The distinction between them is not sharply defined, but incorporated territories were the ones on which Congress had conferred some powers of local government. Four areas had been parts of existing states and were admitted as states by simple acts of admission: Kentucky and West Virginia were formerly part of Virginia, Maine was fashioned from Massachusetts, and Vermont was once part of New York. Texas, which was an independent entity prior to its annexation, came in under a joint resolution setting out its enabling act. California was an unorganized area subject to the authority of the United States Army.[4]

Congress, as the admitting agency, has authority to impose conditions upon prospective states before their admission; but once the state is in the Union it is equal with all others in the political powers it may exercise. This question arose in *Coyle* v. *Smith*[5] which involved the admission of Oklahoma. The act of Congress under which Oklahoma came into the Union provided that the state capital should be temporarily located at Guthrie and should not be changed before 1913 and that meantime no public money should be appropriated for the erection of capital buildings. The admission ordinance further provided for the irrevocable acceptance of the conditions by the constitutional convention of the state. Such acceptance was made; nevertheless, in 1910 Oklahoma passed an act removing the capital to Oklahoma City and appropriating money for buildings. In the case contesting this action, the U.S. Supreme Court ruled that Oklahoma could not be so restricted and said, "The power is to admit 'new states into this Union.' 'This Union' was and is a union of states equal in power, dignity, and authority, each competent to exert that residuum of sovereignty not delegated to the United States by the Constitution itself." The United States may enter into binding contracts with entering states which do not destroy political equality.

Political as well as legal controversies have occurred over the admission of states, and some territories have had to wait as long as sixty-two years, as in the case of New Mexico. Possibly the greatest controversy centered on the admission of Kansas and Nebraska, which became entangled with the slavery issue.

Controversy also raged around the admission of Hawaii because of racial issues and because of the fear of the Democrats that its admission would add two Republicans to the Senate and a Republican to the House of Representatives. This party controversy was finally compromised when the admission of Alaska and Hawaii were tied together in the belief that the former would be Democratic and the latter Republican. Interestingly, tendencies have been in the opposite direction.

On entering the Union, states begin a permanent relationship. They may not withdraw. This was effectively settled at Appomattox Court House, but in *Texas* v. *White* (1869)[6] the Supreme Court, faced with the question of whether Texas ever had been out of the Union, reenforced the verdict of the Civil War with some ringing rhetoric on the nature of the Union:

> The Union of the states was never a purely artificial and arbitrary relation. It began among the colonies, and grew out of common origin, mutual sympathies, kindred principles, similar interests and geographical relations. It was strengthened by the necessities of the war and received definite form, and character, and sanction from the Articles of Confederation. By these the Union was solemnly declared to be perpetual. And when these Articles were found to be inadequate to the exigencies of the country, the Constitution was ordained to "form a more perfect union." It is difficult to convey the idea of indissoluble unity more clearly than by these words. What can be indissoluble if a perpetual union made more perfect is not? When Texas became one of the United States she entered into an indissoluble relation. All the obligations of perpetual union and all the guarantees of republican government in the Union attached at once to the state. Considered therefore as a transaction under the Constitution, the ordinance of sucession, adopted by the convention and ratified by a majority of the citizens, and all the acts of her legislature intended to give effect to that ordinance were absolutely void. Texas continued to be a state.

REPRESENTATION IN THE
FEDERAL SYSTEM

The debates of the Philadelphia Convention revealed one of the concerns of a federal system—equitable representation. The issue of small-state and large-state representation in Congress was settled by the Connecticut Compromise. Other issues, such as who is eligible to vote for representatives, how representatives are apportioned, and the equitability of the districts from which they are selected, have remained to plague us. The handling of these issues illustrates both the continuing evolution of the American federal system and the pragmatic fashion in which decisions concerning the allocation of functions among levels of government are made.

THE CIVIL RIGHTS REVOLUTION

Most observers think of representation and voting rights in terms of the struggles of recent years to insure franchise of blacks. This is much too narrow a view. Since the earliest colonial days, conflict and controversy have existed over the expansion of the guarantee of voting and representation. Under the Constitution, decisions on who shall vote, the boundaries for representative districts, and the conduct of elections are left largely to the states. Consequently, considerable variation among states developed in these matters. Over the years, with starts and stops, the national government has become increasingly involved in all these areas.

Early suffrage requirements were very restrictive. At the time of the ratification of the Constitution approximately 3 percent of the population was eligible to vote. By the time of the Civil War the nation had moved from a position of limited franchise to the point that practically all free adult males could participate in the selection of public officials for all levels of government. Religious requirements were the first to go, followed by those of property ownership.[7] A few taxpaying provisions remained until the present century and numerous localities still allow only property owners to vote in bond or tax millage referenda. The end of racial and sexual restrictions, however, was not easily achieved.

Black Enfranchisement. The painfully slow extension of the suffrage to blacks in some states has its roots in historical and cultural factors. Nevertheless, the existence of a federal system of government, under which differing public values as to who should vote were allowed full play, undoubtedly retarded full voting equality. Some states demonstrated remarkable ingenuity in circumventing constitutional prohibitions against discrimination.

Following the Civil War, Congress enacted a series of laws, including the submission of the Fifteenth Amendment, to insure the right to vote for all male citizens. They were aimed primarily at the recently freed blacks. As a result of narrow judicial interpretation, congressional amendments to those acts stimulated by post-Civil War presidential politics, and public reactions to the excesses of Reconstruction, these laws passed into gradual impotence, leaving the question of franchise again entirely to the states.

Two-thirds of a century later new activities began in this field. The first major recent changes occurred through interest group and court actions. In the case of *Smith* v. *Allwright* (1944) the very effective "white primary" was outlawed as a violation of the equal protection of the laws clause.[8] Later in response to growing public pressure and after bitter controversy, Congress passed the Civil Rights Act of 1957. Thus, for the first time in almost eighty years, the national government moved to enforce universally the basic voting rights of the Constitution, which some states and localities had consistently abridged. Increasing public concern, stimulated by marches, protests, and television coverage that exposed the discrimination for all to see, brought forth adoption of the Twenty-Fourth Amendment. It outlaws the requirement of a poll or capitation tax payment as a prerequisite for voting in national elections in the handful of states still using it. And with the Civil Rights Act of 1960, 1964, and 1965, the national government moved step-by-step into an area of traditional state operation as it sought to extend further and more aggressively the national protection of voting rights. Of particular importance was the establishment of national "referees" or "examiners" to register citizens in areas where the courts find "patterns or practice" of voting discrimination.

The success of these actions is shown in table 3-1 which depicts a major increase in voter registration for blacks in the affected states during the 1964-72 period. Note in particular the Mississippi figures. Overall in the seven states there was a 21.9 percent increase in black registration and a decline of almost 8 percent in white registrants, a reduction in the point spread between the two races of 29.8. Some of this balancing is, of

TABLE 3-1

**VOTER REGISTRATION BY RACE IN THE SOUTHERN
STATES COVERED BY THE VOTING RIGHTS ACT:
1964 VERSUS 1971-72.**

	1964 Percent registered		1971-72 Percent registered	
	White	Black	White	Black
Alabama	70	23	81	57
Georgia	75	44	71	68
Louisiana	81	32	80	59
Mississippi	70	7	72	62
North Carolina	97	47	62	46
South Carolina	79	39	51	48
Virginia	56	46	61	54
TOTAL—7 states	76	35	68	57

SOURCE: Testimony of J. Stanley Pottinger, Assistant Attorney General,
Civil Rights Division, U.S. Department of Justice. **Hearings before the
Subcommittee on Civil and Constitutional Rights, U.S. House of
Representatives, on Extension of the Voting Rights Act.** Ninety-Fourth
Congress, First Session, March 5, 1975 (Washington: Government Printing
Office, 1975), Serial 1, Part 1, p. 243.)

course, a product of recent black political activism as well as of
legal change. The consequences are a dramatic increase in the
number of blacks elected to public office, particularly on the
local level, and a greater responsiveness to minority pressures by
all representatives.

Other Civil Rights Extensions. Just as the extension of civil
rights to blacks has progressed unevenly with advances and
regressions, and with the national government making inputs at
some times and not at others, so has the affording of equal rights
to other groups. The struggle to gain national recognition of
voting rights for women was a long one. Although women voted
for school board members in Kentucky in the 1850s and Montana
sent Jeanette Rankin to Congress in 1917, the Women's Suffrage
Amendment was not ratified until 1920, fifty years after the
Negro Suffrage Amendment. Once the amendment took effect in

1920, however, women experienced little difficulty exercising their franchise, although they still turn out to vote at a rate slightly less than men. This reluctance to "exercise their flabby franchise" to the same degree as men disappears almost completely among women at the higher educational levels and probably results from a socialization process that places little value on political participation by women. Although no legal impediments exist to full participation in voting or other political activities on the basis of sex, acquisition of equal rights for both men and women in all fields may require national intervention to force compliance with constitutional and statutory rights in much the same manner as that necessitated for blacks.

The suffrage was further expanded in 1971 when the minimum age for voting in national elections was fixed at eighteen by the Twenty-Sixth Amendment. Most states before this amendment's ratification had set the voting age at twenty-one, although Alaska, Georgia, Hawaii, and Kentucky had lower minimum age requirements. Subsequently, the minimum age for voting in state and local elections was fixed by the respective states at eighteen.

Lastly, a series of relatively minor state and local limitations to registration and voting in states and localities have been struck down by the courts or legislated out of existence by the Congress and the state legislatures. Registration and voting regulations are still state functions, but, as two observers have noted, the described changes "have moved the United States far toward a nationally defined electorate."[9]

THE REAPPORTIONMENT REVOLUTION

Apportionment refers to the allocation of legislative seats. In the United States the intention was for the United States House of Representatives and the lower houses of the state legislatures to be based on population, generally meaning nearly equal population. Many states employed modifications of the national representation model and apportioned their senates on factors other than population, normally geographic units such as the county or town. Local representation bodies, when elected by districts that were not area-wide, were almost always required to take population into account.

State legislatures have the responsibility to redraw congressional and state legislative district boundaries to reflect population changes reported in the decennial national census. For many years, rurally-controlled state legislatures often failed to enact representation plans and, when they did, they drew district boundaries in a manner designed to maximize their own rural interests. The great population growth and movement of the early part of the current century further aggravated the situation so that by the 1940s the system of representation had become "locked in" to extreme malapportionment.

As urban voters sought equal representation they found a generally closed system. The malapportioned national and state legislatures would not act, and the more sympathetic executives were powerless to offer relief. The state courts for a variety of political and legal reasons offered only occasional and partial relief, while the national courts passed over the whole controversy as being a "political question" to be settled by the legislative branches of government. In the 1946 case of *Colegrove v. Green*, the Supreme Court declared that the courts "ought not to enter this political thicket."[10]

The Colegrove "political thicket" precedent stood until 1962. In that year the Supreme Court stepped in to alleviate the growing disparities in the representation system. In the case of *Baker v. Carr*[11] the Court pointed out that population of districts from which members of the Tennessee House of Representatives were elected ranged from 42,298 to 2,340 and that counties with less than 40 percent of the state's population could elect more than three-fifths of the members of that chamber. Similar and in many cases more extreme disparities existed in other states. The Court rejected the Colegrove guidelines by noting that "the mere fact that the suit seeks protection of a political right does not mean it presents a political question. Such an objection 'is little more than a play upon words'."[12] With this statement the national courts entered a period of aggressive intervention designed to bring equal representation to the federal system.

One year later, giving evidence that equal standards were to apply throughout the country, the Supreme Court outlawed the "county-unit system" in *Gray v. Sanders*.[13] As employed in Georgia and a half dozen other states, the county-unit system provided that the candidate receiving the highest vote in a county garnered one unit vote. In addition, the person with the most unit votes, regardless of total popular votes, was the victor. The Court refused to accept this "winner take all" approach at the state level.

In 1964, the Supreme Court held in *Reynolds v. Sims*[14] that both houses of the state legislature must be apportioned on the basis of equal population. The long-established "little federal system," in which one house was apportioned on a basis other than population, was no longer acceptable. The very structure of the state legislature, the Court ruled, must be changed. In the same year, the justices declared that congressional districts must be based on equal population. In *Wesberry v. Sanders* the Court declared that Georgia, and by precedent other states, must equalize the population of congressional districts.[15] The "one man, one vote" requirement was extended to general-purpose local governments in the case of *Avery v. Midland County, Texas.*[16]

The complete long-range impact of these actions is still uncertain. Despite predictions to the contrary, major and immediate public policy changes have not resulted from the court actions. Intergovernmentally, two major changes are noticeable. First, urban areas are now fairly represented at all levels of government. In the past much of the bypassing of the states and the development of national-local ties was justified on the basis of control of state assemblies by anti-urban rural legislators. The increased state representation of urban interests has led in many cases to a weakening of Washington-city bonds and to a new vitality and responsiveness of the states. Second, the court decisions clearly established the principle of national judicial review and intervention in the federal system's apportionment schemes, an activity that before 1962 was almost exclusively a function of state legislatures.

GENERAL DISTRIBUTION OF POWERS

Many aspects of the relationship between the states and the national government were left vague in the Constitution and there has been a struggle over them ever since. How intense the struggle is a matter of disagreement, as well as one of fluctuation from time to time and from issue to issue. Certainly the states have not always seen eye to eye on states' rights and even the governor and legislature of the same state often disagree. The separation of powers on the national level provides the potential for conflicting presidential and congressional opinions, especially in periods when the two branches of government are controlled by different parties.

The general distribution of powers is determined by the Constitution, and theoretically should remain the same at all times, subject to amendment. However, the interpretation of that document by the Supreme Court has been so liberal as to allow Congress to change the distribution almost unilaterally, subject always to control by the electorate. Congress has not been reluctant to use its powers, and the role of the national government in providing programs has expanded step by step.

The right of the Court to make intergovernmental determinations by reviewing national and local legislation is based on the supremacy clause in Article VI of the Constitution. The Court clearly established the doctrine in *Marbury v. Madison*[17] in 1803, insofar as acts of Congress are concerned, and in *Fletcher v. Peck*[18] in 1810 as it relates to state legislation. The Court's enunciation of the right of judicial review had some background in the review of the acts of the colonial assemblies by the Crown and in previous action by lower national courts, as well as in congressional authorization for the Supreme Court to review state actions.

DELEGATED POWERS

Essentially what the Constitution does is to grant to the national government certain *delegated* powers and to *reserve* to the states all those powers not granted to the national government, unless their exercise by the states is constitutionally restricted or denied. Among the powers delegated to the national government are those of declaring war, making treaties, coining money, regulating interstate commerce and taxing. Others are establishing rules of naturalization, providing for an army and a navy, establishing post offices and post roads, governing the District of Columbia, providing for courts, and many more. Some of these powers such as that of declaring war and coining money are exclusive with the national government; others such as taxing and building roads are exercised concurrently with the states. Some powers are denied to one and not to the other, while others are denied to both. But this is a gross oversimplification of the framework of federalism as it has developed over the years. Through constitutional amendment, court interpretation, congressional action, and custom and usage the relationship has undergone constant change. Also, this relationship is still in the process of modification, particularly as provisions affecting individual liberties are interpreted so as to expand national powers to protect against state interference with individual rights. Federalism is still being forged.

The delegated powers expanded very little through constitutional amendment because most amendments are restrictive rather than additive. The Sixteenth Amendment has special significance, however. By permitting national taxation of incomes, it provided the financial means for the national government to expand its activities, particularly through grants-in-aid.

The development of the doctrine of implied powers set out by the Supreme Court in *McCulloch* v. *Maryland* (1819)[19] has been especially important in the modification process. In this case permitting the national government to establish a bank under its delegated power to control the currency, the Court extended the national powers. It did so by including all those powers that could be reasonably implied from the delegated powers and stipulating that the national government could use whatever means necessary and proper to put them into effect. Chief Justice Marshall wrote:

> Let the end be legitimate, let it be within the scope of the Constitution, and all means which are appropriate, which are plainly adapted to that end, which are not prohibited, but consist of the letter and the spirit of the Constitution, are constitutional.

Congress has increasingly used its implied powers to expand the activities of the national government. This is especially evident with respect to the commerce clause, the war powers, and the authority to tax and to spend. They are discussed in chapter 4.

STATES RIGHTS AND NATIONAL SUPREMACY

The Tenth Amendment appears to specify explicitly the reserved powers of the states. It provides: "The powers not delegated to the United States by the Constitution, nor prohibited by it to the States, are reserved to the States respectively, or to the people." Despite this straightforward statement of reserved powers, the Supreme Court has declared it not to limit the national power but to reiterate "A truism that all is retained which has not been surrendered."[20] This leaves the states with the residual powers—those that remain after the determination of the scope of national power. The states may exercise some powers concurrently with the national government and undertake some other activities in which the national government has not chosen to engage; but their exercise of these powers are not concurrent in the sense of being equal with those of the national government. They are merely exercisable in activities where the national government could replace state action. In effect, then, the Tenth Amendment can be construed to read: "The powers not delegated *or implied* to the United States by the Constitution, nor prohibited by it to the States, are reserved to the States respectively or to the people." Nevertheless, the Court recently declared in *Fry* v. *United States* (1975) that the Amendment was not without significance. It said: "The Amendment expressly declares the constitutional policy that Congress may not exercise power in a fashion that impairs the States' integrity or their ability to function effectively in a federal system. . . ."

Does the grant of power to the national government withdraw it from the states? There is no general answer to this question. The Court has to act as arbiter in each case in controversy. Under the Constitution states share, in some instances, powers delegated to the Congress. States may, for example, exercise some powers over interstate commerce, and state courts share national power to naturalize aliens. The operation of a post office, on the other hand, is an exclusively national function, as are certain aspects of interstate commerce. Sometimes state statutes prevail in a field of national power until they are superseded by national legislation. Along this line, state laws on bankruptcy were recognized until Congress enacted a national bankruptcy law. Should Congress repeal this legislation, any state laws still on the statute books would be revived.

The supremacy clause of the Constitution makes it clear that in the event of conflict the national government is supreme. In Article VI, Section 2, the Constitution reads:

> This Constitution, and the laws of the United States which shall be made in pursuance thereof, and all treaties made, or which shall be made under the authority of the United States, shall be the supreme law of the land; and the judges of every State shall be bound thereby, anything in the Constitution or laws of any State to the contrary notwithstanding.

Placed in the Constitution because of the fear of excessive state power, this clause contributed to the growth of national power, through both legislation and treaties. By making national laws on a matter within congressional jurisdiction superior to those of the states, it has sometimes operated to push state governments out of fields of activity.

Neither the national government nor the states may push their activities to the extent of destroying the federal system. In

McCulloch v. *Maryland* the Court denied Maryland's right to tax a national bank, indicating that a state may not tax a national instrumentality because the power to tax is the power to destroy. If Maryland could tax the bank a reasonable amount, it could tax it out of existence, reasoned the Court. The state could then tax to excess the mails, customhouses, courts, and other national means employed to carry on activities, thus destroying the national government. The indestructability of the states and of the Union was set out in *Texas* v. *White*. Other constitutional protections also are provided to the states.

GUARANTEES TO THE STATES

The states have certain rights guaranteed by the Constitution. As pointed out earlier, they are admitted on an equal basis with every other state, and this equality is reenforced by a section of the amending clause that prohibits amending the Constitution to deprive a state of its equal representation in the Senate. It is doubtful if there is an unamendable clause in the Constitution, but the question is moot because there has never been a serious move to deny this equality of representation. The territorial integrity of states is also protected, as new states may not be formed out of existing states without the consent of the legislatures of the states concerned. Even the Civil War did not prevent compliance with this restriction when the western counties of Virginia refused to secede from the Union and a new state was formed. West Virginia was admitted as a separate state in 1863, after a legislature, composed of representatives of counties loyal to the Union and recognized by the United States as the reconstructed legislature of Virginia, gave its consent to dissolution of bonds with Virginia.

One of the more important but amorphous guarantees is that of a republican form of government for each state. In a strict classical interpretation, republican government means representative government (as contrasted to direct democracy) and no person has a vested interest in office, that is, by blood or title. Over the years since its early Greco-Roman usage the term has become much less precisely defined. The Constitution does not define it, and the courts have refused to do so, by labeling it as a "political question" to be answered by Congress when it seats representatives of a state.

In an interesting case involving the "Dorr Rebellion" in Rhode Island, the question of whether the state had a republican form of government arose after the President had decided to call out the militia to aid the state in suppressing the insurrection. The Court was faced with a possible constitutional crisis if it then decided that the state government, toward which the rebellion was directed and in support of which the President had acted, was not a republican form of government as guaranteed by the Constitution. The Court adroitly decided that this was not a judicial question but a political one. Chief Justice Taney wrote:

> . . . when the senators and representatives of a State are admitted into the council of the Union, the authority of the government under which they are appointed, as well as its republican character, is recognized by the proper constitutional authority. And its decision is binding on every other department of the government, and could not be questioned in a judicial tribunal.[21]

Thus if Congress seats the representatives of a state, the state is deemed to have a republican form of government. The Court again refused to rule on the question of a republican form of government in a case challenging Oregon's mixture of direct citizen participation through the initiative and referendum and legislative representation. The question was to be answered by the Congress when it seated the representatives of the state.[22]

The Second Amendment protects the right of states to maintain a militia for use within their boundaries, and for many years some states refused to allow their militias to be used outside the state. Today the state militia is known as the National Guard, and the national government pays for much of its support and determines minimum requirements. Nevertheless the militia remains under the command of the governor, unless called into the national service by the President. Even though the states have National Guard units, they may receive help from national military forces in the event of an invasion or a domestic uprising. The guarantee of protection against foreign invasion indicates the distrust by the original states of the new national government, as it is difficult to imagine how a state could be invaded without a simultaneous invasion of the United States. This protection, as well as assistance in putting down domestic violence, is at the discretion of the President as commander in chief of the armed forces acting under congressional delegation of authority; and he may or may not send troops on the request of a state legislature or governor. He also has authority to send national troops into a state to protect national property or activities or to enforce an order of the national courts, even over the protest of a governor. Two instances of such occurrences were in the Pullman strike in Chicago in 1894 and in the school desegregation conflict in Little Rock, Arkansas, in 1957.

Because of the controversies involving trade at the time of its adoption, the Constitution guarantees that the ports of a state shall not be the subject of discrimination. This has been interpreted to mean that tariff levies shall be uniform throughout the nation, and the vessels of one state shall not be required to enter, clear, or pay duty in another. These were common practices in the early period of the Republic and contributed to the abandonment of the Articles of Confederation.

The Eleventh Amendment, by removing from the jurisdiction of the national courts cases brought against a state by citizens of another state, guarantees that a state may not be sued by a private citizen in these courts. This amendment followed the outcry resulting from the early Supreme Court decision in *Chisholm v. Georgia* (1793)[23] in which a decision against the state was rendered. The amendment may protect the state against suits by private citizens entirely since the only place left to sue would be in the courts of that state. If the state constitution or legislature does not extend the jurisdiction of the state courts to such cases, the only remedy is legislative action. State immunity from suit by private citizens in the national courts is not absolute. According to the ruling in *Fitzpatrick et al v. Bitzer, Chairman, State Employees Retirement Commission* (1976), national courts may entertain otherwise impermissible suits by private citizens against states. This is done in the context of their being the "appropriate means" selected by Congress for the enforcement of certain other constitutional provisions, such as the Fourteenth Amendment provision for due process.

CONSTITUTIONAL LIMITATIONS ON THE STATES

The most effective limitations on the activities of the states are their own inabilities to act, for one reason or another, and the exercise of authority by Congress which sometimes displaces state action. The Constitution imposes effective limitations, nonetheless, some designed to strengthen the hand of the national government against the state and some to protect individual liberties. Both types have served to deter state action and have occasionally forced unwanted activities on the state. Restraints designed to fortify the national government involve finance and foreign relations.

National control of the currency is protected by prohibitions against states coining money, emitting bills of credit, or making anything but gold or silver coin legal tender in payment of debt. Neither may then levy duties on tonnage, nor impose any duties on imports or exports, except what may be necessary for executing inspection laws, a matter subject to congressional control.

To insure national dominance over foreign relations and war making, states are forbidden to enter into any treaty, alliance, or confederation, or grant letters of marque or reprisal. They may not keep troops of war in peacetime (except a militia) or engage in war unless in such actual danger of invasion as will admit no delay. Compacts with a foreign power require congressional consent. Despite these restrictions, activities of state governments directly influence foreign relations, sometimes to the chagrin and embarrassment of the United States. Refusal of some states to pay off bonds sold to finance internal improvements following the War of 1812 and loans for reconstruction after the Civil War caused international controversy until 1934 when the Principality of Monaco brought suit against Mississippi for payment. The Supreme Court ruled that it had no jurisdiction over cases against a state without that state's permission.[24]

More troublesome instances have occurred. One took place in Louisiana in 1891 when state authorities refused to take action when several Italian nationals were lynched. A second transpired in California in 1906 when Japanese nationals were segregated in schools despite treaty obligations of the United States and Japan. A third developed in 1935 when Americans hauled down a Nazi flag from a German ship and then the local magistrate dismissed charges against five of them with language offensive to the Nazi regime. Certainly state failures to afford full civil liberties to blacks, some of which have inadvertently been applied to diplomats and citizens of African and South Asian nations, made international cooperation more difficult for the national government and adversely affected the image of the United States in large parts of the world.

Other restraints on the states deal with the protection of individual rights. A few of these limitations, such as the prohibition against enacting ex post facto laws and bills of attainder and impairing the obligation of contract, appear in the original Constitution; others have been added by amendment. The Bill of Rights (first eight amendments), proposed by the First Congress, was so worded as to restrict the Congress and not the states, but successive court interpretations through the years have applied most of the bill of rights to the states. In addition, the Civil War amendments impose important restraints. The Thirteenth prohibits slavery and the Fifteenth prohibits the states or the national government from denying the vote to any citizen on account of race, color, or previous condition of servitude. The Nineteenth Amendment prohibits denial of the right to vote because of sex, the Twenty-Fourth outlaws the poll tax as a prerequisite for voting in national elections, and the Twenty-Sixth establishes a uniform voting age of eighteen for national elections.

Important as these amendments are, they have not involved nearly so much litigation as the Fourteenth Amendment. It defines citizenship to include all persons born or naturalized in the United States and subject to the jurisdiction thereof. It further prohibits the states from making or enforcing any law which abridges the privileges or immunities of the citizens of the United States, or which denies any person of life, liberty, or property without due process of law, or of the equal protection of the laws. The due process and the equal protection clauses have served as substantial restraints on the states.[25] The former is the umbrella under which most of the Bill of Rights has been applied to the states by the courts. The latter has been the basis of the school desegregation, busing of students to achieve racially-balanced schools, reapportionment, and voting rights decisions. All these have constrained the freedom of the states to run their schools as they please or to manage elections in whatever way they see fit.

OTHER STATE LIMITATIONS

Too much emphasis can be placed on constitutional restrictions and court rulings in national-state relations. Other very real limitations operate on the states at the same time. These constraints rest in a political culture varying from state to state and often within a state and constricting states in their ability to act in concert even though certain general beliefs seem to pre-vail throughout the country.[26] Even when states agree, they sometimes have difficulties making their voices heard, because no one can speak for all of them. The various public interest organizations, such as the Council of State Governments and the National Governors' Conference, attempt to do this although it can hardly be on an everyday, sustained basis to the same extent that the President speaks for the national government. When state delegations in Congress try to voice the views of their states, they are often divided by party, sectional, or economic interests. The recent establishment of a Washington office for the Governors' Conference has increased the state presence in the capital as has the growth of individual state offices in Washington.

States lack the visibility of the national government in the news media, and often when the spotlight is focused on them it is for their failures rather than their successes. This lack of visibility is evident in a nationwide survey of how up-to-date people perceive themselves to be about what is going on in national, state, and local governments. Table 3-2 summarizes this survey, which was conducted under the auspices of a Senate Subcommittee.

State constitutions are often outmoded, with about one-third having been adopted more than a hundred years ago. Organizationally states are not equipped to act with speed or often with deliberation. Until the late 1960s, many state legislatures were malapportioned. Only recently has a movement developed toward annual legislative sessions. Even so, most legislatures are in session only for short periods and not, like Congress, for most

TABLE 3-2
HOW PEOPLE RATE THEMSELVES ON HOW UP TO DATE THEY ARE ON WHAT IS GOING ON IN GOVERNMENT, BY LEVEL OF GOVERNMENT

Question: How would you rate yourself on how up to date you are on what is going on in the federal government in Washington?
. . . on what is going on in state government in your state capitol? . . . on what is going on in your local government?

	Excellent	Pretty good	Only fair	Poor	Positive	Negative
Knowledge of national government	6%	34%	42%	18%	40%	60%
Knowledge of state government	3	24	49	24	27	73
Knowledge of local government	8	35	38	19	43	57

SOURCE: Adapted from U.S. Senate, Committee on Government Operations, Subcommittee on Intergovernmental Relations, **Confidence and Concern: Citizens View American Government. A Survey of Public Attitude** (Washington, D.C.: Government Printing Office, 1973), part 2, pp. 451-455. Survey conducted by Louis Harris and Associates.

of the year. Sometimes their actions are subject to the initiative or referendum and, when these are invoked, the people frequently take advantage of the only chance they get to vote against more government and higher taxes. Catastrophic events may dissipate state resources and force them to rely on national munificence.

Some state inability to act results from past patterns and "sunk" costs—or money already invested—in activities previously begun. Another factor is a shortage of funds, partially as a result of the national government drawing off large portions of potential tax resources through the income tax and partially from increased demands for more and better services by larger populations. State citizens often are unwilling to impose any more taxes on themselves. Caught in a vise between local cries for assistance and national prodding to administer more and more programs under the grant-in-aid system, the states in the past have often seemed unable to move off dead center and act to solve the burgeoning problems that faced them. Many are now moving to put their houses in order.[27]

CHANGING PATTERNS

Meanwhile groups frustrated by the lethargy of decision makers on the state and local levels look to Congress to rectify inequalities in various fields and to move into new areas needing attention. That branch of government accepts the option provided by the Supreme Court's doctrine of implied powers. According to one student of federalism, Congress can unilaterally change the distribution of powers "within the very broad limits of what the court will accept as appropriate means to enumerated ends."[28] The net result is to permit one level of government to alter the distribution of functions of government between the levels, constitutional provisions notwithstanding. What this means is that there is not a permanent constitutional relationship between the national government and the states. Pragmatic federalism, adjusted to meet the needs as seen by national representatives, is the result.

The intrusion of the national government into fields previously occupied by the states alone does not mean that it has moved into every field. The licensing of professions and domestic relations are fields in which the states operate exclusively. Moreover, education, law enforcement, and other general uses of the police power are still primarily state concerns, although shared with the national government. The primary retention of these areas may be based more on the national government not choosing to act than its legal inability to do so. Indeed, such functions may not lend themselves readily to centralized administration, even if it were so desired.

Large areas of shared activities exist in fields that once were the exclusive province of the states. Sharing meets with public approval as expressed in the Senate Subcommittee survey. The public and its leaders clearly approved participation by more than one government in some activities, while at the same time recognizing separate functions of each governmental level.[29]

OBLIGATIONS OF THE STATES

Without the states, the Union could not operate; and, if they did not exist, some other subdivisions would have to be created on either political or administrative lines. The Constitution places certain responsibilities upon the states. They are required to elect representatives and senators to the Congress, to name electors to choose the President and Vice President of the United States, and to consider amendments to the Constitution. Congress may increase these obligations as long as it does not require states to act outside their field of authority. Congress has not been reluctant to take advantage of this possibility, and often state and local officials are used to enforce national laws. The states have taken on an increased role in national security, for example, both in providing National Guard units for service in foreign military engagements since World War I and in training Reserve Officers' Training Corps students at land grant colleges. The military draft, until its abolition, was enforced to a great extent through state officers.

In less dramatic areas, too, state officials have enforced national laws. In banking, civil rights enforcement, environmental protection and intergovernmental personnel programs, to mention only a few, substantial dependence has been placed on the states. Increasingly the national government is relying on the states for the administration of programs essentially national in character.

EVOLVING FEDERALISM

The main theme which is obvious from this historical overview of the federal system is that both the constitutional arrangements and the patterns of intergovernmental relations are constantly evolving. In a period of two hundred years, this country went from a state-centered to a national-centered federal system that evinces concern for the states. The change in the balance did not occur in a revolutionary manner or in one comprehensive sweep. The passage was incremental and, with one major exception, relatively conflict free. At no time was there a crisis that forced a total reforging of the system. The closest the nation came to catastrophic change was during the Civil War and the Great Depression. In the former case, observers have argued that the federal system did not change radically, although this is a matter of contention. In the latter, the perception of the role of government was the main alteration. This, in turn, produced a series of pragmatic adjustments rather than a major alteration in the system itself. For example, many New Deal programs were financed by the national government and administered by the states and localities.

The next chapter discusses the processes of change and some of the theoretical-philosophical environments in which the changes that have occurred take place. It stresses the same theme set out here—American federalism and intergovernmental relations are almost constantly in a state of change producing pragmatic adjustments to meet new demands.

NOTES

1. Carl Swisher, "The Supreme Court and the Forging of Federalism, 1789-1864," *Nebraska Law Review*, December, 1960, p. 4.
2. Adapted from W. Brooke Graves, *American Intergovernmental Relations* (New York: Charles Scribner's Sons, 1964), p. 51. This section draws heavily from Graves.
3. See, for example, Charles Beard and Mary Beard, *A Basic History of the United States* (New York: New Home Library, 1944), p. 136.
4. This account follows Graves, pp. 94-95.
5. 221 U.S. 559, 55 L.Ed., 858 (1911).
6. 7 Wall. 700.
7. For a detailed account of these changes, see Chilton Williamson, *American Suffrage from Property to Democracy, 1760-1860* (Princeton: Princeton University Press, 1960).
8. 321 U.S. 649. See also U.S. v. Classic, 313 U.S. 229.
9. Marian D. Irish and James W. Prothro, *The Politics of American Democracy*, 5th ed. (Englewood Cliffs, N.J.: Prentice-Hall, Inc., 1971), p. 308.

10. 328 U.S. 549. The decision was not based solely on the "political thicket" issue. In the several opinions written for the case, reference was also made to lack of jurisdiction, standing to sue, inability to offer remedy, and the delicacy of national-state relations. The "political question" position, however, was picked up by national and state courts as the precedent to be followed in their future deliberations.

11. 369 U.S. 186 (1962).

12. *Ibid.*

13. 372 U.S. 368 (1963).

14. 377 U.S. 533 (1964).

15. 376 U.S. 1 (1964).

16. 390 U.S. 474 (1964).

17. 1 Cranch 137 (1803).

18. 6 Cranch 87 (1810).

19. 4 Wheat 316 (1819).

20. U.S. v. Darby Lumber Company, 312 U.S. 100 (1941).

21. Luther v. Borden, 7 How. 1, 41, 12 L. Ed. 581 (1849).

22. Pacific States Telegraph and Telephone Company v. Oregon, 223 U.S. 118 (1912).

23. 2 Dall. 419 (1793).

24. Monaco v. Mississippi, 29 U.S. 313 (1934). See W. Brooke Graves, *American State Government* (Lexington, Mass.: D.C. Heath and Company, 1953), pp. 38-41, for elaboration of the topic of states in foreign relations.

25. Historically the Fourteenth Amendment's role has been equally if not more important in the economic sphere in preventing populist attempts to control the implications of the Industrial Revolution at the state level. Thus our economic and industrial systems were maintained as *national* systems.

26. See Daniel J. Elazar, *American Federalism: A View from the States* (New York: Thomas Y. Crowell Co., 1966) for a discussion of different state cultural patterns and Donald J. Devine, *The Political Culture of the United States* (Boston: Little, Brown and Co., 1972) for a discussion of belief systems.

27. Ira Sharkansky, *The Maligned States* (New York: McGraw-Hill Book Co., 1972, and Terry Sanford, *Storm Over the States* (New York: McGraw-Hill Book Co., 1967) are strong defenders of the states.

28. Michael D. Reagan, *The New Federalism* (New York: Oxford University Press, 1972), p. 10.

29. A differently worded question in the same survey, centering more on the question of trust and including the private sector, also indicates substantial approval of sharing, but shows that the public does not necessarily *trust* the same level to perform a function that

it thinks *should* handle it. For example, in table 1-2, in response to a question on which level *should* handle drug abuse problems, 55 percent selected the national government, 43 percent the states, 38 percent local governments. (Multiple responses were possible.) Comparative figures for the "trust" question, "Who would you *trust* to do something about the problem?" were 26 percent national, 14 percent state, and 46 percent local, the remainder divided between the private sector and "no answer/no response." This difference could be explained by the wording of the question or by the timing of the survey—raising the "trust" question during the Watergate controversy. For the trust survey see U.S. Senate Committee on Government Operations, Subcommittee on Intergovernmental Relations, *Confidence and Concern: Citizens View American Government* (Washington, D.C.: Government Printing Office, 1973), Part I, p. 298.

4

National-State Relations: Change and Accommodation

Since the beginning of the Republic, relationships between the central government and the states have constantly undergone change and adjustments as Americans attempted to solve their problems and achieve their potential. American history reflects the disagreements that have occurred over the proper role for each. The starts and stops and shifting patterns can be seen in executive actions, judicial decisions, legislative enactments and, above all, in the administrative changes which have taken place over the years. What has emerged is a federal system which would be hardly recognizable by its creators—a system still changing and adjusting as governments on all levels are forced to accommodate to meet demands.

EXPANDING NATIONAL ROLE

No development in American government has been more marked or has produced more telling consequences than the expanding role of the national government. This growth has been fed by more sophisticated technology that increased the geographical area of problems at the same time that it improved the means of dealing with them. The explosion in communications technology, to the point where anyone anywhere can view the same telecast or hear the same broadcast simultaneously (and from the viewpoint of the same broadcaster), affected in a homogenizing way the attitudes of the American public. Constant crises occurred on either the international or economic front. Several wars and increased international responsibilities expanded national activities and powers enormously. Sky-rocketing population growth created at once new problems and new demands on government. The nation became increasingly accustomed to a national government which promised to respond when other governments did not. All these develop-ments contributed to the reversal of the situation existing at the outset of the Republic and substituted for constitutional federalism a pragmatic federalism which adjusts anew for each problem, particularly in an administrative sense.

The national government moved into new fields, not in a conscious effort to increase its power at state expense, but as a consequence of public demands. William Anderson pointed to a little realized fact when he wrote in 1960:

> Here is no power assault upon the states by the national government, but instead the actions of numerous individual candidates for Congress and members of Congress trying to meet the demands of their constituents in the only way they can, by promising to work for national action and national aid—for they obviously cannot promise action by the state governments.[1]

STATE REACTION TO NATIONAL GROWTH

Growing national power does not always produce an adverse reaction from the states. A substantial portion of the national power came from the expanded use of grants-in-aid, which are welcomed and even sought much of the time. The picture is mixed. Just as the President, the Congress, and the national courts seldom regard national-state relations in an identical light, so is there a mixed reaction from governors and legislatures. National money is more welcome than national interference with the ways states do things. Efforts to enforce voting rights, desegregation, and busing provisions are often met with cries of protest from some state officials. And when grants-in-aid are withheld to force compliance with national standards, the furor increases.

CHANGES IN ORGANIZATION AND POLICIES

States responded to the growth of national activity and especially to the lure of the fisc (money) by gearing their governmental policies and machinery to maximize their oppor-tunities. Legislatures passed enabling statutes permitting them to take advantage of national assistance and shifted appropriations and policy emphasis to programs receiving national financial support. Recent administrative reorganizations demonstrate a tendency to establish state structures that correspond to the national departments. For example, several states have replaced highway departments with departments of transportation which handle varied transportation programs and resemble the national model. In addition, there has been a proliferation of planning and substate regional organizations encouraged by national grants.

State responses to a growing national role also have included increases in their efforts to influence the national government through lobbying. Part of this effort has been channeled through the Council of State Governments, in which they all participate, and other public interest groups. Another facet of increased lobbying has been the establishment and growth of state liaison offices in Washington.

STATE WASHINGTON OFFICES[2]

Twenty-three states now maintain liaison offices in Washington. They exist for states in the immediate proximity of the national capitol as well as for more distant states, and are most likely to service the more populous states. Tenure for these establishments is somewhat erratic, and some states have created and later abolished them. Usually a Washington-based extension of the governor's office, their effectiveness depends largely on his support.

The Washington offices provide a wide range of services to their states and often to localities within them as well. Among their more important activities are: (1) the collection and distribution of a variety of data to their states, including proposed legislation, regulations, and government actions; (2) provisions of communication and coordination services facilitating the exchange of views between the state and national levels; (3) arrangement of appointments for officials, organizations, and groups within the state with national personnel; (4) service as spokesmen for state interests with congressional staff or executive agency staff; (5) promotion of tourism in the home state through the distribution of brochures and other information; (6) encouragement to out-of-state businesses to locate in the state through provision of information; and (7) arrangement of travel, dining, theater, and lodging reservations for officials journeying to Washington. Not all offices perform all these services.

How much a state benefits from the establishment of a liaison office in Washington remains to be determined. Research indicates that there is little relationship between whether a state operates such an office and its success in influencing national policy. Furthermore, states with these agencies are not among the most successful in receiving national financial assistance. No causal effect should be inferred, however. It may be that the low fiscal success results from the less favored states creating the offices for that reason, or it may be a matter of size, industrialization, or other factors. The offices seem to facilitate intergovernmental relations. For example, Washington offices were in a position to alert their respective states when the Office of Management and Budget decided that private contributions for social services would not be matched by national grants. Furthermore, they help to provide a state counterbalance to local demands on Washington which have been growing in intensity in recent years. The Washington offices work closely with the National Governors' Conference.

THE COURTS AS CHANGE AGENTS

Courts on both the state and national levels have played a major part in shaping the federal system. More than any other institution they have given thought and enunciated theories about the relationships of the federal parts. Since cases that ultimately end in the United States Supreme Court can begin in either the state or national courts, both share in the initial stages of the court actions.

The activities of the Supreme Court have been particularly important in the evolution of the federal system. Prior to 1937, the Court showed little reluctance to strike down both national and state actions in the sphere of social regulation. This was especially true of the fifty years bracketing 1900, a period of great social experimentation by the states. It can be argued that this led to a shift in demands for action—a shift which concentrated pressures at the national level rather than on the states and which led to a later willingness (after 1937) to allow both national and state actions in the social sphere. Nevertheless, despite the circuitous path taken by the Court, the end reached to date is an increasingly strong national role. Many years ago Professor Oliver P. Field commented in the following vein:

> The Supreme Court of the United States has been as impartial an umpire in national-state disputes as one of the members of two opposing teams could be expected to be. This is not to impugn the wisdom or the fairness of the Supreme Court, but it is to say that the Supreme Court has been partial to the national government . . . . The States, as members of the federal system have had to play against the umpire as well as against the national government itself.
>
> * * *
>
> This increase in Federal power and this place of dominance of the national government in the Federal system, has been aided by the Supreme Court. For the time being, such changes do not necessarily mean that the states lose power, although they have already lost position, so far as the Federal system is concerned.[3]

STATE LIMITATIONS: NATIONAL EXPANSION

Once the Supreme Court established the doctrine of judicial review of state laws and court decisions involving the Constitution, it has, with starts and stops and varying rates of speed, proceeded to limit the states in some fields through interpreting certain constitutional clauses so as to make the national jurisdiction exclusive. At the same time it has broadened the authority of the central government in activities traditionally performed by the states. The Marshall Court's sweeping interpretation began the development of federalism toward its present position, where it is largely up to Congress to determine which powers will be exercised by Washington. The Jeffersonians and Jacksonians advanced the idea of an inherent state right to control certain local matters through setting up a reservation of powers for the states in the Tenth Amendment. The Jacksonian Court developed the concept of "police power" which the states could use to buttress their positions to regulate matters particularly local. There being no basis for interpretation of what was "intrinsically local," the Court was free to allow national power or to strike it down as it saw fit. This was the prevailing attitude from the third quarter of the last century until 1937.[4] During the 1930s, a tremendous fight over the Supreme Court occurred, largely from the lag between the Court's thinking and that of the public. Franklin Roosevelt's effort to pack the court by enlarging it failed; but the same result was eventually achieved by changes in court personnel over time.

The justices since that period have reverted to the expansionist, interventionist, activist decisions of the Federalist period. This was especially true of the Warren Court during the 1950s and 1960s, with its decisions broadening the base of civil rights and representation with a consequent diminution of state powers to interfere with them. President Richard Nixon announced his intention to return the Court to a stricter interpretation of the Constitution, and his appointments underlined this resolve. In one important case, at least, the Berger Court struck a blow for the states. The 1976 decision in *National League of Cities* v. *Usury* declared as a violation of states' rights Congress's exercise of its commerce powers to set wage and hour standards for state and local employees. In the same week, however, the Court held in *Elrod, Sheriff v. Burns* that state and local employees who did not make policy could not be discharged for partisan reasons when the opposition party came to power, thus outlawing a practice widely followed since the Jackson Administration. In contrast to the National League of Cities case, *Elrod* placed another restriction on state and local control of their personnel. The full impact of the Nixon appointees on the Court is yet to be determined and, in any event, justices sometimes vote contrary to presidential and public expectations once they are on the Court. Chief Justice Earl Warren is a clear example of this; his record was more liberal than the President who appointed him and more liberal than the public expected.

The transition from one set of Supreme Court justices to another has not always been smooth and easy. Sometimes public opinion has been very critical of the Court, with some groups calling for impeachment when they objected to particular decisions. There were, for instance, cries of "Impeach Earl Warren" for decisions of the Court about school desegregation and prescribed prayer in public school cases. The Court, for its part, has hemmed and hawed back and forth on the expansion of the national role, although the trend over time has been expansionist and since 1937 almost exclusively so. Much of the increase in national power came from the Supreme Court's development of the doctrine of implied powers. This has been most evident in the application of this doctrine to the war powers, the power to regulate interstate commerce, and the power to tax and spend for the general welfare, although other specifically delegated powers often are used as a basis of national action.

While the Supreme Court as the court of last resort on constitutional issues has set the tone for judicial action, the lower national courts have also made substantial contributions to change. This has been especially true of the U.S.District Courts which have played an expanded administrative role in developing desegregation and apportionment plans. Judges of these courts have felt the heat of local opposition to their decisions. In some instances, particularly in states such as California and Arizona, state judges have been the precursors of change but, for the most part, they seem not to be the trend setters.

CONGRESSIONAL ACTION

Congress eagerly shed its reticence to use its powers to expand the activities of the national government. Wartime powers are easily directed toward this end. During war, the national government may find it necessary to marshal the total resources of the country to destroy the warmaking capacity of the enemy. The national government is almost unlimited in its power to direct the lives and requisition the property of its citizens toward this end. President Franklin Roosevelt went so far as to inter American citizens of Japanese origin living on the West Coast during World War II. In an era when war is no longer "declared" but ordered by the executive, when the military capacity to destroy civilization completely is at hand and might be arbitrarily used, and when constant defense readiness becomes a way of life, national activities which were expanded when an official state of war existed do not shrink when hostilities cease. The President exercises most of these powers, even the power to make war if not to "declare" it. The question of the legitimacy of the President committing American troops abroad without congressional consent—a power recent presidents have exercised—is still unresolved.

COMMERCE CLAUSE

The commerce clause of the Constitution has been mighty in the expansion of national powers. Under this provision Congress has authority to regulate commerce that affects more than one state. Judicial interpretation of the "commerce clause" enabled national extension of its activities into fields once believed to be the exclusive realm of the states. Congress has regulated not only the production of goods intended for interstate commerce such as those produced in prison industries, but has prohibited certain crimes such as kidnapping and white slavery, which it would be unable to deal with otherwise. It also has regulated labor-management disputes and used the commerce clause to protect the civil rights of black citizens to access to public transportation and accommodations, and to jobs. These are only a few of the broad uses of this important power. The *National League of Cities v. Usury* case, discussed above, was the first important court restriction on the use of the commerce power in forty years.

TAXING AND SPENDING

It may be argued that the power to tax and spend for the general welfare is the clause under which Congress achieved the most in its relations with the states. It may be further argued that this power is the one most responsible for alterations in the balance of national-state powers. Congress uses its authority to tax as a constitutional base to regulate in areas previously controlled by the states. Also, the development of grants-in-aid, through which the central government gives money to the states for specified purposes, enables it to (1) effectuate national purposes locally, (2) stimulate numerous state and local activities and exercise unprecedented administrative supervision over them, (3) influence the budgeting priorities of these units, and (4) instigate an increasing number of intergovernmental interactions. This topic will be discussed in detail in chapter 5. It is important to stress here that fiscal arrangements developing primarily since the 1930s and the rash of grant-in-aid programs of the 1960s implemented the cooperative nature of the federal system and simultaneously provided increasing opportunities for friction. The national government broadened its bounty with one hand and imposed restrictions on its use with the other. These restrictions ran the gamut of state activities, reaching down into what were once considered the bastions of state and local powers—education, law enforcement, land use, and welfare services. Recent national legislation relating to Medicaid requires states to waive their immunity to suits in the national courts (conferred by the Eleventh Amendment) or lose 10 percent of the national Medicaid funds. A class action suit to stop the cutoff of national funds to states that fail to sign the waiver was filed by Pennsylvania in behalf of several other states.

TREATY POWER

The treaty-making power has been used to broaden the base of national power. Interpretation of the supremacy clause of the Constitution allowed Congress to undertake functions to effectuate treaties which it might otherwise have had no authority to perform. For instance, Congress enacted a law pursuant to a 1916 treaty with Great Britain in which the two nations agreed on closed seasons on the killing of migratory birds flying between the United States and Canada. The Supreme Court upheld the law although a previous national statute regulating the killing of migratory birds had been held unconstitutional by lower national courts before the enactment of the treaty.[5] In the same case, the Court recognized the inherent powers of the national government to act in matters of national concerns in which every civilized government is empowered to act. These include war powers, control over foreign relations, ability to acquire territory, and authority to exclude and deport aliens. Acquisition of national power by prescription—that is, by exercising it over a long period without challenge—has also been recognized by the Court.[6]

LIMITATIONS ON NATIONAL POWER

National power has not grown unhindered and unopposed. There are constitutional limitations on its use, especially in the Bill of Rights. In addition, court rulings have limited it in some instances, although the courts generally tend toward liberal interpretation of national powers. Other limitations operate at the same time, some perhaps more important. There is, in the first place, a philosophical bent of the American people for decentralization. Dating back to the Jeffersonian model of an agricultural republic is a widely-respected belief in the wisdom of small, self-governing rural communities, sometimes referred to as "grass roots." As Roscoe C. Martin puts it, "One who rejects or ignores a grass-roots incantation does so at his peril, for the public mind does not entertain the alternative of grass-roots fallability."[7]

PUBLIC OPINION AND ESTABLISHED INTERESTS

National public opinion polls show a trust of state government that serves to restrain, to some extent, the expansion of the national role. A survey by the Institute for Social Research at the University of Michigan indicated that while no level of government was rated "very good" in serving the people, on a rating scale from 0 to 8 both the states with 4.57 and the local governments with 4.33 ranked higher than the national government with 3.86.[8] Responses to a U.S. Senate Subcommittee survey show quite clearly that citizens would prefer to strengthen local and state governments and reduce national power (note table 4-1), although responses to questions of this type are not always consistent. It also should be remembered that these surveys were made as the Watergate scandals began to unfold. Furthermore, in some specific policy areas support for national performance is substantial. (On this last named point, see table 1-1 in chapter 1.)

Past actions further serve to constrain national expansion. Around a service performed at another level of government is built up a constituency of interests that have access to the decision makers and resist change. With the increased professionalism in most functional areas, however, this factor would seem to have more leverage in opting for transfer of a function to the national level than for keeping it with the states.

TABLE 4-1
DESIRED CHANGES IN STRENGTH OF LEVELS
OF GOVERNMENT IN THE AMERICAN FEDERAL SYSTEM

Question: How strong do you think the following should be made? Local Government? State Government? National Government?

	Made stronger	Power taken away	Kept as is	Not sure
Local government	61%	8%	23%	8%
State government	59	11	22	8
National government	32	42	17	9

SOURCE: U. S. Senate, Committee on Government Operations, Subcommittee on Intergovernmental Relations. **Confidence and Concern: Citizens View American Government. A Survey of Public Attitudes.** 93rd Congress, 2nd Session, Committee Print (Washington, D.C.: U.S. Government Printing Office, 1973), Part I, p. 299. Survey conducted by Louis Harris and Associates, 1973.

POLITICAL PARTIES

Very real constraints exist in the political party and electoral system. Anyone who has spent much time in Washington knows that the real basis of political power is back in Sacramento, Austin, Columbus, or Chicago. National officials, from the President on down, depend upon state centers of political power for their support—particularly as they relate to campaign activities. The center is not necessarily the state capital but it does include state and local party organizations and the vote which comes from throughout the country. Were this not so, such substantial amounts of time would not be spent by national figures, when they are out of the nation's capital, visiting governors, party officials, and other political leaders, and speaking before party-oriented groups. This does not mean that all states present unified power bases. Often they are honey-combed with factions. But with their local components they exert a powerful force in national affairs.

Representatives and senators in Congress are particularly sensitive to state and local supportive structures. They may receive some help from the national committees of their parties, or even more from the concerned national congressional or senatorial campaign committee, but they rely more heavily on the party organization within their state or district. This is not to say that they do not often set up their own campaign committees or sometimes operate independently of the state and local party organization. It does mean that they try not to alienate the party organization, for the relationships maintained within the constituency are crucial to the success of the candidate.

A state party is often in a position to influence voting by members of the House or Senate for political purposes back home. This influence extends not only to legislative issues, but also to votes which approve presidential appointments, elect the President and Vice President when no majority develops in the Electoral College, impeach and remove civil officers on conviction, and fill a vacancy in the office of the Vice President (as in the selection of Gerald Ford and Nelson Rockefeller). Constituency public opinion, as expressed by party leaders as well as by citizens themselves, can often be determinative on all of these actions. What must be kept in mind when considering the effect of party as a limitation on national power, or on any other aspect of American government, is the confusing complexity that exists within the system, both as its organization appears on paper and as it functions. Parties display unpredictable degrees of autonomy and cohesion.

The uncentralized nature of the party system was discussed in chapter 2. The argument continues as to whether the uncentralized party maintains the federal bargain as Riker contends or whether the federal system contributes to an uncentralized party organization as put forth by David Truman.[9] Whatever the ultimate truth may be, little doubt exists that the interrelationship is crucial.

STATE OPTIONS

State options in the administration of certain national programs can provide additional limitations on national power. For example, not all states employ grant-in-aid programs to the same degree, and their decisions to use or not to use them affect the extent of national influence accompanying the program. Furthermore, the enthusiasm with which states accept national standards and regulations, or indeed whether they do anything about them at all, circumscribes national power.

Other constraints effectively hinder government expansion on the national level. The Bill of Rights limits all government movement into certain areas, and belief systems affect activities in some fields (for example, prohibiting aid to private schools, and protecting the right of private property). Probably only a small segment of the American public would support general government ownership of the means of production.[10]

DUAL FEDERALISM

People wishing to restrain national dominance in the federal system have been reenforced by the doctrine of dual federalism. It emphasizes the clear delineation between the powers of the national government and those of the states, and the conflict between these two levels of government. This doctrine has given way to a theory of cooperative federalism in recent years, but it still enjoys substantial public support, especially in the South.

Dual federalism is used to signify a view of federalism that (1) sees a clear demarcation between the powers of the two levels of government, (2) stresses the reserved powers of the states as well as a limited, strict interpretation of the delegated powers to the national government, and (3) believes that the distribution of powers within the federal arrangement can be altered only by formal amendment to the Constitution. Further, the delegated powers of the central government were to be understood as if the Tenth Amendment used the term "expressly delegated," even though that terminology was explicitly rejected by the 1780 Congress which drafted the Amendment.

The term "dual federalism" came into prominence through the writings of Edward S. Corwin during the early part of the present century. However, the unnamed concept had served as the center of political controversy since the beginning of the Republic and as a guideline for judicial interpretation of the Constitution as early as the Taney Court (1836-1864). As Corwin notes, from 1837 on, the Court based many of its constitutional rulings on the following theory.

> Sovereignty in the United States was divided between two centers, the States and the National Government, both of which operated over a common territory and a common citizenship for distinct purposes; each of which was completely equipped with the organs necessary for the discharge of its functions and neither of which was dependent upon or subordinate to the other, save in one particular which did not alter the theory of the system. For while an organ of the National Government, the Supreme Court, construed the Constitution finally, yet it did so under the Constitution which recognized the sovereignty and independence of the States within the range of their powers.[11]

Judicial reliance on this approach continued until the mid-1930s. One of the most explicit statements of a Tenth Amendment-based dual federalism is found in the 1918 case of *Hammer* v. *Dagenhart*. In this decision the Court invalidated Congress' attempt to prohibit interstate shipment of items made by children. Noting that the legislation involved the powers reserved to the states, the Court wrote that "In interpreting the Constitution, it must never be forgotten that the nation is made up of states to which are entrusted the powers of local government. *And to them and to the people the powers not expressly delegated to the national government are reserved.*"[12] (Emphasis added.) The Tenth Amendment was still being invoked in this manner for the important New Deal decisions of *A. L. A. Schecter Poultry Corporation* v. *United States* (1935),[13] *United States* v. *Butler* (1936),[14] and *Carter* v. *Carter Coal Company* (1936).[15]

During the 1936-1942 period, however, the Court, fighting for survival in its existing form in the face of Roosevelt's Court-packing plan and mounting public criticism, made a series of decisions that undid the judicial endorsement of dual federalism based on the Tenth Amendment. In the major decision of this brief, but crucial period of judicial backtracking, the Court wrote that the Amendment states "a truism." It was nothing "more than declaratory of the relationship between the national and state governments as it had been established by the Constitution before the Amendment. . . ."[16]

Notwithstanding the Court's remarkable turnabout rejection of dual federalism, the concept did, and in some ways still does, play an important part in the federal system. Dual federalism has been implemented in the political arena through the devices of secession, nullification, and interposition, and states' rights philosophies. Secession is no longer seriously considered for the American federal system. However, nullification and interposition are still occasionally raised as barriers to national action, and the states' rights approach continues to be strongly endorsed by many political leaders and theorists and apparently, by large segments of the public.

SECESSION

Secession is defined as a voluntarily withdrawal from a union. The definition suggests a peaceful dissolution. However, as is sadly obvious, secession, whether or not successful, is rarely a peaceful process. Fratricidal wars over the "perpetuality of the union" are commonplace throughout the world.[17] The recent bloody secession efforts in Pakistan and Nigeria, the former successful and the latter not, suggest the high costs of such efforts.

Hans Kelsen observes in his monumental work, *Allgemeine Staatslehre*, the widely held theory that peaceful secession from a confederation is possible under certain conditions, but secession from a federal union is never possible.[18] Although this distinction is logically and legally untenable, Kelsen notes that it has been argued for centuries by students of federalism. This was a major distinction made in the early debates about the American arrangement. Did the states retain their sovereignty in a type of confederal agreement among equal sovereigns, and therefore retain the right to determine their continued association with the Union? Or did they give up that sovereignty in "order to form a more perfect union"? Theorists such as John C. Calhoun, Jefferson Davis, Bernard J. Sage, and Alexander H. Stephens argued the first of these two points. Calhoun, for one, hoped that a serious threat of secession would be sufficient to force compromise on the Union to avoid dissolution.

Although in the end the question of secession became a southern issue, that course of action had been proposed by other groups. The earliest effort was the attempt to form the Northern Confederation (1803), and the most famous, other than the Civil War, was probably Aaron Burr's infamous action designed to end the Union.[19] As W. Brooke Graves points out at the conclusion of his review of secession, "While sentiment for union evolved rather slowly, separatist sentiment was easily stimulated."[20] These earlier efforts aside, the question of the indestructibility of the Union, and in theory the question of the location of the sovereign, were settled by the Civil War. Although most observers would agree with Graves' comment, "It would seem clear that a State has no right, under any circumstances, to withdraw from the Union,"[21] a few contemporary theorists still argue that a state, primarily through the guarantees of the Tenth Amendment, possesses the right of secession.[22]

As a final comment on the use of the secession, the question should be asked: What changes in the federal agreement occurred because of the use of this extreme instrument of dual federalism? An early and generally prevailing view is that the Civil War was a great centralizing event for the Republic and some scholars still hold to this view. We went into that conflict as a rather loosely formed confederation, it is argued, and emerged as a relatively centralized Union. Recent studies, however, suggest that this may not have been the case. Elazar argues that very little actually changed as a direct result of the War.[23] The Union was preserved, some economic issues were temporarily settled or set aside, and the blacks were emancipated, although kept in a condition of near bondage for many decades thereafter. Certainly these were not radical changes considering the violence of that conflict. As Elazar observes:

> The most intriguing thing about the Civil War is that American federalism emerged from it intact as a system and substantially as it was before the war began. It is all the more intriguing when one stops to consider that whatever the composite of causes leading to war, it was the existence of federalism ... that gave the Southern secessionists the form through which to mount their rebellion and the arguments by which to justify it.[24]

The reasons for the continuation of substantially the same federal agreement range from the maintenance of the same forms of government throughout the conflict—state governments were unchanged and the Confederacy was amazingly similar in structure to the Union—to the reappearance of the Supreme Court as a major defender of federalism after the excesses of Reconstruction. Of major importance was "the deeply imbedded political consensus of the American people, North and South, which is founded on commitment to the federal principle."[25] The net result, according to Elazar, was that

> the existence of federalism prevented the victorious North from confronting the defeated South with an "either-or" proposition, namely, demanding that the Southerners accept reunification on the North's terms alone or forever be denied their rights as Americans, this despite the desire of some Northern radicals to do just that. The existence of federalism made it possible for the South to accept those minimal terms which the North could not help but demand—abjuration of secession and slavery and minimal recognition of the Negroes' civil rights while retaining much of its own way of life and regaining the right to be the master of its future.
>
> More specifically, the fact that the Southern states were left intact allowed Southerners to reidentify with the Union which had humbled them, destroyed their institutions and property, and killed their sons, without accepting the Northern interpretation of the meaning of the war.[26]

A similar aftermath was recorded for the more recent Biafran secession attempt from Nigeria. Of that conflict, one study concludes that "its resolution has not only reaffirmed Nigerian unity but its unity on a federal basis."[27]

NULLIFICATION

Many persons who have stressed that the Republic is a union of sovereign states have advanced the concept of nullification. That is, as a sovereign, a state may declare a national law null and void and therefore not binding upon its citizens. Nullification, like other mechanisms of more extreme states' rights views, has traditionally been associated with the South and its pre- and post-Civil War struggle with questions of racial equality. Interestingly, nullification was first advanced in New England, and when first expounded by a southern state it was over economic, not racial, issues.

In the southern example the state of South Carolina was objecting to trade and tariff policies which it believed to be enriching the northern states at the expense of the South. Nullification had been alluded to earlier by both Virginia and

Kentucky in their protest of the Alien and Sedition Acts of 1798. The Kentucky Resolutions noted that the Federalist-inspired Acts were "altogether void and of no force." Interestingly, some states' rights advocates supported the more extreme doctrine of secession but rejected nullification. Alexander H. Stephens argued, for instance, that a sovereign state had the right to leave the Union, but if it elected to stay, it must abide by the collective legitimate decisions since to do otherwise would be too dysfunctional to the federal agreement.[28]

John C. Calhoun was the main apologist for the doctrine of nullification. His views were based on the firmly held conviction that the Union was composed of individual sovereign entities which were autonomous and equal as a result of the break with England, and which did not give up that sovereignty upon entering the Union. Therefore, the Constitution was but a statement of a compact among states—not individuals. As a condition of that compact the sovereign states retained the right to review the actions and laws of the central government and, if need be, to declare them "null and void" and not binding on the people of the state. Calhoun's perception of the federal arrangement was unlike earlier definitions. As one student of his work summarizes,

> Calhoun declared the central government of the United States to be a federal government in contradistinction to a national government on the one hand and to a confederacy on the other. It was federal and not national because it was a government of states united in a political union, not a government of individuals socially united by what was usually called a social compact.[29]

In defense of this position Calhoun observed that the colonies had each cast one vote to approve the Declaration of Independence and the Articles of Confederation, and in both proposing and ratifying the Constitution states voted as units, casting a single vote apiece. That is, the states were acting as single sovereign entities. Calhoun, one of the few American original political theorists, advanced his major theories in his *Disquisition on Government* and *Discourse on the Constitution and Government of the United States,* both of which still serve as basic references for advocates of nullification.

INTERPOSITION

A milder form of state resistance to national action is found in the doctrine of interposition. This concept holds that a state may place (interpose) itself between its citizens and actions of the national government so as to prevent the enforcement of a perceived illegal or unjust national action. In this milder instance the state need not actually declare the national law "null and void," but merely interposes its authority and resources to prevent effective enforcement.

As in the case of nullification, the act of interposition finds its basis in a dual-federalism orientation to the federal agreement which stresses state sovereignty and residual powers. Associated with the doctrines of secession and nullification, interposition today is primarily linked with the South, the Civil War, and post-World War II resistance to integration. The doctrine, however, has most often been invoked by non-southern states and for non-racial issues. Massachusetts, for example, adopted a report against the embargo legislation associated with the War of 1812, stating in part, "Whenever the national compact is violated, and the citizens of this state are oppressed by cruel and unauthorized laws, this legislature is bound to interpose its power, and wrest from the oppressor its victim."[30] Similar positions were taken by Rhode Island over the same controversy, by Connecticut over the use of that state's militia in the War of 1812, by Virginia and Kentucky over the Alien and Sedition Acts, and by Pennsylvania over the extent of national judicial power, to name simply a few instances.

The overtness and direct challenge to the maintenance of the system of actions taken under the doctrines of secession and nullification make them ineffective. Interposition, on the other hand, while dysfunctional to a smoothly functioning federal system, has been relatively effective. The reason is that interposition often does not call for a direct confrontation, but rather a nebulous and more subtle interposing of state authority. One study goes so far as to assert that "from its early history to this date, interposition has always succeeded in the hands of a Governor or a State court that has had the desire and the courage to use it with determination."[31] While this view is obviously extreme and untrue, the doctrine has been effective. Witness the long delays created by southern states' use of interposition to delay meaningful integration. On issues of this type, victory may not lay in a total reversal of national policy but in protracted delays.

It is often thought that the doctrines of nullification and interposition are exhausted mechanisms of the nineteenth century. This is not so as the following statement of nullification and interposition, adopted in 1950 by the Alabama Legislature, illustrates.

> RESOLVED By The Legislature of Alabama, Both Houses Thereof Concurring:
> That until the issue between the State of Alabama and the General Government is decided by the submission to the states, pursuant to Article V of the Constitution, of a suitable constitutional amendment that would declare, in plain and unequivocal language, that the states do surrender their power to maintain public schools and other public facilities on a basis of separation as to race, the Legislature of Alabama declares the decisions and orders of the Supreme Court of the United States relating to separation of races in the public schools are as a matter of right, null, void, and of no effect; and the Legislature of Alabama declares to all men as a matter of right, this State is not bound to abide thereby; we declare, further, our firm intention to take all appropriate measures honorably and constitutionally available to us, to avoid this illegal encroachment upon our rights, and to urge upon our sister states their prompt and deliberate efforts to check further encroachment by the General Government, through judicial legislation, upon the reserved powers of all states.[32]

Statements of nullification and interposition generally received widespread support in the South during this period as illustrated by the signatures on the famous "Southern Manifesto." Congressional delegations from eleven southern states signed that document of resistance to school integration.

STATES' RIGHTS

During the first century of the Union's existence the doctrine of states' rights served as a source of bitterness and conflict. In more contemporary times, the states' rights philosophy is still very much alive. However, it is now perceived by many of its advocates as a positive force which has helped to: (1) maintain the federal bargain; (2) prevent total centralization of political and governmental powers; and (3) develop the responsibilities of the states.

To understand the durability of the states' rights philosophy, it is necessary to appreciate the pre-eminent position of the states at the time of the forming of the nation. For centuries prior to the American Revolution, the colonists had as the focus for loyalty and identity the individual colony or the Crown. As tensions with England mounted, the main identification was transferred to the respective colony. The emphasis was on being a

Virginian, New Yorker, or Pennsylvanian. With the dissolution of the relationship with Great Britain, it was the state loyalties that were intensified, not the allegiance to a new central government. The great competition among states and among regions during the first seventy-five years of the Republic served to heighten these feelings of state identification.

While the states' rights position often relied on the devices of threatened secession, nullification, or interposition, the general bankruptcy of these mechanisms did not lead to the total decline of the states' rights philosophy. It is often forgotten that many modern theorists still subscribe to earlier views that stress the dominant position of the states and their crucial residual powers. James J. Kilpatrick, a leading contemporary "states'-righter," observes that

> It is astonishing how many persons in public life never have grasped—or even thought about—the origin and abiding location of political power in the United States. This power now flows from fifty identical springs, filling fifty separate but identical reservoirs. And whatever powers may be vested, now or hereafter, in the central government, these powers must flow upward from the State reservoirs. The flow never goes the other way. If beginning students of the Constitution were asked to understand one truth only of their government, they could not do better than to begin with this: *The Constitution acts upon the States in a prohibitory fashion only.*[33] (Emphasis in original.)

Although most Americans may not think in these terms the survey data used throughout this book do indicate a continued strong support for decentralization of functions and a viable federalism, meaning strong states and localities. The stress on the positive part of the states' rights philosophy is found in the "New Federalism" approach as developed during the Nixon Administration. Emphasis was on: (1) decentralizing national power; (2) returning functions and responsibilities to the states and localities where local options could prevail and adequate administration occur; and (3) increasing the financial viability of state and local government, especially through the use of general and special revenue sharing. The philosophy of the New Federalism comes through in President Nixon's remarks upon signing the State and Local Fiscal Assistance Act of 1972 (Revenue Sharing) in Philadelphia.

> As we sign this historic document ... today, we are carrying on the work which started here in Independence Square—where independence was declared, where the Constitution was written,

and where the Bill of Rights was formally added to the
Constitution. . . . They came here in the 18th century to establish
the federal system. We return here in the 20th century to renew
the federal system. They came here to create a balance between
the various levels of government. We come here to restore that
balance. . . . This program will mean both a new source of revenue
for state and local governments—and a new sense of responsibility.

New Federalism, then, is a positive embodiment of an early
often negative states' rights doctrine.[34] As former White House
staff member William Safire noted at the time:

A sea-change in the approach to the limitation of centralized
power—part of what is "new" in the new Federalism—is that
"States' rights" have now become rights of first refusal. Local
authority will now regain the right to meet local needs of its
citizens. States' rights are now more accurately described as
States' duties; this is a fundamental change in Federalism,
removing its great fault without undermining its essential
local-first character. . . .[35] (Emphasis in original.)

In stressing the positive responsibilities aspect of states' rights,
the New Federalism moved the philosophy from a reliance on
dual federalism to a view which emphasizes a viable, balanced
system relying on cooperative interaction of all levels of
government.

NATIONAL-STATE CONFLICTS

An on-going dispute is present among scholars of federalism
as to whether the nature of the nation-state relationship is one of
cooperation or conflict. Considerable evidence exists that recent
years have seen an increase in the amount of cooperation, even if
such a situation has not always been so. Considerably less evidence
exists to indicate that the amount of friction has decreased,
although the increasing cooperation should mitigate some of it. A
1973 nationwide survey of state officials reveals that 40 percent of
them regard intergovernmental red tape as an important obstacle
impeding the performance of their jobs. When the views of
executives were separated from those of legislators, 53 percent of
the executives expressed this view.[36] Earlier, more localized
surveys by two scholars reflected little conflict, however. R. Bruce
Carroll reported in 1963 that almost four-fifths of those officials
queried thought that no points of conflict or tension had developed

in intergovernmental dealings.[37] Edward Weidner's 1960 mail survey of Minnesota officials on all levels showed that state and local officials regarded national administrators as generally cooperative.[38]

ADMINISTRATIVE CONFLICT

Most of the friction which exists is in the day-to-day administration of programs because that is where most of the interaction occurs. Rarely does conflict erupt into publicized intransigence by either set of officials. Sometimes, however, national grants are withheld or delayed when local officials or administrators fail to comply with national guidelines or neglect to file environmental impact statements for such activities as highway construction or sewage treatment facilities. This action is self-defeating, of course, because the withdrawal of funds insures a failure of the national objective. The courts may be called into play in some instances—for example, to force voting rights compliance on the part of a state, or conversely to adjudicate a case brought by a state to force the national government to turn over money for environmental control to which the state feels entitled. In other cases, political pressure may be exerted on the Congress or the President to change or modify a program. Additionally, one level of government will attempt to solve a problem in a particular way because of distrust of the other. A study of the Potomac River Basin Compact illustrates that the governors of the concerned states believed that the states bordering the Potomac must get together to establish an interstate organization before the national government stepped into the case.[39]

In the studies of intergovernmental relations in Minnesota, William Anderson found that points of potential friction involved personnel standards, service regulations, audits, and inspection, together with difficulties in state budgeting of national grants-in-aid.[40] Certainly almost every functional area of government activity could be included on the list.

TAXATION CONFLICT

Conflicts over taxation plagued the country from the time of the adoption of the Constitution. Hamilton and Madison disagreed as to whether the grant of authority to Congress "to lay and collect taxes ... to provide for ... the general welfare" was in addition to the enumerated powers or a modification of them. That is, can Congress tax and spend to accomplish those purposes enumerated in the Constitution or spend to achieve other purposes not enumerated, so long as those purposes were for the "general welfare"? Hamilton's early view that this conferred additional power on Congress was at first adopted by the courts and then went into eclipse until the late 1930s when it again emerged. There was no clearcut judicial confrontation on this point until *U.S.* v. *Butler* in 1936 when Justice Roberts wrote that the taxing and spending powers were in addition to other powers granted by the Constitution. Nevertheless, in that case the Court refused to allow Congress to use its taxing and spending power to regulate agriculture.[41] Shortly thereafter, the Court upheld a wide variety of programs, such as Tennessee Valley Authority and Social Security, which recognized congressional omnipotence in regard to revenue and appropriations.[42] Neither the states nor private citizens has been able to stem the tide of national taxation.

CONFLICT ON CIVIL RIGHTS

Another important conflict between the national government and the states has involved national protection of civil rights and the states' exercise of their police power to protect the health, safety, and morals of their citizens. Climactic in the 1960s with civil rights marches, campus protests, urban rioting, and strikes of public employees, it poses a problem difficult of resolution. In an effort to protect the civil rights of the blacks, chicanos, and the less affluent, the national government resorted to various means. They consisted of persuasion, legislation, granting money, withholding of funds, court action, appointment of national officials to perform certain activities once performed in the states (i.e., voting registrars), and armed force. While most states generally complied with national attempts in this area, a few of them turned to counter legislation, resolutions, court action, refusal to accept national funds, and outright defiance. They saw these as appropriate activities to protect the freedom of action and free use of property of their citizens.

An inherent conflict often exists between two civil rights, such as the right to a trial by an impartial jury and the right of a free press, both guaranteed by the Constitution from both state and national interference. But when the power of the state to legislate and regulate for the protection of its citizens in their freedom of action and free use of their property is introduced, the situation becomes complicated indeed.

Racial integration and law enforcement are probably the most troublesome areas, although the nation has experienced considerable difficulty with abortion, pornography, and other matters. In law enforcement, for example, necessary national court rulings protecting the rights of defendants in criminal cases have sometimes resulted in the release of hardened criminals to prey upon the public. State and local law enforcement officials have been thwarted in their efforts to clear the streets of repeated offenders and thus fulfill their obligations to protect the lives and property of their citizens. Further, the United States Department of Justice occasionally has entered a case as a "friend of the court" in a school desegregation controversy. Also, since the passage of voting rights legislation during the 1960s, the department has instigated cases on behalf of those deprived of their voting rights.

This is not to say that the general position of the states has been in opposition to civil rights. Resistance to some national legislation, executive orders, and court decisions regarding rights of minorities and defendants has come from some states not in agreement with the national norms of the times. Sometimes the conflicts in law enforcement have occurred over who had jurisdiction, as in President Kennedy's assassination in Dallas where the dispute concerned the removal of his body without going through the required legal processes in Texas. Sometimes the conflict is a contest between the Federal Bureau of Investigation and state police over investigation or criminal custody in a particular case.

STATE COMPLIANCE

The question of state compliance with national laws, rules, and regulations, and court decisions has arisen frequently in recent years, spurred by the Warren Court's expansion of individual rights. State authority is sometimes asserted in counterpoise to national action and, because state officials do retain some powers, confrontation can result. Persuasion is the usual device for convincing a state to comply, and it is not always easy to do so. At times when the matter comes before the Court, it tries to sidestep the issue. Samuel Krislov writes:

In the face of determined state opposition to a decision the Court has followed the same tactics of delay. Rather than risk an affront to their moral authority, the justices have usually accepted half a loaf or even a gesture, assuming that time would produce acquiescence or at least diminish the intensity of opposition. In stressing the continuity of its moral authority even at the risk of foregoing a victory the Court follows the pattern of other institutions like the Catholic Church, which instills respect through its moral standing rather than through the imposition of sanctions. The Court, like the Church, has not sought to challenge and test the limits of its power, preferring to display the impression of power.[43]

Not all showdowns have been averted, and the national government pointedly emphasizes that challenges to the Court's authority will be met. Power has usually been directed at the weakest point in the state armor, that is, subordinates rather than governors; but in the desegregation cases governors were dealt with directly. Because of their defiance of court orders, two governors of Mississippi were found guilty of contempt.

Organized local opinion against the rulings of the Court present the greatest problems. Compliance to law is ordinarily so traditional that disobedience must be created, usually by a forceful leader such as a governor, before it can be sustained. If the governor asserts that "The law will be enforced," prospects for mass disobedience are unlikely. This happened in several states during the desegregation controversy. In West Virginia, Governor William Marland threatened to "fill the jails" with those who attempted to thwart the Court's desegregation orders, and Governor A.B. "Happy" Chandler of Kentucky sent the Kentucky National Guard into Sturgis to see that legal requirements were met. Delaware officials also insisted on enforcement of the ruling. South Carolina, although under pressure, complied. As a consequence, these states had less difficulty with school integration than those in which the governors led public opinion in defying the courts, such as in Georgia, Mississippi, Alabama, and Arkansas. In the more recent conflicts over forced busing to achieve racial integration, governors have not promoted resistance. The remarks of other opinion leaders, however, such as Louise Day Hicks of Boston, a former congresswoman, school board member, and city council member, have lent legitimacy to defiance.

Some feeling of legitimacy for state defiance of national action still obtains in the United States and encourages state officials to speak out for their prerogatives. Once a state has defied national authority, it will be easier the second time since the legitimacy of obedience has been devalued. For example, southern forces, never known for complete acceptance of national actions without question, have attacked the Court on grounds other than desegregation. They have criticized the Court for its decisions on prayer in schools and protection of defendants' rights, and on general interference with states' rights in such matters as apportionment. While at one time their position drew broad support, their coalition seems to have disintegrated.[44] State and local officials are the keys to opposition to court rulings, and they also are the keys to compliance. Sometimes court rulings are simply ignored as in the case of school prayer decisions in religiously homogeneous communities. In any event, most decisions relative to free speech, holding rallies, and law enforcement are made on the state and local level. The support or criticism received by officials from citizens of their communities significantly influence public actions.

NATIONAL-STATE COOPERATION

Prominent scholars of American federalism propound the theory that the relationship of the national government and the states has continually functioned on a cooperative basis. Morton Grodzins, whose work *The American System* is the bible of cooperative federalism, reasoned that the American government was a "single mechanism" in which the powers and functions of nation and state were intermeshed in a "marble cake," an analogy adopted from Joseph E. McLean, rather than in a "layer cake" fashion as proponents of dual federalism claimed.[45]

HISTORIC COOPERATION THEORY

Daniel J. Elazar presents evidence in *The American Partnership* that cooperation existed from the early days of the Republic. He examined the activities of Virginia, New Hampshire, Colorado, and Minnesota during the nineteenth century, particularly as they related to internal improvements, finance, and education, and concluded that the American system has always been a partnership. He writes:

> ... The American federal system has been fundamentally a cooperative partnership of federal, state, and local governments

since the early days of the Republic. Within a dualistic structural pattern, the governments of the United States have developed a broadly institutionalized system of collaboration, based on the implicit premise that virtually all functions of government must be shared by virtually all governments in order to fulfill the demands of American democracy for both public service and private access. More specifically, the evidence presented . . . indicates that the relative balance between the federal government and the states has not significantly shifted over the past one hundred and seventy-five years.[46]

Elazar cites many examples of cooperation. Some are informal cooperation between the second Bank of the United States and the various states in the development of a national monetary system, cooperation between the Army Corps of Engineers and state and local authorities in the construction and maintenance of river and harbor improvements, shared responsibility for implementing parts of a jointly produced state-federal plan for internal transportation and communications systems. Others are reimbursement of states for money spent on behalf of the national government for defense purposes, and grants-in-aid in the form of land grants, grants of material, cash grants based upon land sales, and direct cash grants.

Elazar sees American federalism as evolving over three historical periods, identified by the forms of intergovernmental collaboration predominant in each. The first period encompasses the formative years of the Republic and the federal system, beginning with the convening of the second Continental Congress in 1775 and lasting until the Mexican War. The basic procedure for cooperation during this time was outlined in the Articles of Confederation and refined under the Constitution. The chief vehicles of intergovernmental collaboration were the joint-stock company for long-term projects such as the Dismal Swamp Canal, and the cooperative survey carried out with the use of national technicians by the states. Thus, national services-in-aid were provided to the states.

The second period, according to Elazar, began during Jackson's administration and was marked by the use of the land grant as the predominant means of cooperation. The highlight was the Land Grant College Act of 1862 which provided land grants to all states. This period lasted until the end of the nineteenth century. The third period, which started about 1913, is regarded as the era of cooperative federalism. During this time cooperation was refined to the extent that many believed it began with this period.[47] Other scholars have adopted the cooperative view.

COOPERATION NOT HISTORIC

As is usual in such complicated matters, all scholars are not in agreement, however. For example, Harry N. Scheiber disputes this analysis in his *Condition of American Federalism: An Historian's View*.[48] Scheiber grants that occasional instances of cooperation did exist, but denies that this was the general pattern. He contends, instead, that American federalism has gone through a series of stages before emerging to its existing state. He defines the first period, extending from 1790 to 1860, as one of "rivalistic state mercantilism" in which "dual federalism, involving effective separation of powers, became the basic framework for a pervasive rivalism among the individual states and among local communities within the States."[49] The power center gradually shifted to a period of "centralizing federalism" from 1860 to 1933. During this time the national government gradually preempted functions formerly lodged in the states. The third period was the "New Deal and new federalism" era from 1933 to 1941 when the shaping of modern cooperative federalism occurred. There was a dramatic centralization of powers as the national government moved to respond to the crisis of the Depression and the Supreme Court overturned landmark cases. Scheiber's final period dates from 1941 to 1966, the latter date being when the study was published. World War II began to involve state and local officials in national activities, such as the military draft and rationing. The years after this war committed the national government to growing welfare programs as the states found difficulty in maintaining their traditional levels of services. There also came a renewal of emphasis upon intergovernmental effort, a significant increase in grants-in-aid, and important shifts in purposes for which grants are distributed.

PRESENT COOPERATION

Whether or not one agrees that the national-state relationship has always been cooperative—and we believe a pragmatic federalism has and does exist, with conflict and cooperation varying from function to function, from time to time, and from one official or bureaucrat to another—it must be admitted that at present substantial cooperation exists in the administrative aspects of American government at all levels. This cooperation reflects the accommodations government officials have made to public demands for resolving conflict situations and to change. Congress, because of its local constituency orientation, has chosen many times to effectuate a program through state administration rather than by direct administration by the national bureaucracy. The proliferation of grants-in-aid in areas clearly within the constitutional authority of Congress, such as the construction of roads, is firm evidence of this.

It is currently difficult to think of program areas which do not involve both the national and state governments. The day-to-day consultation going on among administrators testifies to the spirit of accommodation that often exists. Many problems are solved or actions expedited by their telephone calls, letters, luncheon meetings, and the somewhat more structured interactions in hearings, conferences, and investigations.

At the same time, the lobbying efforts of public interest groups bring administrators face to face, particularly those of organizations such as the Council of State Governments and the groups under its umbrella, such as the National Governors' Conference, the National Conference of State Legislatures, and the Council's Intergovernmental Relations Committee whose primary concern is national-state relations. The functions of these groups as representatives of the state interest was formally recognized by the national Office of Management and Budget Circular A-85 in accordance with the Intergovernmental Cooperation Act of 1968. It provides that national agencies should consult with public interest groups before adopting guidelines and regulations. While the consultations do not always occur and, when they do, are sometimes too late to provide an effective voice for the interests concerned, they often bring to light conflicts among units of government. When that happens, the disagreements are reconciled or some groups acquiesce before the guidelines are issued.

Other intergovernmental cooperation occurs through a wide range of devices. Included are emergency aid, the giving of technical advice and assistance, joint use of facilities and personnel, joint enforcement of laws and regulations, legislation supporting the laws of the other level or making an offense on one level an offense on the other. Other devices are the acceptance of joint standards, compacts and other contracts, and national-interstate commissions. Still others are the establishment of commissions on intergovernmental relations, fiscal assistance in the form of grants, loans, and revenue sharing, and national expenditures in the states. Recent intergovernmental cooperation acts, passed by Congress, furthered such cooperation and oiled some "squeak points." Grants-in-aid are the most prominent device through which the national government encourages the cooperation of the states, and these grants provoked a pronounced change in national-state relations. Because of the importance of financial programs to the entire question of intergovernmental relations, they will be given extensive treatment in chapter 5, which is on fiscal federalism.

EMERGENCY AID

Emergencies can occur anywhere and, when they do, they often require more manpower and assistance than are at hand. Those on a large scale emanating from natural disasters, such as tornadoes, floods, or earthquakes, usually result in the President declaring the location a "disaster area," making it eligible for wide ranging assistance of all types—from loans at low interest rates to national aid in restoring essential service. These are discussed in some detail in chapter 8.

Other emergencies with which the state cannot cope are usually human-made civil insurrections such as strikes, demonstrations, and riots. The nation went through a rash of them during the civil rights and peace protests of the 1960s and early 1970s. State law enforcement officials are often involved, especially in those conflicts widespread enough to involve more than one community. State police are usually sent first to help local officials and then, if they are unable to quell the disorders, the governor will dispatch the national guard. If the guard is otherwise deployed or cannot cope with the situation, the state legislature if in session or, if not, the governor, will call on the President of the United States for troops.

The President, as commander in chief of the armed forces, has complete discretion as to whether or not he will comply with the request. If he feels that the situation is too much for the state to handle, he may send them. In fact, he may dispatch them to a state on his own initiative if national property needs protection or national activities are subject to interference. This has happened and usually aggravates the relationship between the national government and the state. Most of the time, however, the state is reluctant to call for help, and the President is reluctant to send it. No governor likes to admit that his administration cannot maintain order, and armed force is not a politically popular device for the President to employ. Even when both of these officials are willing to cooperate, arguments sometimes ensue about jurisdiction, timing, and other matters. Note the controversy between Governor George Romney of Michigan and President Lyndon B. Johnson over that state's request for assistance at the onset of riots in Detroit in 1967. The Governor claimed the president was slow in responding, and the President accused the Governor of delaying the request.

TECHNICAL ADVICE AND ASSISTANCE

The exchange of technical advice and assistance occurs every day on a multitude of occasions. Observers are most likely to notice the assistance which goes from the national government to the states and, in fact, this is the route of most of it. But the path runs in both directions and states frequently provide such help to agencies of the national government. Several states, such as Pennsylvania, Connecticut, California, and New York got into the superhighway business long before the adoption of the national interstate highway program and were in a position to offer substantial advice on its planning and design elements. State officials are often called for advice when new legislation is being drafted, by both the national bureaucracy and the congressional committees concerned, in order that administration of the programs will be smoother. This practice is also likely to be followed in the preparation of guidelines for the administration of national programs.

From the national government may come technical advice in many fields. That offered by the United States Department of Agriculture is wide-ranging and long-standing. Agriculture is a field in which much cooperation exists. Another example of the type of assistance the states can expect is offered by the Department of Housing and Urban Development. That agency maintains an office devoted primarily to providing management assistance to state and local governments in federally-assisted housing programs. The United States Civil Service Commission is empowered by the Intergovernmental Personnel Act of 1970 to furnish both operational and consultative services. That is, this commission can refer names for appointment to state jobs from its own register of eligible personnel, engage in joint recruiting and examining with states and localities, and help to train their employees. On a consulting basis, it is authorized to provide service by its own staff, ranging from one day to several months in duration.

Another illustration of cooperation under the Intergovernmental Personnel Act is temporary assignments of employees of one level to another. A high-ranking civil servant in the national Department of Commerce, for example, may be temporarily released for duty as head of a state agency dealing with commerce upon the request of the state. Or a state law enforcement officer may serve for a short period in the national Law Enforcement Assistance Administration because he has special skills or viewpoints not available on the national level. Officials from both levels will consult on guidelines for carrying out national-state programs, may be invited to assist in training by teaching classes or giving demonstrations, or may seek and give advice on the environmental impacts of a particular project. One of the best examples of intergovernmental personnel arrangements is that of the county farm agent who is simultaneously an employee of the national, state, and local governments. He receives his salary from all three levels of government and must abide by the policies of all three. Or, someone in the health department of a city or county may perform functions for all levels of government as part of a daily routine.

TABLE 4-2

INITIAL ASSIGNMENTS UNDER THE INTERGOVERNMENTAL PERSONNEL ACT, MAY 1971 to JUNE 1976

Assignments from national agencies		Assignments to national agencies	
To states	739	From states	339
To local governments	534	From local governments	125
To institutions of higher education	291	From institutions of higher education	992
To Indian tribes	27	From Indian tribes	2
Sub-Total	1,591	Sub-Total	1,458

TOTAL 3,049

SOURCE: U. S. Civil Service Commission, Bureau of Intergovernmental Personnel Programs.

JOINT USE OF FACILITIES

The states and the national government not infrequently engage in the joint use of facilities as well as of personnel. Campuses of state universities were used during World War II for the training of military forces. One entire section of the Chapel Hill campus of the University of North Carolina was blocked off for use in naval pre-flight training and on other parts of the campus both University facilities and faculty were employed in teaching officer candidates for the Army and Navy. This was not an unusual situation.

Even during peacetime the military services may contract with public (or private) universities for the education of selected personnel. This is fairly routine and in addition to ROTC training. The University of Maryland, for example, offers classes at the Pentagon in Washington and at nearby military bases, as well as overseas, as a convenience for military personnel and their dependents. The United States Department of Agriculture may use state agricultural experiment stations, financed in part from national funds, for agricultural research.

COOPERATIVE LAW ENFORCEMENT

It is well known that law enforcement agencies of the states often enforce national as well as state laws and that the Federal Bureau of Investigation often assists state and local officials. Other agencies of both levels also are involved in this kind of cooperation. The states cooperate with the Bureau of the Census in supplying vital statistics. State officials aid in the enforcement of food and drug regulations, meat inspection, and banking laws; and coal mining safety is a cooperative effort of both state and national inspectors. Court cases involving national issues often are tried in state courts, and national courts apply state statutes in certain instances including those involving crimes committed by persons on national enclaves (e.g., national forests or parks) within a state.

SUPPORTING LEGISLATION

Concurrently with joint law enforcement, one level of government may enact laws supporting those of the other jurisdiction; for example, it is a national crime to transport alcoholic beverages into a state where their sale is prohibited. Congress also legislated to cover the interstate aspects of other crimes—use of the mails to defraud, interstate flight to avoid criminal prosecution, kidnapping, and white slavery, for instance. Furthermore, Congress occasionally refers to or adopts the common law of various states; thus, in passing laws relating to ships in interstate or foreign commerce, Congress recognizes laws of several states regarding pilotage.

The use of state election laws for national elections is generally recognized through the absence of national laws covering most procedures, although some national election laws do exist. The states condone national laws by statute and by use, also; for instance, they recognize the United States mails as transmitters of legal documents and use census data for classification of cities. Either the state or national legislatures may adopt standards set by the other if uniform regulation is desirable. In addition, Congress attempts to protect one state from another; for example, national laws on inheritance and estate taxes prevent some states from becoming havens for people wishing to escape these taxes by moving their places of residence.

COOPERATION BY CONTRACT

The states and the national government enter into all kinds of agreements of a contractual nature, including compacts. Contracts are made on a routine, day-to-day basis. The ordinary variety includes such agreements as national-state contracts on the temporary incarceration of national prisoners in state or local correctional institutions, on national research at a state university, or on the disposal of surplus equipment or real estate. Often land no longer needed for national purposes will be turned over to the state for a nominal fee. All kinds of arrangements of this sort exist between the two levels of government.

Compacts, which are agreements transferring political power, were long used solely as an interstate device, but in recent years, especially in river basin development, the national government has entered as a party to the compact and participates in its administration. Its entry into the Delaware River Basin Compact was an innovative development, and the Susquehanna and Potomac River Basin compacts contain similar provisions.

INTERGOVERNMENTAL ORGANIZATIONS

Other innovative developments include the creation of

national-interstate commissions, which are rapidly growing in number (discussed in chapter 6), and the establishment of intergovernmental commissions created for the purposes of suggesting solutions for intergovernmental problems and generating harmony. The use of the latter organizations is not new, but the establishment of the Advisory Commission on Intergovernmental Relations in 1959 as a permanent body was innovative, since previous commissions had enjoyed only temporary existence. This *national* agency is composed of representatives of the executive and legislative branches of the national, state, and local governments and the general public. It maintains a continuing review of the federal system, makes recommendations for its improvement, and issues reports. The reports provide a wealth of information on the operation of the federal system. ACIR's consistent support aided the cause of revenue sharing legislation aimed at restoring the balance in the federal system by financially strengthening states and localities.

Overall, the attempts at intergovernmental cooperation seem to be increasing in scope and in intensity. There is growing recognition of the interdependence of national, state, and local agencies as they attempt to determine public policy.

CHANGE AND ACCOMMODATION

Like the society that spawns it, the emerging federal system is a dynamic one. It is a fluid system adjusting on a day-to-day, issue-by-issue basis as its governments strain and change to meet the demands of an increasingly urbanized and technological society. In relationships that are sometimes cooperative, sometimes conflicting, and sometimes both at once, efforts are made to work out individual solutions to each major problem that will meet the requirements of adequate service delivery, financial solvency, conflicting interests, and public support.

The system has adjusted as the national government increased its activities manyfold, sometimes at state expense but often because it undertook programs which previously engaged no government. Each adjustment required further adjustment throughout the system as officials strove to accommodate to them. Little remains the same. It is as though the batter for McLean's marble cake had never been baked to solidify it into a permanent pattern but was still in the process of being mixed, with ingredients added and subtracted as the occasion required.

NOTES

1. William Anderson, *Intergovernmental Relations in Review* (Minneapolis: University of Minnesota Press, 1960), p. 159.
2. Information in this section is drawn from Nicholas B. Wilson, "Enhancing Federal-State Relations: State Liaison Offices in Washington," Ph.D. Dissertation, University of Maryland, College Park, 1975. For a discussion of state lobbying through public interest groups, see Donald H. Haider, *When Governments Come to Washington* (New York: The Free Press, 1974).
3. "States versus Nation and the Supreme Court," *American Political Science Review*, April, 1934, pp. 233 and 244-245.
4. Samuel Krislov, *The Supreme Court and the Political Process* (New York: The Macmillan Company, 1965), pp. 80-81.
5. Missouri v. Holland, 252 U.S. 416 (1920).
6. U.S. v. Midwest Oil Company, 236 U.S. 459 (1915); Inland Waterways Corporation v. Young, 309 U.S. 517 (1940).
7. Roscoe C. Martin, *Grass Roots* (University, Ala.: University of Alabama Press, 1957), p. 5.
8. *Washington Post*, May 9, 1974, p. A-1. For a discussion of citizens' attitudes toward levels of government, see Mavis Mann Reeves and Parris N. Glendening, "Areal Federalism and Public Opinion," *Publius: The Journal of Federalism*, Vol. 6, No. 2 (Spring, 1976), pp. 135-67.
9. William H. Riker, *Federalism: Origin, Operation, Significance* (Boston: Little, Brown and Company, 1964); David B. Truman, "Federalism and the Party System," in *Federalism: Mature and Emergent*, edited by Arthur W. MacMahon (New York: Russell and Russell, Inc., 1962), pp. 113-136.
10. Donald J. Devine, *The Political Culture of the United States* (Boston: Little, Brown and Company, 1972), pp. 211-212.
11. Edward S. Corwin, *National Supremacy* (New York: Henry Holt and Co., 1913), pp. 108-109.
12. 247 U.S. 251.
13. 295 U.S. 495
14. 297 U.S. 1.
15. 298 U.S. 23.
16. United States v. Darby, 312 U.S. 100, (1941). For an excellent summary of these interpretations, see Walter Hartwell Bennett, *American Theories of Federalism* (University, Ala.: University of Alabama Press, 1964), pp. 179-220.
17. For an interesting discussion of the reasons for the dissolutions of federal arrangements, see Thomas M. Franck, editor, *Why Federations Fail: An Inquiry Into the Requisites for Successful Federalism* (New York: New York University Press, 1968).

18. For a discussion of Kelsen's complex but critical theories on federalism, see Sobei Mogi, *The Problem of Federalism: A Study in the History of Political Theory*, Vol. II (London: George Allen and Unwin Ltd., 1931), pp. 965-1056.

19. A good review of several early attempts to seceed is found in Edward P. Powell's *Nullification and Secession in the United States* (New York: G. P. Putnam's Sons, 1898).

20. W. Brooke Graves, *American Intergovernmental Relations* (New York: Charles Scribner's Sons, 1964), p. 127.

21. *Ibid.*, p. 126.

22. See, for example, M. B. Holifield, "Secession: A Right Reserved to the States," *Kentucky State Bar Journal* (September, 1954), pp. 160-173; and H. N. Morse, "Study in Legalities of Doctrines of Nullification and Secession," *Journal of the Bar Association of the District of Columbia*, March, 1950, pp. 130-142, and April, 1950, pp. 182-193.

23. Daniel J. Elazar, "Civil War and the Preservation of American Federalism," *Publius*, Vol. 1 (1971), pp. 39-58.

24. *Ibid.*, pp. 39-40. Elazar's evaluation of the limited impact of the Civil War focuses on the constitutional and, to a lesser extent, political structure of the American system. Not addressed are the major fiscal, social, and functional changes that grew out of that conflict. Most observers would agree that in these areas, at least, the Civil War had a major impact on the American system.

25. *Ibid.*, p. 51.

26. *Ibid.*, p. 55. Concerning the last point, Elazar facetiously notes that "Given the popular response to Confederate symbols in the intervening century, the South may even have won the war of myth and interpretation."

27. John A. A. Ayoade, "Secession Threat as a Redressive Mechanism in Nigerian Federalism," *Publius*, Vol. 3 (Spring, 1973), p. 74.

28. Alexander H. Stephens, *A Constitutional View of the Late War Between the States*, 2 Vols. (Philadelphia: 1868, 1870). See especially Vol. I, pp. 421ff.

29. Bennett, p. 132.

30. Quoted in *ibid.*, p. 103.

31. Drew L. Smith, *Interposition: The Neglected Weapon* (New Orleans: Federation for Constitutional Government, 1959) as quoted in Graves, *American Intergovernmental Relations*, p. 115.

32. Alabama Legislature, Act No. 42, February 2, 1950. See also Mississippi Legislature, Senate Concurrent Resolution No. 125, February 29, 1956, and the statement of Congressman John Bell Williams of Mississippi before the U.S. House of Representatives, January 25, 1956.

33. James Jackson Kilpatrick, "The Case for 'States' Rights'," in Robert

A. Goldwin, editor, *A Nation of States: Essays on the American Federal System* (2nd ed.; Chicago: Rand McNally and Co., 1974), p. 97.

34. For further analysis of New Federalism, see: Leigh E. Grosenick, editor, *The Administration of the New Federalism: Objectives and Issues* (Washington, D.C.: American Society for Public Administration, 1973); "The New Federalism: Theory, Practice, Problems," special report of *National Journal*, March, 1973; Richard P. Nathan, "The New Federalism versus the Emerging New Structuralism," *Publius: The Journal of Federalism*, Vol. 5, No. 3 (Summer, 1975), pp. 111-129; and, especially, "The Publius Symposium on the Future of American Federalism," *ibid.*, Vol. 2, No. 1 (Spring, 1972), which reprints a collection of papers written by four members of the Nixon Administration: William Safire, Tom Huston, Richard Nathan, and Wendell Hulcher.

35. *Ibid.*, p. 99. See also Zell Miller's "A New Definition of States' Rights," *State Government*, Vol. XLVIV (Winter, 1976) pp. 31-33. Miller speaks of states' rights not "as an abstract notion of political science or as a code word for something else, but a new division of responsibilities among levels of American government—a vital idea whose time has arrived." (p. 32.)

36. U.S. Senate Committee on Government Operations, Subcommittee on Intergovernmental Relations, *Confidence and Concern: Citizens View American Government. Survey of Public Attitudes* (Washinton D.C.: Government Printing Office, 1973), Part I, p. 296 (Committee Print).

37. R. Bruce Carroll, "Intergovernmental Administrative Relations," in *Cooperation and Conflict: Readings in American Federalism* edited by Daniel J. Elazar, R. Bruce Carroll, E. Lester Levine, and Douglas St. Angelo (Itasca, Ill.: F. E. Peacock Publishers, Inc., 1969), pp. 310-311.

38. Edward R. Weidner, *Intergovernmental Relations As Seen by Public Officials* (Minneapolis: University of Minnesota Press, 1960), pp. 91-96.

39. James A. Mederios, "The Politics of Water Resources Development: The Potomac Experience," Unpublished Ph.D. Dissertation, University of Maryland, College Park, 1969, pp. 113ff.

40. Anderson, p. 62.

41. 297 U.S. 1.

42. Krislov, p. 84.

43. *Ibid.*, pp. 145-146.

44. *Ibid.*, p. 148.

45. Morton Grodzins, *The American System: A New View of Government in the United States*, edited by Daniel J. Elazar (Chicago: Rand McNally and Co., 1966). For McLean's usage, see Joseph E.

McLean, *Politics is What You Make It*. Public Affairs Pamphlet, No. 181 (Washington, D.C.: Public Affairs Press, April, 1952), p. 5.

46. *The American Partnership: Intergovernmental Cooperation in the Nineteenth Century* (Chicago: University of Chicago Press, 1962), p. 297.

47. *Ibid.*, pp. 312-317.

48. A Study submitted by the Committee on Government Operations, Subcommittee on Intergovernmental Relations, U.S. Senate, 89th Congress, 1966. Now out of print this heavily documented study is most readily available in Mavis Mann Reeves and Parris N. Glendening, *Controversies of State and Local Political Systems* (Boston: Allyn and Bacon, Inc., 1972), pp. 64-92.

49. *Ibid.*, p. 69.

5

Fiscal Federalism

Fiscal relations in the American federal system are a myriad of confusing, changing, and accommodating interactions among governments. The system operates within a context of over-lapping, competing, and duplicating tax structures which permits more wealthy communities to accumulate surpluses in their public coffers, while poorer neighboring governments are unable to provide minimum public services. It is a system that generates different emotions. From the academicians and students of public finance comes confusion and from the elected officials and public administrators there is often frustration. While the citizen waiting for an unprovided service emotes despair and hopelessness, the taxpayer increasingly is given to outbursts of anger over perceptions of wasted public monies and increasingly higher taxation.

And yet within this often painted dark picture general positive images clearly stand out. Most important is that the system works, albeit with occasionally significant problems. Revenues are collected and expenditures are made while most state and local governments stay far from the abyss of total financial collapse predicted by the strongest critics of American fiscal federalism. Further, it has been argued that the lack of a more centralized, ordered—perhaps, even rational—system of fiscal relations promotes certain values crucial to American federalism, for example, diversity and decentralization. As a leading student of American public finance, L. L. Ecker-Racz, observes

Federal democracies aspire to decentralized decision-making in both taxing and spending. They want to leave maximum responsibility for domestic government in the hands of those close to the people—at the local level, if possible; at the state level, if necessary; but rarely at the federal level. With this goes a preference for each level of government to raise its own revenues so that the responsibility for taxing can go hand in hand with that for spending. We are reassured when those who have the pleasure of spending have to suffer the pain of imposing taxes.[1]

Lastly, the present revenue raising system, all its short-comings notwithstanding, finds a defense in its acceptance by the American people. It is a reluctant and begrudging acceptance to be sure, but one that stands firm in the face of proposals for sweeping reordering of revenue-collecting responsibilities. Perhaps the public in some vague way recognizes that a major restructuring of the revenue collection system poses a potential threat to inherited values and traditions. Perhaps the defense of the current fiscal arrangements comes more from a visceral conservatism of the American electorate than from implicit or explicit consideration of the United States' political theory heritage.[2]

Whatever the cause, it seems clear that a major restructuring of the revenue-collection system will not take place in the near future. Change will come, as it has in the past, in incremental and limited steps, rather than an immediate, major overhaul. Even the much heralded national revenue-sharing program enacted in 1972 or the emergence of the block-grant approach in the mid-1970s must be evaluated as relatively minor changes when viewed in the context of the total American fiscal federal system.

THE CONSTITUTIONAL BASIS

The current array of revenue-raising efforts and fiscal interactions among governments has its genesis in the broad grants of taxation powers found in the national and state basic laws. The power to tax is defined as the ability to extract compulsory contributions to be used for public purposes by a government. In the American system both the national and state governments have indigenous taxing powers. These powers are subject to both formal legal and informal political limitations.

NATIONAL TAXING POWERS AND LIMITATIONS

The United States Congress has almost unlimited taxing

power. In large part this constitutional grant of power grew out of the difficult financial situation facing the central government under the Articles of Confederation. Under that document the national government lacked the power to levy taxes. Instead, the states were to supply revenues to the United States treasury in proportion to the land occupied in each state. Not suprisingly, states soon fell far behind in their contributions to the national government, leaving it financially impotent. In this environment, the members of the Constitutional Convention stood nearly unanimous in their demand that the new national legislature be given broad powers to raise its own revenues.

Accordingly, the first part of the eighth section of Article I of the Constitution states that "the Congress shall have power to lay and collect taxes, duties, imposts and excises, to pay the debts and provide for the common defense and general welfare of the United States. . . ." This is, indeed, a broad open-ended grant of taxing power. The Supreme Court has strengthened and broadened this authority even further by consistently asserting that the Congress itself is the sole interpreter of what is "necessary and proper" in providing "for the common defense and general welfare of the United States." According to the Court,

> The discretion, however, is not confided to the Courts. The discretion belongs to Congress, unless the choice is clearly wrong, a display of arbitrary power, not an exercise of judgment. This is now familiar law. "When such a contention comes here we naturally require a showing that by no reasonable possibility can the challenged legislation fall within the wide range of discretion permitted to Congress." Nor is the concept of the general welfare static. Needs that were narrow or parochial a century ago may be interwoven in our day with the well-being of the Nation. What is critical or urgent changes with the times.[3]

Most authorities today agree that the wording of Article I, Section 8, in tandem with Court interpretations, gives Congress practically unlimited taxing powers.

Is there any limitation to the national taxing power? The Constitution explicitly specifies a few limitations. Article I, Section 8, provides that all duties, imposts, and excises shall be uniform, meaning geographic uniformity, throughout the United States. Further, Section 9 of the same Article prohibits preference to one state's ports over those of another and forbids the levying of an export tax. Also, taxation methods that violate the due process standard would obviously be in violation of the

Fifth Amendment. These few restrictions have placed no real obstacle on congressional taxing ability.

The judicial branch of government has looked carefully at national taxing power and, with the exceptions of restrictions on taxation of state and local governments, has not found the occasion to add substantially to limitations on this authority. Demonstrating the extent of the acceptance of nearly open-ended interpretation of national taxing powers, the Court has ruled that a national taxpayer, because he pays taxes to support a particular program, does not automatically gain standing to sue (that is, a direct personal interest necessary to enter the courts) to stop a national government expenditure.[4] Further, Congress can use its taxing powers to regulate in social and economic areas traditionally viewed as state prerogatives. The unlimited power of Congress to regulate in these areas (e.g., narcotic, marijuana, and gambling controls) and to intervene in accepted areas of state police powers has been with a few notable exceptions,[5] repeatedly affirmed by the Court.

An area in which the national government's taxing ability has been restrained by the judicial branch concerns its powers to tax other governments. *McCulloch* v. *Maryland* provided the headwater for a stream of judicial decisions addressed to the question of intergovernmental immunity from taxation.[6] Growing out of an attempt by the 1818 Maryland state legislature to tax the Baltimore branch of the Bank of the United States, this decision, written by Chief Justice Marshall, set the tone for future consideration of attempts by one government to tax another government. It declared "that the power to tax involves the power to destroy, that the power to destroy may defeat and render useless the power to create, that there is a plain repugnancy in conferring on one government a power to control the constitutional measures of another. . . ."[7] Marshall's opinion was based largely on his strongly-voiced view of the supremacy of the national government.

> The American people have declared their constitution and the laws made in pursuance thereof, to be supreme; but this principle [of state taxation of national activities] would transfer the supremacy, in fact, to the states. If the states may tax one instrument, employed by the government in the execution of its powers, they may tax any and every other instrument. They may tax the mail; they may tax the mint; they may tax patent rights; they may tax the papers of the custom-house; they may tax judicial process; they may tax all the means employed by the government, to an excess which would defeat all the ends of

government. This was not intended by the American people. They did not design to make their government dependent on the states.[8]

In a dictum contained within the decision, Marshall, demonstrating his concern for national supremacy, argued that while the national government was immune from state taxes, state activity may in turn be taxed by the central government. This view was rejected by later courts which moved to a position of reciprocal immunity, thus offering both the national government and the states immunity from intergovernmental taxation.[9] The principle of reciprocal immunity—attempting to assure the equality and integrity of both levels of government—did more than exempt from taxation property and activities of both the national and state governments. It also exempted the salaries of national, state, and local employees, private businesses for that part of their activity dealing with a government, and the interest on national, state, and local bonds.

Starting in the late 1930s the Court released a series of opinions that has gradually eroded the principle of reciprocal immunity. The rule today is that intergovernmental taxes are generally prohibited if they are seen as providing an obstacle to the performance of another government's activities. At present, reciprocal immunity has been sufficiently eroded to the point that it serves as a rather weak limitation on national taxing power, or for that matter on state taxing power. The physical facilities of one government are still exempt from taxation by another government. However, taxes may be levied on other governmental concerns provided they do not harm the taxed government's ability to perform its functions. For example, a national judge living in New York City is subject to state and city income taxes on his public wages, just as a New York state legislator pays an income tax to the national government. In neither case does the tax interfere with the official's ability to perform his job.

A major controversial exception to the end of tax immunities is the continued exemption of municipal bonds from the national government's income tax. (The controversy, however, is centered on questions of equity, rather than a concern about intergovernmental taxing relations.) A last "gray area," which still has not been entirely cleared by the courts, concerns taxing state or local activities that are not exclusively governmental in character. In 1905, for example, the Court upheld a tax on South Carolina's liquor-dispensing business.[10] What of other services that are *sold* to the public, rather than supported by general taxes, such as water or mass transit? Are such sales taxable? The Court has not yet given a definite response.

Thus, a long history of judicial review of these concerns—the standing of a taxpayer to sue, the propriety of regulation through use of the taxing power, and intergovernmental taxing immunity—has produced only a few limited restrictions on national taxing authority. Meaningful limitations on congressional revenue-raising activities comes, as will be shown below, from the political arena rather than from the Constitution or the courts.

STATE TAXING POWERS AND LIMITATIONS

In theory, the state taxing power is even greater than that of the national government. The authority of the central government to raise revenues, as great as it is, is still a specific enumerated grant of power. As pointed out elsewhere, however, the states possess residual powers, that is, those "powers not delegated to the United States by the Constitution, nor prohibited by it to the States."

Although a broad grant of taxing power has been specifically delegated to the national government, it is not an exclusive grant of power and, therefore, as in other functional areas, is shared concurrently with the states. The states, however, since they are not prohibited from taxing by the national constitution, possess an open-ended authority to tax. Because this power is residual and open-ended, the best way to understand it is to examine the limitations placed on the states' taxing authority. What is left free of those limitations provides a fairly strong reservoir of powers.

The limitations on a state's revenue-raising authority come from three sources: the United States Constitution, the state's own basic law, and political realities. The national Constitution contains several restrictive measures against state activity in the tax area. Article I, Section 10, provides that "No state shall, without the consent of the Congress, lay any imposts or duties on imports or exports, except what may be absolutely necessary for executing its inspection laws: and the net product of all duties and imposts, laid by any state on imports or exports, shall be for the use of the treasury of the United States and all such laws shall be subject to the revision and control of the Congress." Further, "No state shall, without the consent of Congress, lay any duty on tonnage. . . ."

Other limitations come from that same section's prohibition against state "law impairing the obligation of contracts," Article IV's "privileges and immunities" clause prohibiting discrimination against nonresidents of a state, Article I, Section 8's "commerce clause", and the Fourteenth Amendment's "equal protection" and "due process" standards. All these provisions have limited the states' ability to tax. A voluminous number of Supreme Court decisions have attempted to define the extent of these limitations.

The sum of almost two hundred years' interpretation of these vague, but crucial limitations on state taxing power is that a state tax may not (1) impair interstate commerce, (2) discriminate against citizens of other states, (3) deny equal protection and due process to its own citizens nor those of other states, or (4) conflict with national legislation. While the acceptable limits of the state taxing authority are still not clearly defined, Congress and the courts have shown a liberal and flexible attitude toward state powers of taxation.

The states' constitutions are not nearly as liberal and flexible about the power of the states to tax. Nor are their provisions as complex and nebulous as those limitations imposed by the United States Constitution and the Supreme Court's interpretations of that document.

State constitutions adopted soon after independence placed relatively few limitations on the legislatures' taxing powers. As a result of excessive spending and taxing, incurrence of debts, and repeated scandals and corruption, particularly during the last half of the nineteenth century, state constitutions were rewritten to restrict substantially the legislatures' taxing abilities.

All states' basic laws provide for certain outright exemptions for particular types of properties. Land and facilities owned by public agencies are uniformly exempted throughout the United States. In addition, most states exempt from all taxation property and income used for educational, religious, and charitable purposes. Approximately 20 percent of all land in the United States falls into one of these exempted categories, including that land exempted by way of public ownership. Many states grant a "homestead exemption" (e.g., the first $5,000 of assessed value of a private home) to their residents. In some cases this latter limitation applies only to certain groups of properties, such as that owned by the elderly. Some state constitutions place an absolute ban on taxation of income, either personal or corporate, or both.

In addition to these exemptions, most state constitutions specify certain types of limitations on the rate of taxation. Industrial and agricultural property is often required to be taxed at a lower rate than other properties in a state. This mandated tax differential is designed to promote industry and jobs. In the case of the agricultural limitations—the so-called "greenbelt" laws— the promotion is aimed not only at agricultural, ranching, and forestry interests, but also increasingly at preserving open-space and reducing land speculation in urbanizing areas. The limitations and exemptions found in state basic law, when combined with those imposed by the national charter and with political restrictions, greatly reduce the taxing power of the states.

LOCAL TAXING POWERS AND LIMITATIONS

Of the three levels of government, the local level has the least taxing power. Being creatures of the states, municipalities, counties, townships, and special districts do not possess indigenous authority in this area. Instead, they must rely on grants of particular taxing powers from the states. The grant of revenue— raising powers to localities is a restrictive and very controlled process throughout the Republic. Even those local governments enjoying home rule, whether statutory or constitutional, find that their discretionary power in the area of taxation is carefully circumscribed.

This very minimal taxing authority is further limited by the same national and state constitutional strictures that affect state power of taxation. Further, many states place by constitution or statute maximum tax rates (mills) on local government property taxes, which is their major source of revenue. The maximum millage may be set according to function, e.g., 10 mills for roads, 25 mills for education, and so on, or there may be a stated total millage for all functions combined. To their dismay, local officials find that variations of this approach are becoming increasingly popular as state legislatures seek to subdue the "taxpayers' revolt" which is generally focused on local property taxes.

As with the national and state governments, local units find that major obstacles to their revenue-raising capabilities come from the political arena. This may be even more true at the local level because of the proximity of the voters' wrath and because of the great unpopularity of the property tax.

EXTRA-CONSTITUTIONAL LIMITATIONS ON TAXING POWERS

All three levels of government are subject to major limitations on their taxing powers beyond the formal constitutional strictures. In many ways, the informal, extra-constitutional limitations may be more determinant of the amount and location of revenues that are available to the fiscal federal system than all the discussed constitutional-legal restrictions combined.

The most important and most powerful of these informal limitations is that imposed by the growing opposition of the American public to new and higher taxes. While the dissatisfaction has not yet reached the proportion of the Whiskey Rebellion's protest (1791-1794) over excise taxation, during which President Washington had to use national troops to restore order, public officeholders are aware that politically the results can be just as deadly.

How real is the public dissatisfaction? The Harris survey reported in 1971 that almost 70 percent of those interviewed in a nationwide sample said they would sympathize with a "taxpayers' revolt." This is 26 percent more than felt the same way only two years before (table 5-1). This observation is reinforced by survey data which indicate that 64 percent of the public believes that the tax burden has "reached the breaking point," an increase of 10 percent in two years (table 5-2).

TABLE 5-1

SYMPATHY FOR REVOLT OF TAXPAYERS

Question: Can you foresee the time when taxes in this country would reach the point where you would sympathize with a taxpayers' revolt where people would refuse to pay any more taxes unless taxes and spending were reduced, or don't you think you would sympathize with it?

	1971	1969
Would sympathize	69%	43%
Would not sympathize	17	41
Not sure	14	16

SOURCE: Adapted from "The Harris Survey." Reported in **The Washington Post,** April 18, 1971, p. G-4.

TABLE 5-2

TAX BURDEN ATTITUDES

Question: As far as you and your family are concerned, do you feel you have reached the breaking point on the amount of taxes you pay, or not?

	1971	**1970**	**1969**
Reached breaking point	64%	60%	54%
Not reached breaking point	25	29	34
Not sure	11	11	12

SOURCE: "The Harris Survey." Reported in **The Washington Post,** April 18, 1971, p. G-4.

The elected officials' reactions have been mixed. Some have moved to hold the level of taxes constant or reduce them, generally, however, at another level of government. Thus, the state legislator introduces a bill to freeze the millage or the assessment levels for local governments. Others seek relief through the transfer of expensive functions to different levels of government. Witness in this respect efforts to make welfare assistance a national responsibility or to make capital construction for schools a state responsibility. Still others seek relief from intergovernmental revenues, as in the support of revenue sharing or demands for larger state grants-in-aid to the local governments. All these efforts have impact on the intergovernmental fiscal system and largely account for its great state of flux. Unfortunately few reactions by the officials resolve the dilemma of higher taxes or reduced service levels, a dilemma involving choices that neither the elected officials nor the public appears eager to make.

Another limitation of governmental taxing power is found in established patterns that maintain existing types of revenues among levels of government. States, for example, at one time levied high taxes on property, but now leave that area almost entirely to local governments. Likewise, long traditions of tax exemptions, such as those given to religious or charitable groups, are hard to overcome. Many states have established patterns of high or low tax efforts or long-existing limitations on certain kinds of taxes, e.g., avoidance of personal income taxes or of a sales tax on food and medicine. In some instances these "traditions" are carefully cultivated by vested interests who benefit from them; other times the traditional patterns are just recognized by the people as "the way things are done."

In line with this restraint by tradition, governments often find themselves limited by the deference they show to the tax needs of other partners in the federal system. The national government, for instance, has for a variety of reasons, including deference for state revenue needs, avoided major reliance on direct national sales taxes. In a similar manner, the states have avoided weakening the fiscal capacity of local governments by minimizing reliance on state property taxes. Accordingly, although the states received more than 50 percent of their tax revenue from that source at the turn of the present century, by 1970 state property taxes accounted for only 2.3 percent of state-collected taxes. The same attitude is shown by local governments when they avoid, for the most part, attempts to tax residents of neighboring jurisdictions through devices such as the commuter tax or the nonresident income tax. This avoidance in part comes from legal and political restrictions, including the likelihood of retaliatory action by nearby jurisdictions, but also comes from a deference to the sovereignty and needs of other units.

Both states and localities often find their revenue-raising abilities muted by perceptions of government competition with nearby governments. These perceptions see large cities within a state in competition with each other for industry, business, and the "right kind" of citizens, generally meaning the upper-middle and upper-income strata of society. Similar rivalries exist between central cities and suburbs and among states within a region. The competition is often given as the reason for avoiding higher taxes or certain kinds of taxes. While it is questionable what weight individuals or businesses give to lower taxes compared to adequate government services and amenities of public life, the perception of this type of competition has often influenced public finance decisions.[11]

Another explanation of limitations on revenue-raising capabilities of the state and local portion of the federal system comes from recent policy analysis research indicating that legal and political considerations may be of secondary importance in determining state and local governments' abilities in this area. Socio-economic variables, geographic region, past taxing and spending patterns, and intergovernmental aid are increasingly offered as inputs that are more likely to affect taxing and spending activities than are constitutional, structural, or political variables. While the full extent of the import of these variables and the way they affect the public finance system is still not completely understood, it has been demonstrated that certain arrangements of these variables are correlated with particular taxing and spending patterns.[12]

TAX OVERLAPPING IN THE FEDERAL SYSTEM

The American federal system is characterized by tax duplication and overlapping to an extent not found elsewhere in the world. Despite the deference shown by one level of government to another, with very few exceptions all levels of government utilize the same taxes. There is a national tax on liquor and tobacco, a state tax and, depending on the municipality or county, a local sales tax on those products. Likewise, it is possible to pay taxes on one's wages to the national, state and local governments. This duplication exists for all the major taxes and most of the minor ones. The one real exception is the customs tax which is reserved for the national government, and that, in today's world, is an increasingly insignificant portion of national revenues.

In addition to the vertical duplication within the federal system, there is great overlapping of taxes on the horizontal plane, especially within the more urbanized areas. It is possible to have property taxed by the municipal government, the county, the school district and perhaps three or four special districts. The overlapping may not be immediately obvious to the taxpayer because of the practice of letting one government, generally the county, assess, bill, and collect taxes for all property in the area with subsequent distribution to the taxing bodies, but the impact is just the same.

A serial tax duplication also will add many taxes to one item. A home appliance, for example, may have its base metals taxed at the mines, be the subject of a levy at the manufacturing level, be taxed indirectly through motor fuel levies as it is transported during the manufacturing process and to the point of sale, be subjected to an inventory tax as it waits in the warehouse, and finally, in a last ignoble act, provide the occasion for the imposition of sales taxes for the state and the municipality.

TRENDS IN THE FISCAL FEDERAL SYSTEM

The fiscal arrangements of the federal system were not always so complex. In the early years of the Republic the public sector did far less than is expected of it today. At the national level, for instance, most functions now associated with the Departments of Health, Education and Welfare, Housing and Urban Development, Labor, and Transportation, were then firmly rooted in the private sector. Similarly, many services now routinely expected from the state and local governments, e.g., water and sewage disposal or transportation, were rarely performed by public bodies in the early period. Equally important, at that time the governments of the federal system were somewhat isolated from one another in terms of the functions performed and financial interactions. The relatively limited demands on government in general and the governments' fiscal isolation insured fairly small budgets and a great deal of tax concentration. The national government's budget in 1789, for example, was only $4.4 million, of which 99.6 percent came from customs collections. As late as 1862, the national government received 94.4 percent of its $51.9 million receipts from the customs tax.

Beginning with the Civil War dramatic changes started to take place in the size of governmental budgets and sources of income. The national treasury, for instance, went into that conflict with $41.5 million total receipts; by 1866 this skyrocketed to $558 million. More importantly, perhaps, only 32 percent of the 1866 income came from the previously dominant customs tax, the other 68 percent coming from a multitude of new national taxes. While the central income declined somewhat after the fratricidal conflict, a gradual increase in the national budget began after the turn of the twentieth century, accelerated under the demands of World War I, leveled off again after that struggle, and then realized extraordinary increases during and after World War II.[13]

As a result of new international responsibilities assumed by the United States at the end of World War II and as a consequence of the emergence of "a more positive" view of the role of government following the Depression of the 1930s, the national budget began an inexorable pattern of growth which by the Bicentennial brought it to over $400 billion. A similar outline of growth, decline, spurts forward and then unrelenting expansion could be traced for state and local revenues. The main point is that the old system of limited governments operating in a relatively autonomous tax-raising sphere has been replaced by a public sector requiring ever-increasing income and which, as a result, constantly adds to the complexity of the system through new taxes and expanding patterns of intergovernmental fiscal relations. A brief examination of a few clear trends will help to explain where the fiscal federal system is and where it is headed.

THE TREND OF INCREASED TAXES

An obvious trend to the taxpayer, the elected official, and the student of fiscal federal relations is that recent years have seen a phenomenal demand for new taxes. Whether measured by per capita tax rates or by public revenues as a percent of the gross national product, the upward trend is unmistakable.

Looking at the first mentioned index, the combined per capita tax receipts for all governments of the federal system was only $18 at the turn of the present century ($7 national, $2 state, and $9 local). At that time 51 percent of the collected taxes went to local governments. As table 5-3 shows, by the beginning of World War II, the per capita tax amount had multiplied almost tenfold to $172 and by 1974 it had increased tenfold again, to $1,869 per capita. That is, over $1,800 in taxes was raised for every man, woman, and child in the United States in 1974. Also of importance to note from this same table is that the national share of these taxes increased to 64 percent while the local share declined from a majority at the start of the twentieth century to a current 15 percent.

Table 5-4 shows the federal system's total expenditures as a percentage of the gross national product (GNP). In the twenty-year period from 1954 to 1974 combined public sector expenditures grew from $47 billion to $354 billion, or from 26.5 percent to 32.8 percent of the gross national product. Given the public debate about defense budgets, it is worth observing that defense expenditures are steadily accounting for less of a proportion of the gross national product. National, state, and local domestic expenditures explain the increasing importance of public sector expenditures. (These data are presented graphically in figure 5-1.) Not all of this growth is the result of tax increases or new taxes. Natural growth of the economy, inflation, and other factors explain some of the increased governmental revenues.[14]

TABLE 5-3

FEDERAL, STATE, AND LOCAL TAX RECEIPTS: PER CAPITA AND PERCENTAGE DISTRIBUTION, SELECTED FISCAL YEARS, 1902-1974

Year	Per capita				Percentage distribution			
	Total	National	State	Local	Total	National	State	Local
1902	$18	$7	$2	$9	100.0	37.4	11.4	51.3
1913	24	7	3	14	100.0	29.2	13.3	57.6
1922	68	31	9	28	100.0	45.6	12.8	41.5
1927	80	28	14	38	100.0	35.6	17.0	47.4
1932	64	15	15	34	100.0	22.7	23.7	53.6
1934	70	23	16	31	100.0	33.2	22.4	44.4
1936	83	30	21	32	100.0	36.6	24.9	38.5
1938	110	45	30	35	100.0	41.4	27.0	31.6
1940	108	42	32	34	100.0	39.2	29.2	31.6
1942	172	100	37	35	100.0	58.1	21.7	20.2
1944	389	313	40	35	100.0	80.6	10.4	9.0
1946	357	276	44	38	100.0	77.3	12.2	10.5
1948	377	277	54	46	100.0	73.6	14.3	12.1
1950	365	252	60	53	100.0	69.1	16.3	14.6
1952	548	414	73	61	100.0	75.5	13.3	11.2
1953	571	429	76	66	100.0	75.2	13.3	11.5
1954	569	423	77	69	100.0	74.3	13.6	12.1
1955	539	388	78	73	100.0	72.0	14.5	13.5
1956	602	436	88	78	100.0	72.3	14.7	13.0
1957	637	457	95	85	100.0	71.8	14.9	13.3
1958	631	446	95	90	100.0	70.6	15.1	14.2
1959	630	435	100	94	100.0	69.1	15.9	15.0
1960	709	495	113	101	100.0	69.8	15.9	14.3
1961	724	497	118	109	100.0	68.7	16.3	15.1
1962	756	516	126	114	100.0	68.3	16.6	15.1
1963	794	543	134	117	100.0	68.4	16.9	14.7
1964	834	567	144	124	100.0	67.9	17.2	14.9
1965	861	578	151	132	100.0	67.1	17.6	15.4
1966	949	642	167	141	100.0	67.6	17.5	14.8
1967	1,057	731	177	149	100.0	69.1	16.8	14.1
1968	1,096	743	196	157	100.0	67.8	17.9	14.3
1969	1,297	901	222	174	100.0	69.5	17.1	13.4
1970	1,357	916	249	192	100.0	67.5	18.4	14.1
1971	1,354	879	263	212	100.0	64.9	19.4	15.6
1972	1,515	975	304	236	100.0	64.4	20.0	15.6
1973	1,667	1,066	347	254	100.0	64.0	20.8	15.2
1974	1,869	1,198	390	280	100.0	64.1	20.9	15.0

SOURCE: Tax Foundation, Inc., **Facts and Figures on Government Finance,** 18th edition (N.Y.: The Foundation, 1975), p. 21.

TABLE 5-4

THE GROWING PUBLIC SECTOR: PUBLIC EXPENDITURES AS A PERCENT OF THE GROSS NATIONAL PRODUCT, 1954, 1964, and 1969 THROUGH 1974

AS A PERCENT OF THE GROSS NATIONAL PRODUCT

Calendar year	Total public sector (billions)	Total public sector	Domestic (National, state, local)	Defense	National domestic expenditure[1]	State-local expenditure
1954	$46.9	26.5	12.9	13.7	5.5	7.4
1964	110.8	27.8	17.5	10.3	8.4	9.1
1969	191.6	31.1	20.6	10.6	10.0	10.6
1970	215.8	32.0	22.1	9.9	11.0	11.1
1971	245.2	32.2	23.2	9.0	11.9	11.4
1972	278.2	32.1	24.0	8.1	13.0	11.0
1973	310.8	31.5	24.0	7.5	12.9	11.1
1974 est.	354.0	32.8	25.4	7.4	13.8	11.6

1. Excludes expenditure by the national government for national defense, international affairs and finance, space research and technology, and the estimated portion of net interest attributable to these functions. Includes Social Security (OASDHI) and all national aid to state and local governments including general revenue-sharing payments.

SOURCE: Adapted from Advisory Commission on Intergovernmental Relations, **Trends in Fiscal Federalism, 1954-1974** (Washington, D.C.: The Commission, Feb., 1975), pp. 9-11.

FIGURE 5-1

THE GROWING PUBLIC SECTOR
1954-1974

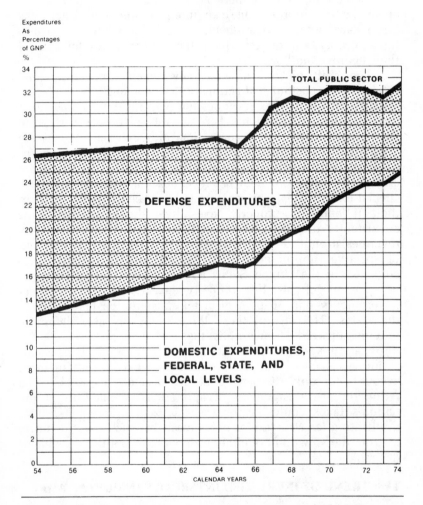

SOURCE: Advisory Commission on Intergovernmental Relations, **Trends in Fiscal Federalsim, 1954-1974** (Washington, D.C.: The Commission, Feb., 1975), p. 8.

THE TREND OF SPECIALIZATION OF TAXATION

This chapter began by discussing the myriad of overlapping, duplicating taxes that exist in the fiscal federal system. While that perception is true, there is, however, a great deal of tax specialization in the American intergovernmental system. As Ecker-Racz notes, "governments at each level have one work-horse, one type of tax on which they generally rely for most of their tax revenue."[15]

The shift by the national government from near total reliance on custom collections (99.6 percent) to a similar reliance on income tax revenues (90 percent) demonstrates that the "workhorse" to which Ecker-Racz refers has been part of the fiscal federal system for some time although new horses are occasionally lassoed. The states abandoned the property tax for an increasing dependence on consumption taxes, and now get almost three-fifths of their tax revenues from general sales and special excise taxes. The local units have been more constant in their reliance on property taxes; over the years they have consistently drawn about four-fifths of their locally-raised tax revenues from *ad valorem* taxes. Viewed from a different perspective, approximately 90 percent of all income taxes collected in the United States go to the national government, 98 percent of all the property taxes goes to the local governments, and 56 percent of all consumption taxes goes to the states. The last of these three figures is also definitely moving upward. Concerning the earlier comments on tax duplication and the observation of concentrated tax speciali-zation, it is clear that the jungle of tangled duplicated taxes accounts for only 20 percent of the system's tax intake. The reduction or reassignment of approximately one-fifth of the nation's taxes could assure a specialized, orderly, and non-duplicating tax structure. It is not clear that such a restructuring is, from the viewpoint of either economics or politics, feasible or desirable.

THE TREND OF INCREASED INTERGOVERNMENTAL AID

One of the most important trends—and many observers would argue *the* most important trend—within the fiscal federal system has been the great growth of intergovernmental aid, both from the national government to states and localities and from states to their local units. The increase in national assistance to state and local governments is shown graphically in figure 5-2.

FIGURE 5-2

NATIONAL GRANTS TO STATE
AND LOCAL GOVERNMENTS,
1967-1977

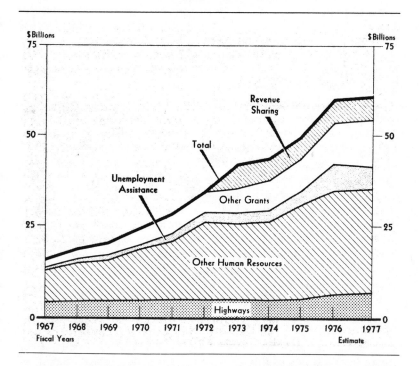

SOURCE: Office of Management and Budget, **Special Analyses: Budget of the United States Government, Fiscal Year 1977** (Washington, D.C.: Government Printing Office, 1976), p. 255.

In 1950, per capita national aid to other governments was $16. A decade later this figure had more than doubled to $39. That figure doubled again by 1967, and by 1975 the national government was contributing $233 per capita to other governments.[16] This national average or $233 per capita in national aid has great regional variations; for example, federal region V (Illinois, Indiana, Michigan, Ohio, Wisconsin, and Minnesota) received the lowest per capita amount ($195) in fiscal year 1975; while the states in federal region II (New York, New Jersey,

Puerto Rico, and the Virgin Islands) received almost $100 more per capita ($283). There are equally great variations among the states within regions. These differences are based on many factors including a state's per capita income, education level, population density, and land holdings of the national government. A state with greater concentrations of poor individuals, for example, generally receives more grants from the Department of Health, Education and Welfare, while states with low population density but large geographic area, such as those in the Rocky Mountain region, will generally receive higher per-capita grants from the Department of Transportation.

Table 5-5 gives three indexes of the growth and impact of national government assistance. National aid, in absolute terms, has increased from $2.2 billion in 1950 to $60.5 billion in 1977. Since 1960 alone national aid has grown by $53.5 billion. Much of that increase, over $40 billion, occurred after 1968 when President Nixon began his New Federalism programs with their emphasis on state and local power.

Columns 2, 3, and 4 of table 5-5 place these absolute figures in perspective. As of the Bicentennial, national government aid represented 16 percent of the total national budget and nearly 22 percent of the national domestic budget. Further, national assistance accounted for approximately one-fourth of all state and local expenditures.

Another major change is the new emphasis on national aid to large urban areas. In 1961, the metropolitan areas received $3.89 billion from the national government. By 1974, national monies, either directly granted to local governments or passed through the states to the localities in the 269 metropolitan areas, had increased to $31.42 billion. Extraordinarily, if one expected that the 70 percent of the population living in metropolitan America should receive a proportion of national aid equal to their numbers, $31.37 billion should have been spent in those areas in 1974, an amount only minutely in excess of the ideal projection. Approximately 15 percent of national grants is transmitted directly to local government. An indeterminable, but much larger amount, however, goes to the states to be passed through to the localities.

The states give considerable amounts of their own resources as intergovernmental aid. Accounting for only 6 percent of the revenues of local governments at the beginning of the present century, by 1974 state aid provided 58 percent of local general revenue, an extraordinary figure considering the public fixation

TABLE 5-5

NATIONAL AID OUTLAYS IN RELATION TO TOTAL FEDERAL OUTLAYS, FEDERAL DOMESTIC OUTLAYS, AND STATE-LOCAL EXPENDITURES, SELECTED YEARS 1950-1977

		National grants as a percent of		
		National outlays		State and local expenditures[2]
	Grants (in millions)	Total	Domestic[1]	
1950	$2,253	5.3	8.8	10.4
1955	3,207	4.7	12.1	10.1
1960	7,020	7.6	15.9	14.7
1965	10,904	9.2	16.6	15.3
1969	20,255	11.0	20.1	18.0
1970	24,018	12.2	21.1	19.4
1971	28,109	13.3	21.4	19.9
1972	34,372	14.8	22.8	22.0
1973	41,832	17.0	24.8	24.3
1974	43,308	16.1	23.3	22.7
1975	49,723	15.3	21.3	23.4
TQ estimate[3]	15,561	15.9	21.7	24.3
1976 estimate	59,787	16.0	21.7	25.2
1977 estimate	60,523	15.4	21.1	23.0

1. Defined here as excluding national defense and international programs.
2. As defined in the National Income Accounts.
3. TQ—transition quarter from July 1 to September 30, 1976, caused by change in start of fiscal year to October 1.

SOURCE: Office of Management and Budget, **Special Analyses: Budget of the United States Government, Fiscal Year 1977** (Washington, D.C.: Government Printing Office, 1976), p. 264.

TABLE 5-6

STATE AID TO LOCAL GOVERNMENT, 1902-1974, BY SELECTED YEARS

	Total state intergovernmental aid (in millions)	State intergovernmental aid as a percent of total general revenue
1902	$ 52	6.1%
1927	596	10.1
1934	1,318	22.7
1948	3,283	28.9
1967	19,056	32.4
1970	28,892	56.2
1971	32.640	57.3
1972	36,759	57.0
1973	40,822	57.9
1974 est.	45,000	57.5

SOURCE: Adapted from U.S. Bureau of Census, **1967 Census of Governments,** Vol. 6 **State Payments to Local Governments.** Updated from data in Advisory Commission on Intergovernmental Relations, **Trends in Fiscal Federalism, 1954-1974** (Washington, D.C.: The Commission, Feb., 1975), p. 29.

with national governmental aid (table 5-6). State aid to local government is of two types—grants-in-aid and shared taxes. The former are appropriations specifically authorized by the state legislature or national funds being passed through the state government to its political subdivisions. The shared taxes are monies collected by the state, such as an extra penny "local government" sales tax or a portion of the state gasoline tax. The money is shared with the local governments either on an allocation formula or according to place of origin.

Other trends in fiscal federal arrangements could be isolated concerning increased reliance on deficit financing by all levels of government, shifts in functional allocations in intergovernmental aid, increased direct national fiscal involvement in domestic programs, and changes in the relative tax effort and fiscal capability of various governments, to name only a few. However, they are not as important from an intergovernmental viewpoint as those that have been discussed. A few conclusions are evident from the reviewed trends: (1) the system is in a dynamic state of fluctuation and change; (2) while patterns are evident, the lasting impact of those patterns on the continued viability of all participants in the federal agreement is not so readily understood; and (3) for all its strengths, the fiscal federal system still has some major inequities, stress points that appear to be weakening, and potential pitfalls. These observations will be discussed in more detail later in this chapter.

At present there is evidence of some important modifications of the reviewed trends and of some further changes in the fiscal federal system. Most startling to many students of federalism is the apparent renewed financial strength of the states. Long considered the weak link in the fiscal federal chain, the states, beginning about 1972-1973, suddenly showed a renewed fiscal vigor. As the national government reeled under the combined weight of massive deficits, inflation, and balance of payments problems, the states began showing several years of consecutive surpluses and balanced budgets. Indeed, an observer who viewed the system only from 1970 onward would come to a markedly different conclusion than those generally reached in fiscal federal analysis. To this new observer, the states would be clearly the healthier partner. The years ahead will determine if this period marks only a temporary aberration or "breather" for the states or the beginning of a significant new trend.

As a natural followthrough to this new fiscal strength of the middle units of the federal system, two other somewhat surprising changes are apparent. For the first time in many years federal intergovernmental assistance as a proportion of state and local revenues actually showed a slight decline in fiscal years 1973 and 1977. The 1973 decrease is almost certainly a peculiarity resulting from the unique payment schedule of the 1972 revenue-sharing funds in 1973; even the 1977 decrease probably does not signal a reversal of long-established trends. Second, the states have made major efforts to improve the revenue posture of their local governments. This includes not only greater state assistance to localities as outlined above, but also efforts to integrate local and state revenue systems. To this end, approximately one-third of the states restructured their local property tax arrangements in the past decade.

PUBLIC OPINION AND FISCAL FEDERALISM

The direction of some of the trends described above is likely to cause long-run misgivings with the American public. Elected officials are well aware of the public's opposition to "big government" and especially to centralized "big government." While public opinion data concerning this area are scarce, the available survey resources seem to support what most politicians, even those serving in Washington, "know."

For example, despite a general loss of confidence in the national government, more people feel they get more for their money from this unit than from state and local governments. Table 5-7 shows a 10 percent decline in the standing of the national government between 1972 and 1974, but a dramatic climb to 38 percent in 1975, and then a slight drop in the next year. The Advisory Commission on Intergovernmental Relations makes the following evaluation of the reversal of the first three polls' downward trend:

> The upturn in public favor for the Federal government appears to be attributable in large part to nonfiscal factors, primarily the end of the Watergate crisis and the related upswing in public confidence in the Presidency.
>
> It may also be attributed in part to the fact that the Federal government enjoys certain fiscal advantages over state and local governments, particularly in periods of recession. Because of its ability to engage in deficit financing, only the Federal government is in a position both to expand its spending and cut its taxes. In sharp contrast, many state and local governments have to take highly unpopular action—either increase taxes or decrease services, or both.[17]

Confidence in the ability of state government to spend wisely fluctuated over the three-year period. The lack of confidence in local spending varied little during this time.

Interestingly, an increase in education level is associated with stated feelings that state and local governments give "the most for the money," i.e., the less education a person has, the more likely he believes he gets the most from the national governmental level. This difference is minor, however. Conversely and more striking is the greater confidence college-educated individuals have in the fiscal management abilities of local governments when contrasted with those who have not completed high school (29 percent versus 19 percent).

TABLE 5-7

WHICH LEVEL OF GOVERNMENT SPENDS MOST WISELY

Question: "From which level of government do you feel you get the most for your money—federal, state, or local?"

	March 1972	May 1973	April 1974	May 1975	March 1976
Federal (National)	39%	35%	29%	38%	36%
State	24	18	24	20	25
Local	28	25	28	25	20
Don't know	19	22	19	17	19

SOURCE: Advisory Commission on Intergovernmental Relations, **Changing Public Attitudes on Governments and Taxes: 1976** (Washington: The Commission, July 1976), p. 2.

TABLE 5-8

RATING OF THE FEDERAL INCOME TAX LEVEL

Question: Do you consider the amount of federal (national government) income tax you have to pay as too high, about right, or too low?

	Percent saying "too high"		Percent saying "too high"
1941	54%	1961	46%
1948	57	1962	48
1949	43	1963	52
1950	56	1964	55
1951	52	1966	52
1952	71	1967	58
1953	58	1969	69
1957	61	1973	65
1959	51		

SOURCE: **Gallup Opinion Index** (March, 1973), p. 5. Summary of trend of years past from **The Washington Post,** April 14, 1973, p. A-13.

One focus of the taxpayer's wrath is the level of national income tax. That tax has been considered too high by more than two-thirds of the public since 1969. Indeed, even though national income tax rates have not increased in recent years and have actually seen some reductions, Gallup found strong dissatisfaction with the amount of national government taxes paid (table 5-8). The 1973 "too high" response was greater, except for the two years of 1952 and 1969, than at any time during the past thirty-two years.

The feeling that national government income taxes are too high is spread fairly uniformly throughout the sample, with a couple of exceptions. Both the very low-income respondents and those over fifty years old generally gave significantly less "too high" answers than the other interviewees, often 10 to 20 percent less.[18]

Other levels of government also receive criticism for their tax levels. There is some dissatisfaction with state taxes. Gallup found in 1973 that about half of the population felt their state income tax was too high, while 56 percent believed the state sales tax was excessive. The latter figure actually represents a slight decline from four years before (60 percent). When asked what was the best method of raising state taxes if it had to be done, 46 percent of a 1972 U.S. Advisory Commission on Intergovernmental Relations survey looked to an increase in the state sales tax, 25 percent to the state income tax, and 14 percent to the state property tax.[19]

Financially, the states apparently occupy a rather enviable position in the federal arrangement. They do not bear nearly as much attention or hostility toward their tax base as do the national government and local governments. The latter are often cited as the real target of the "Taxpayers' Revolt." Most of the outcry about tax levels in recent years has centered on the dramatic increase in local ad valorem property taxes. Caught between inflation-produced rising assessments and skyrocketing local government costs, resulting from the labor-intensive nature of that level of government, most property owners are facing almost annual increases in their ad valorem tax bills. In a 1973 Gallup poll 65 percent of the respondents reported their property taxes were "too high," an increase of 6 percent since 1969. Similarly, when the Watts and Free study asked which tax should be utilized—income, sales, or real estate—if a tax increase became absolutely necessary, an increase in the real estate tax was received least favorably.[20] A parallel question asked in an

Urban Observatory project showed that in eight of ten cities an increase in the property tax was the least desirable of five alternatives (property, income, utilities, sales, and car owner's tax). In the other two cities property taxes were the next-to-last choice.[21]

In opposition to the findings of other polls, the Urban Observatory's inquiry did not find universal agreement that property taxes were too high. In only four of the ten survey cities did a majority think the local taxes were too high (Baltimore; Boston; Kansas City, Kansas; and Milwaukee). Indeed, in four cities (Albuquerque, Atlanta, Denver, and San Diego) there was a majority feeling that the local taxes were "about right."[22] The different finding is undoubtedly, in part, a result of lumping all local taxes rather than centering on property taxes as did the other surveys.

CHANGE AND ACCOMMODATION IN THE FISCAL FEDERAL SYSTEM

The operation of the fiscal federal system has generated a number of concerns. Some are practical considerations affecting day-to-day living such as fears about higher taxes or complaints about inadequate service levels in vital areas such as education or law enforcement. Others are overtly political—partisan and personal. And some misgivings are expressed on a more theoretical and philosophical plane, for example, debates about the Founding Fathers' likely reaction to today's interpretation and utilization of the general taxing power.

While not minimizing the importance of these considerations, most observers feel that the system's ability to deal with one area of concern will probably determine its future. That is the concern over disparities and inequities—viewed from both the revenue and expenditure perspective—that abound in the federal system today.

The system's fiscal disparity and inequity problems can be viewed from three perspectives. Vertically, there is an inadequate resource base for the state and local governments, especially when viewed relative to the very elastic and potentially unlimited source of national revenue—the personal and corporate income tax. The limited yield resulting from this resource base, of course, may be grounded as much in lack of political will and inadequate legal powers as on economic considerations.

The second area of concern is on the horizontal axis of the federal system, namely, the disparities and inequities among the several states. Simply stated, there are very rich states and there are very poor states. The median family income for Connecticut (1970) of $12,011 is almost twice Mississippi's $7,577. Given the importance of the impact of many of the state and local functions on an individual's future (e.g., health care or education), can the United States long tolerate a type of federal lottery system in which one person receives more and better basic services because, by accident of birth, he or she was lucky enough to live in a relatively affluent state-local system? Should state boundaries artificially segregate resources and perpetuate disparities?

These questions, probably in a more extreme form, are also applicable to the third area of concern, that of interlocal resource disparities. The imbalance of resources among the states is relatively minor compared to that among local governments. Wealthy communities with an abundance of human and financial resources are separated from less affluent neighbors by the legal stricture of municipal and county boundary lines. By every major index, e.g., tax base, functional expenditure, socio-economic characteristics, the disparity between central cities and their suburbs is steadily increasing.[23]

With the political system taking only limited actions to alleviate these conditions, the courts have begun to intervene to relieve the grossest of inequities. In the area of school financing courts in California, Michigan, Minnesota, New Jersey, and Texas have ordered the states to take necessary steps to alleviate the inequities among school districts that result from local reliance on property taxes for school financing. In the precedent-making case of *Serrano* v. *Priest*, the California Supreme Court ruled that state and local governments could not allocate funds solely on the basis of a school district's wealth.[24] In Los Angeles County, for example, the Beverly Hills School District had a per pupil assessed property base of $50,885 and a per student expenditure of $1,232; in the Baldwin Park District the assessed value was only $3,706 per student and the expenditure was $577, less than half of that of Beverly Hills. This disparity existed despite the fact that the Baldwin District had a much higher tax rate. The Court turned down the state's defense of the existing arrangement in the following words:

More basically, however, we reject the defendants' underlying thesis that classification by wealth is constitutional so long as the wealth is that of the district, not the individual. We think that discrimination on the basis of district wealth is equally invalid. The commercial and industrial property which augments a district's tax base is distributed unevenly throughout the state. To allot more educational dollars to the children of one district than to those of another merely because of the fortuitous presence of such property is to make the equality of a child's education dependent upon location of private commercial and industrial establishments. Surely, this is to rely on the most irrelevant of factors as the basis for educational funding.[25]

Even though the United States Supreme Court has refused to follow the lead of the state courts and even though some state courts, such as New York's, have rejected Serrano-type arguments, continued judicial intervention to reduce these inequities appears inevitable for two reasons. First, many cases have been successfully argued on the basis of the Fourteenth Amendment's comprehensive and far-reaching equal protection provisions. Second, the courts are viewing the extreme disparities of some basic services such as education with care because of what the Minnesota Federal District Court called the "fundamental interest" of essential state and local services. For example, that Court ruled in Van Dusartz v. Hatfield that education "has a unique impact on the mind, personality and future role of the individual child. It is basic to the functioning of a free society and thereby evokes special judicial solicitude."[26]

A variety of devices have been proposed or implemented in an attempt to reduce these three types of inequities and disparities within the federal system. One of the more imaginative state actions designed to reduce metropolitan fiscal disparities is the Minnesota Metropolitan Revenue Act of 1971 that provides for local government sharing of the growth in the commercial-industrial tax base in the seven-county Twin Cities area. However, most approaches center on providing more national funds to assist the lower-level governments. Among the more famous proposals are (1) reduced national taxes; (2) direct national assumption of functions; (3) tax credits; (4) grant-in-aid reform; and (5) revenue sharing.

REDUCED NATIONAL TAXES

One of the least complicated proposals for fiscal adjustment is the often repeated suggestion that the national government reduce its taxes. The intention is that the state and local governments will take up the "tax slack" through their own tax increases. After all, it is argued, the primary obstacle to higher taxes at the state-local level is political, not economic, since most industrial nations of the world have taxes far higher than those of the United States. The political difficulties, it is believed, would be lessened if at the time of a national tax decrease, the Congress and the President announce that it is hoped and intended that the state-local sector will pick up all or the greater portion of that decrease. This method of fiscal adjustment would give the maximum flexibility to the state and local officials to determine how they wish to secure the new tax revenues, if indeed they do seek a tax increase, and how they will spend the new funds.

The past utilization of this approach has had mixed success. The elimination of national excise taxes has not automatically meant a state expansion in those areas. The reduction of national government taxes on amusement admissions, utilities, and telephone services was not greatly absorbed by other levels, perhaps because "an industry with enough political influence to persuade Congress to give it tax relief is likely to have the capability to restrain states or cities from increasing their taxes on it."[27]

Success with income tax reduction has been more notable. Not only may states pick up the "slack" through tax increases but also when states permit deduction of national tax payments in the computation of state income taxes, less national taxes mean a smaller deduction and, therefore, more state tax yield. Senator Jacob Javits (Republican, N.Y.) estimated that as much as one-third of the $6.5 billion 1964 national tax reduction ended up in the state coffers.[28] Perhaps more predictably a national tax reduction will almost certainly stimulate the economy and, therefore, because of the natural elasticity of many state and local taxes, give a higher revenue yield.

Critics of this approach argue that there is no guarantee that other governments will pick up national tax reductions. Such action is therefore sometimes seen as a "gimmick" designed by conservatives to reduce public expenditures rather than to transfer revenues within the federal system. Second, it is asked, from where will the national monies come? In these days of continuous national deficit a significant tax reduction must mean a decrease in national programs, probably those designed to aid state and local governments since they are the cause of the national tax deduction. The net effect may be to cancel out any advantage to the state and local governments. Lastly, it is strongly and justifiably pointed out that even if such a transfer of revenues does take place, it will not alleviate the disparities within the horizontal levels of the system. The wealthy jurisdictions will get more; the poorer ones will get less.

DIRECT NATIONAL EXPENDITURE

The financial problems of the state and local governments and the disparities among governments can be lessened by direct national expenditure, that is, the transfer of certain functions to the national government. Direct expenditures have been expanding markedly in recent years. Nearly 70 percent of the $155 billion in the 1976 national budget goes to the traditional areas of retirement and disability (Social Security); however, new direct expenditures such as Medicare, food stamps and family assistance, account for increasing portions of recent national budgets.

Similar transfers of functions are under way at other levels of government. For example, an increasing number of states pay directly all or part of certain education costs, such as capital construction, and many counties, especially the larger ones, are assuming functions from the smaller municipalities, such as police and fire protection. The main effort in this area currently is to have the national government assume responsibility for all public assistance costs. This is argued on the grounds of justice as well as fiscal adjustment because benefit disparities among the states are most evident in the area of welfare payments. The major shortcoming to this approach is that it insures a continuous process of centralization. How many transfers to higher governments can the system absorb and still remain a viable federalism?

TAX CREDITS

This third adaptive device would regularize the stimulus that would be available under the national tax reduction approach and would encourage state and local officials to increase taxes. In simplest terms, the tax credit permits a taxpayer to subtract, that is, credit, from his national income tax responsibility a set percentage of his total state and local taxes. For example, if a citizen has paid $800 in local property taxes, and $700 in assorted state taxes, and he owes $2,500 to the national treasury, assuming a 50 percent tax credit, he would substract $750 from the amount owed the national government. This serves as a stimulus for greater state-local tax effort. If in this hypothetical case a 50 percent credit were given, it would be politically more acceptable to raise taxes since 50 percent of the increase would come off national taxes. The computation for the above example before and after a tax increase is as shown:

Before Tax Increase	After State and Local Tax Increase ($100 each)
$ 800 local taxes	$ 900 local taxes
+ 700 state taxes	+ 800 state taxes
1,500 total state and local	1,700 total state and local
× 50% assumed tax credit rate	× 50% assumed tax credit rate
$ 750 national tax credit	$ 850 national tax credit
$2,500 national taxes due	$2,500 national taxes due
− 750 tax credit	− 850 tax credit
$1,750 owed national government	$1,650 owed national government

This method, strongly preferred by many economists, has two major disadvantages. It does not reduce interjurisdictional disparities; and, second, a large enough credit, without an upper limit, will soon substantially reduce national revenues. If the credit is set too low, for example, at 10 or 20 percent, or if there is a maximum deduction, its effectiveness will rapidly dissipate.

The tax credit approach has been successfully utilized in a few select national areas, e.g., inheritance tax credits and unemployment insurance tax deductions, as well as by many states. In the latter case, credits are normally given for select excise taxes paid at the local level such as a local tax on cigarettes.

GRANT-IN-AID REFORM

The official definition of a grant-in-aid is "the payment of funds by one level of government to be expended by another level for a specified purpose, usually on a matching basis and in accordance with prescribed standards or requirements."[29] Grants can be divided into three groupings—categorical, consolidated, and block. The categorical grant is used for a specific, carefully-defined purpose such as construction of a particular type of highway, or assistance for graduate programs in speech therapy. Today over 95 percent of all national grants-in-aid fall into this class. A consolidated grant is the result of a grouping or combining of several categorical grants. An example of the consolidated grant is the Partnership in Health Act of 1966 that consolidated more than a dozen categorical grants in the disease control area to establish a single health care grant. The use of this approach is increasingly common. The 1977 national budget, for example, suggested several major grant consolidations. Included were $10 billion for the Financial Assistance for Health Care Act that would consolidate Medicaid and fifteen other health programs, $3.3 billion for the Financial Assistance for Elementary and Secondary Education Act that would consolidate twenty-seven separate grant programs, and the Child Nutrition Reform Act that would combine fifteen complex and overlapping child nutrition programs.

The block grant is funded for a broad functional area, much broader than the consolidated grant. The 1968 Omnibus Crime Control and Safe Streets Act and the Housing and Community Development Act of 1975 are examples of major block grants. Many observers see increasingly less difference between block and consolidated grants, viewing it only as a question of scope. Thus, they see a dichotomy between categorical grants and block or consolidated grants with the latter terms being used interchangeably.

Further, all grants can be divided into a formula or project allocation approach. The former are grants which all eligible jurisdictions, states, counties, and so on are allotted funds according to a congressionally-set formula. A government must, on the other hand, prepare a detailed application for a project grant. Within certain congressional guidelines, the discretion for allocation of project grants is normally left to a national administrator who decides each grant application, or project, on its merits. An awareness of these different types of grants is important in understanding the problems with and the proposed reforms of the existing grant-in-aid program.

The national-grant approach has its antecedent in the pre-Constitution land ordinance of 1785, which provided that some centrally-owned lands be given to the states for the support of state and local education efforts. The 1914 Smith-Lever Act, which established the cooperative agriculture extension program, is generally thought to be the basis of the modern national grant-in-aid system. As outlined earlier in this chapter, from these modest starts sprang the massive program of over $40 billion with approximately 500 separate grant alternatives, a program so massive that the *Annual Catalog of Federal Domestic Assistance* now runs well over 800 pages. (Grant data also have been computerized for more convenient information retrieval.)

As a result of this growth, many criticisms and fears have been voiced about the operation and impact of the grant-in-aid system. These concerns can be classified as administrative or systemic.[30]

The former group of concerns centers on the manner in which national grants are administered. Much criticism is directed at the proliferation of grant programs. The sheer number of programs can awe and overwhelm state and local officials to the point that they are often unaware of grant money for which they may be eligible. This is especially true of smaller jurisdictions that lack specialized staffs to deal with grants. Further, great irritation is expressed about the technical and administrative requirements for most programs. From first application—often running several hundred pages—to required periodic statements of use, to final audit, a massive amount of expertise and paperwork is required. To illustrate, until recently HEW annually required over 7,000 pages of documentation from the states about the use of that Department's grants. The increasing complexity of the grant-in-aid processes has generated occasional humor as in figure 5-3; the more common reaction, however, is one of bewilderment and frustration.[31] The complex requirements have led to the emergence of specialists who play the "game of grantsmanship." Most states and large cities and counties have special offices of intergovernmental aid exclusively assigned to procurement and coordination of national grants. Increasingly, these governments are establishing special Washington offices to facilitate the awarding of national money. The smaller and poorer jurisdictions complain that they, who most need the assistance, cannot afford such expertise although some smaller jurisdictions have pooled their resources to produce a regional source of grantsmanship expertise.

The systemic concerns center on the long-range impact on American federalism of the national government's grant-in-aid program. For example, the current grant system has had, according to most observers, a major impact on state and local policymaking. This is most obviously true with reference to the

FIGURE 5-3

STAGES OF A GRANT-IN-AID PROJECT AS IT
ADVANCES THROUGH THE APPROVAL PROCESS

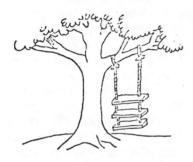

As proposed by the project sponsor

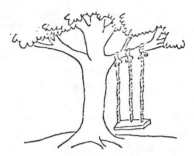

As specified in the project request.

As designed by the senior analyst.

As produced by the programmers.

As installed at the user's site.

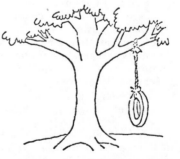

What the user wanted.

Adapted from **Front Lines,** a publication of the U.S. Agency for International Development.

state and local budgetary processes. Budgets have been influenced both with regard to level of expenditures and relative functional allocation. Strouse and Jones find, as an example, a very high association between national aid and states' expenditures in the areas of welfare, education, and highways.[32]

With regard to total state and local revenues, the national grant-in-aid policy has obviously stimulated new demands whose political implications are evident. Less evident but perhaps more important is the pressure to pick and choose among areas of expenditure according to the availability of national aid funds, rather than according to a more ideal democratic process. One million dollars spent for a non-aided function will give the public one million dollars of services (assuming a pure input-output system). One million dollars expended on an aided function may produce anywhere from two to ten million dollars in services, depending on the matching formula. An Illinois state official saw the situation as being one which produces decisions without real alternatives, which are not decisions at all but delusions of decisions. "The trappings of Constitutional sovereignty exist, but the expenditure decisions made under this protective umbrella are not the decisions of a sovereign."[33] The policy consequences of the grant system have been well summarized by Deil Wright:

> The lesser financial sacrifice required to undertake aided rather than non-aided programs alters the agenda of state and local policy issues. The priorities of state and local units are revised or made less clear. Moreover, decisions about the number of programs to pursue and the service levels to maintain for the various programs become more complex.
> ... grants set conditions in which federal administrative officials may substantially restrict the policy action and discretion of elected state and local officials. Given the financial inducements and conditions attached to grants, the states and their local units are all but required to adjust their behavior to fit specified nationally-prescribed constraints.
> Federal grants bring about a direct confrontation between conflicting national and state (or local) policy preferences.[34]

Further, it is argued that the detailed prerequisites for national funds have created a situation of close rapport and professional interaction among grant administrators at all levels that tends to weaken the power of elected executives.

People concerned about the systemic impact of massive amounts of intergovernmental transfers through the grant-in-aid device are particularly suspect of the continued ability of the state-local sector to maintain its relative autonomy and viability as increasingly large portions of its budget come from the central government. For example, K. C. Wheare's authoritative work on federalism notes that to be effective and viable on a continuing basis all the component units of a federal system must

> possess sufficient economic resources to support both an independent general government and independent regional governments. It is not enough that the general government should be able to finance itself; it is essential also that the regional governments should be able to do likewise.[35]

Commenting on this observation, Michael D. Reagan, after reviewing the growing dependence of the state and local governments in the American federal system, writes that

> the state-local governments are by no means financially independent. Furthermore, it seems beyond cavil that this financial dependence will increase further over time.... If Wheare's requirements are accurate, then the fiscal facts ... suggest that federalism in the United States is dead.[36]

Reagan goes on to distinguish between *financial dependence* and *programmatic dependence*. The loss of the latter would surely mean the end of viable federalism, but it is not clear that programmatic dependence always follows the loss of financial independence. Unfortunately, our understanding of the probable impact of the recent changes is very meager. The outlook for continued independence, however, is occasionally bleak. Witness the success of the national government's efforts to enforce "busing" school children for the purposes of racial balance, a success that was not based as in earlier years on the use of national marshals and national guardsmen, but rather a success based on the *threat* to end national school assistance funds.

Lastly, there are growing concern and opposition by state officials to the increasing number of national grants bypassing the states and going directly to the local governments, and even to private groups or individuals. This growth of "direct federalism" and "private federalism" is seen as substantially weakening the ability of the states to maintain long-established patterns of relations with their political subdivisions.

All these concerns, administrative and systemic, have prompted many proposals for change and reform in the grant-in-aid system. Numerically, most of them focus on procedural and technical administrative changes to reduce the need for lengthy grant applications and the many paperwork and red-tape requirements. Some of these proposals have met with success. For example, the national government no longer routinely requires a separate audit for the use of national funds nor does it require as many periodic reports on the expenditure of grant money. Further, much of the post-grant review and evaluation is now left up to the discretion of the recipient unit. Many of these administrative proposals were incorporated into the Intergovernmental Cooperation Act of 1968[37] and its subsequent amendments.

Other proposals for change have centered on the structure of the grant system itself.[38] There is strong support for the reduction in the number of categorical grants and for an increase in the use of consolidated or block grants. The popularity of the block grant approach under the Omnibus Crime Control and Safe Streets Act of 1968 has been encouraging for advocates of this reform. A variation of this approach is found in the proposals for joint funding simplification (JFS). Under this plan a state or local government undertaking a project involving many categorical grants could designate one national agency as the lead agency to process all the grant applications and to secure simultaneous approval of the grants. Further, that unit could serve as the single management and review organization, thereby eliminating the need for duplicate paperwork to many agencies.

The question of grant reform is not one-sided. Congress has a variety of purposes in creating and funding the multiplicity of grants that it does. They include the desire to stimulate a particular activity, insure minimum service levels, equalize interjurisdictional differences, and promote economic stabilization and development. Others are to provide special hardship relief, promote experimental or demonstration projects, and encourage planning and coordination.[39] What will be the impact, for example, of wide use of block or consolidated grants on the congressional wish to stimulate greater activity in a specified functional area? While the state and local officials may gain under block grants, much of the original purpose of the categoric grant-in-aid will be lost. That is, block grants will not provide stimulus for particular types of functions, narrowly defined. The net political balance may well be, then, that state and local officials gain some increase in policy choice, while Congress loses one of the major underlying purposes of the grant-in-aid approach. This consideration lends weight to the joint funding simplification approach over the block grant alternative.

REVENUE SHARING

The most recent addition to the many devices for eliminating fiscal disparities within the federal system is revenue
sharing. Basically, this approach provides for the distribution of
a sum of national money to the states and the local governments,
with the distributed funds having no national requirements as to
expenditure other than those required by the Constitution and
law (e.g., cannot be used to promote discrimination). Revenue
sharing is used by most federal systems in the world,[40] and
occasionally has been utilized in the United States to dispose of
early national budget surpluses and more recently to share
certain limited funds (generally in the natural resource area and
amounting to less than $500 million per year). However, revenue
sharing had its modern beginning in the United States in 1958
when then Representative Melvin Laird introduced a tax-sharing
bill in the House of Representatives.[41] Even though tax sharing
had been long used by the states as the major method of assisting
the localities, Laird's proposal became controversial enough to
take thirteen years to be enacted.

The plan received a major boost in 1964 when it was
endorsed by famed economist, and then chairman of the
President's Council of Economic Advisors, Walter Heller. In
early debates on revenue sharing, as a result of the strong
endorsement, the approach was often referred to as "the Heller
Plan." Debate over this program became intense in 1967, perhaps
as a result of the upcoming election, and resulted in many
variations of the tax-sharing plan being introduced into
Congress. Finally, in 1972 the State and Local Fiscal Assistance
Act was passed. The legislation provided for a total of $30.2
billion to be distributed to the states and localities over a
five-year period with appropriations growing from $5.3 billion
in 1972 (including 1971 retroactive payments) to $6.5 billion in
1976. The act was subsequently extended.

During the 1964-1972 period headlines such as "Mayors
Endorse Revenue Sharing," "State Lawmakers Clamor for
Revenue Sharing," and "Revenue Sharing: Toward a 'Great
Goal'," were commonplace.[42] Further, as table 5-9 indicates,
there was continuing overwhelming popular support for the plan,
support that transcended party lines with 77 percent of the
Democrats, 81 percent of the Republicans, and 73 percent of the
Independents in favor. Why, then, the long delay before
adoption? In addition to continuing partisan divisions largely

TABLE 5-9
PUBLIC SUPPORT FOR REVENUE SHARING

Question: It has been suggested that 3 percent of the money which Washington collects in federal income taxes be returned to the states and local governments to be used by these states and local governments as they see fit. Do you favor or oppose this idea?

	Favor	Oppose	No opinion
January, 1967	70%	18%	12%
April, 1967	70	15	15
July, 1967	72	17	11
January, 1969	71	17	12
March, 1971	77	14	9

SOURCE: **Gallup Opinion Index** (March, 1971), p. 13.

centering on which party or presidential candidate was to receive credit for coming to the rescue of state and local governments—with what was subsequently to become known as the Nixon Plan—there were deep divisions about how to implement the program. Was the amount to be shared to be a percentage of total national revenues, a percentage of collected personal income, or a set absolute amount? Who was to receive the money? The states? The cities? Other local jurisdictions? What was to be the distribution formula? Per capita? By tax effort? According to need or some other variable? What requirements or strings, if any, were to be attached to the money? And perhaps most important, from where was the money to come? Was this "new money" or a reduction in other existing state and local aid?

These very real differences were settled by one of the major compromise pieces of legislation of the past several decades. Under the State and Local Fiscal Assistance Act an absolute sum of money was authorized ($30.2 billion) to be distributed to both the state and local governments. The entitlement of each state is determined by a formula which includes population, tax effort, and the inverse of per capita income. Allocations are made automatically by the Office of Revenue Sharing in the Department of the Treasury based on data prepared by the Department of Commerce. No expensive and time consuming applications are necessary.

The cities and counties receive two-thirds of the money allocated to each state with distribution determined by formulas similar to that used for state allocation, although states may provide for some variation in the formula. There are no limitations or "strings" on state use of revenue-sharing funds other than those common to the use of all national monies, such as the prohibitions against using national money as the state's contribution to match grants-in-aid or the violation of civil rights by discriminatory use of national funds. Further, there are only broad guidelines for the localities. The local governments must spend their funds within the wide priority groupings of public safety, social services, environmental protection, sanitation, public transportation, health, recreation, libraries, and "ordinary and necessary capital expenditures."

With the plan just under way headlines such as "Democractic Governors Wary on Tax Sharing," "Revenue Sharing Snubs Suburbs," and "Revenue Sharing Plans Called Unfair to States Without Income Tax," became increasingly commonplace.[43] The change was based on a variety of criticisms about the plan, many of which are still being heard. Among these are:

1. It is believed that revenue-sharing money is coming from prior grant-in-aid funds and that there is not a major increase in total revenues going to the states and localities as was promised.

2. Some jurisdictions, because of the formula used for the revenue-sharing allocation and a general cut in certain grant programs, are receiving less funds than before 1972.

3. If in fact money is coming or will come from the grant-in-aid program, it is likely to hurt the poor and minorities who have received continued special assistance under the grant approach.[44]

4. There is evidence of the beginning of a series of administrative requirements ("strings") and reports that must be met to participate in the program. As of 1973, for example, local jurisdictions had to submit a "planned use program" which had been presented to the public through hearings and newspaper advertisements. Many critics feel this is the start of a bureaucratic maze of paperwork similar to that now existing under the grant-in-aid program. At least one small city, Templesville, Maryland, rejected its claim to revenue-sharing funds as being too expensive and time consuming.

5. Revenue sharing supports the continuation of the fragmented governmental structure in the metropolis by giving financial support to smaller governments which might otherwise seek unification because of financial pressures.

6. The demand for revenue-sharing funds is certain to increase, thereby creating a drain on the national treasury and a further dependency for state and local governments. As a recognized authority on fiscal federalism, William Anderson, observes, revenue sharing may be

> a pork barrel to out-pork-barrel anything ever proposed. And of course the barrel will never be large enough to satisfy the appetites of the state spenders. It looks like "easy money" but easy come can also be easy go—or else Uncle Sam will have to control the states' expenditures as never before.
>
> This "tax-sharing"... is not just a fiscal matter. Its ramifications are beyond calculation and prediction. I think [it] is as bad for the states as it is for the income taxpayers.[45]

There is strong evidence to support this fear. In a National Science Foundation-sponsored survey on revenue sharing, for example, 73 percent of the mayors interviewed believed that funds available through revenue sharing should be increased.[46]

7. Many critics complain that revenue sharing was first debated when the national coffers were relatively affluent and the states and localities were in desperate financial straits. Now, it can be argued, the situation is reversed, with the states, in particular, being in a very healthy fiscal position. Therefore, revenue sharing ought to be declared a success and terminated. Congressman Jack Brooks (D-Tex), a strong advocate of this point of view, referred to revenue sharing as "a little monster" and a "snake" that should be killed. He justified this conclusion in this manner:

> It is bad because we are trying to gain control over the federal budget but can't in less than about three years because too many mandatory spending programs such as revenue sharing are built into the budget.
>
> ... America cannot at this time afford a five-year commitment to federal revenue sharing. As long as the federal budget is in deficit there are, by definition, no revenues to share.
>
> ... Since revenue sharing started in 1972 we have never had a surplus in the federal budget. We could have reduced our total deficits since then by at least $35 billion if it had not been for revenue sharing, and, during 1972, 1973, and 1974 the states ran a unified budget surplus of over $36 billion.[47]

The initial experience with revenue sharing has apparently been successful. In a 1973 survey of chief administrative officers of cities of 50,000 or more, it was reported that 46 percent of the respondents were "very satisfied" with the revenue-sharing program, 32 percent were "somewhat satisfied," while only 6 percent were "somewhat dissatisfied," and 3 percent were "greatly dissatisfied."[48] Interestingly, in light of the criticism of the revenue sharing approach outlined above, especially critiques 1, 2, and 3, when the respondents were asked to assess the effect of revenue sharing on total federal aid to cities, 43 percent felt that there would be an overall increase, 23 percent believed there would be no change, and 35 percent noted that there would likely be a decrease.[49] A later study found that more than 94 percent of the local officials strongly supported the program.[50]

Public support for revenue sharing has fluctuated in recent years. In 1973, 56 percent of a nationwide survey supported the program. The following year that figure increased to 65 percent, but declined to 55 percent in 1975. The strongest support comes from the Northeast region of the country, where cities are known to be in financial difficulties.[51]

A sample of local governments' use of revenue-sharing funds reveals that most expenditures went for public safety (39 percent) and capital outlays (33 percent). These two major areas of use were followed by expenditures for public transportation (9 percent), environmental protection (6 percent), and health services (5 percent).[52] Different reporting requirements and procedures make it more difficult to assess state initial use of revenue funds. However, it is clear that both the states and localities have utilized this new source of revenue to hold the line on tax rates and in some cases to reduce taxes. Officials of eighteen states reported that revenue sharing funds would help permit some form of tax relief, fourteen of these indicating that property tax reduction would be the major thrust.[53] Likewise, three-fourths of the responding local governments expected their funds to reduce taxes or relieve pressures for tax increases.[54] The 1976 National Science Foundation study found, among other things, that (1) "the principal impact of the program was to expand the capital outlays of local governments, and to expand the transfer payments of State governments"; (2) "more revenue-sharing funds were used to maintain or expand operating programs than to reduce or stabilize taxes"; and (3) "both at the local and State level, GRS funds appear to have been used primarily to support ongoing activities, with only modest amounts of revenue-sharing monies going to activities that would be appropriately characterized as innovative."[55]

As an extension of the revenue-sharing program and as a response to the criticisms of the categorical grant program,

President Nixon proposed a *special* revenue sharing program to supplement the *general* revenue-sharing funds. This program would have replaced many categorical grants with flexible funding. The purpose of this approach, according to the national Office of Management and Budget, is that special revenue sharing

> emphasized the belief that in many cases State and local governments are in a better position than the Federal Government to design and implement responsive and effective programs which meet local conditions and priorities. Eliminating or reducing the Federal administrative role in these programs will relieve State and local governments of many federally imposed requirements and limitations, including in most cases, the elimination of matching requirements.[56]

The concept of special revenue sharing was not accepted by Congress, although, as noted above, much greater use is made currently of block and consolidated grants which in some cases approach being a type of special revenue sharing. That trend is almost certain to continue.

In 1976, after much debate, intensive lobbying by public interest groups, and several close votes in congressional committees, the revenue-sharing program was extended beyond its original five-year authorization. Twenty-five billion dollars was authorized for a three and three-fourths year continuation of the program.

WHO FARES BEST?

Throughout all the attempts at cooperation and efforts to devise formulas for grants-in-aid and revenue sharing that will be "equitable," obviously some states are likely to benefit more than others in the federal system. Some will find national policies more acceptable to them than others will. Some will subsidize others because they pay relatively more money into the national treasury in proportion to what they receive in national assistance or direct expenditures within their boundaries. What are the factors that determine which states will be most satisfied with the policy and fiscal outcomes at the national level?

Numerous suggestions have been made as to the determinants of state success with national fiscal and policy matters. Some of them are size and wealth of the state, party competition, civil service arrangements, personality of state leaders, state representation in the national leadership structure, political culture, and policy preferences in an individual state. Additional determinants proposed have included national administrative factors and modernized state governmental machinery.

Richard Lehne, in an interesting study of policy and fiscal success in which he analyzed the amounts paid to and received from various states and compared the states' congressional vote on key issues, found some intriguing correlations.[57] States profiting financially were those with low incomes and traditional political cultures, frequently agrarian, and those whose representatives in Congress possess high seniority. Wealthy states with innovative bureaucracies, strong governors, professionally-staffed legislatures, and substantial representation in the national executive and judicial cadre tend to lose and to subsidize the remaining states. This is not to say that they lose because they have these characteristics, but there is a positive correlation between states with these characteristics and financial loss. These traits are often associated with relatively affluent and rapid growth states. It is probable that wealth and growth are the more important determinants.

The picture is almost reversed in regard to success in achieving national policies in areas other than fiscal matters desired by the state. Those states that experience fiscal success do not generally meet the same degree of success in getting favorable policies adopted. States whose delegations have high seniority in Congress do not have much success in having policies they favor enacted. Wealthy states, characterized by highly competitive party systems, professionally-staffed legislatures, strong governors and substantial leadership, are winners when it comes to having Congress adopt policies with which they agree. More culturally diverse states, reflecting the heterogeneity of the nation, are generally more successful in having Congress adopt their policy preferences as reflected in the votes of their congressional delegations. According to Lehne's research, some states achieve the policies they desire but have to provide financial support for other states, while the latter benefit financially but have to accept policies with which they disagree.

Just as states fare differently in the amount of national aid received, so do local governments. A 1969 survey by Morley Segal and A. Lee Fritschler, for example, showed that while the average for all responding cities was $52.25 per capita in national grants-in-aid, there existed great disparities among cities.[58]

Population size was related to which cities fared best. While the largest municipalities (over 500,000) received slightly more ($55.87) than the average, the real winners were the smaller jurisdictions. Those in the 25,000 to 50,000 range received $65.26 per capita and those in the 10,000 to 25,000 group collected $58.64. Of interest, given the often repeated opinion of the national government's bias toward big cities, is the poor showing of larger cities. Only $38.74 went to those cities in the 250,000 to 500,000 population range.

Other factors that Segal and Fritschler found to be important were location and region. For the former, cities outside of metropolitan areas received far more per capita ($80.43) than did central cities ($50.68) or suburbs ($37.17). Concerning regions, the New England municipalities fared best ($92.76 per capita), followed by those of the Mid-Atlantic region ($72.74). Cities in the West South Central area (Arkansas, Louisiana, Oklahoma, and Texas) did the poorest, receiving a per-capita return of only $25.80.

Other factors that Segal and Fritschler, and other researchers, have determined to be significant are the existence of a municipal national liaison office, or grant coordination office, the attitude of local officials toward grants, and the knowledge of local administrators, especially city managers, of the grant process and grant availability.[59] Although it is uncertain exactly why such great disparities occur, it is clear that some municipalities consistently fare better than others in receiving national monies.

PRAGMATIC FEDERALISM AND FISCAL ADJUSTMENT

The study of American fiscal federalism demonstrates the pragmatic adjustment processes of the federal system. A summary of the major points of this chapter clearly shows the system's ability to accommodate to change and to meet new demands placed on it. These accommodations were not the result of a comprehensive reworking of the federal structure. Rather, they were—and are, as the system continues to evolve—the outcome of literally thousands of relatively minor pragmatic and incremental requirements. For example, the constitutional basis of the taxing powers of all levels of government has been gradually reworked and expanded over the years to permit the raising of revenues sufficient to meet the tasks of modern government. The new taxing powers of any particular government still may not be enough to meet its needs; however, the change in the revenue-raising capabilities and distribution patterns of all governments would astound the constitutional writers of two hundred years ago and would certainly amaze the students of American federalism of only thirty or forty years ago.

Similarly, the trends reviewed herein, e.g., that of specialization of taxation or of increased intergovernmental aid, demonstrate clearly the process of change and adjustment. Recent experimentation in the use and administration of national grants-in-aid and revenue sharing emphasizes the contemporary continuation of historical change processes. It is probably true that fiscal federalism more than any other sector of American intergovernmental relations demonstrates pragmatic federalism in action.

NOTES

1. L. L. Ecker-Racz, *The Politics and Economics of State-Local Finance* (Englewood Cliffs, N.J.: Prentice-Hall, Inc., © 1970), p. 152.
2. Acceptance of the current fiscal federal arrangements should not be equated with acceptance of current tax laws. The former can be accepted while at the same time calling for comprehensive tax reform to eliminate the perceived inequities in current tax law and tax administration.
3. Helvering v. Davis, 301 U.S. 619 (1937), pp. 641-642. See also Steward Machine Company v. Davis, 301 U.S. 548 (1937).
4. Frothingham v. Mellon, 262 U.S. 447. For a major exception to this position, see Flast v. Cohen, (392 U.S. 83) in which the Court ruled that because of the overriding importance of the First Amendment's establishment of religion clause, a taxpayer can urge more than his general interest in the expenditure of funds.
5. These exceptions were largely the product of a conservative Court in the 1920s and the 1930s and do not serve as a basis for judicial approach today. See, for example, Bailey v. Drexel Furniture Company, 259 U.S. 20 (1922); and United States v. Butler, 297 U.S. 1 (1936). Justice Frankfurter wrote a scathing dissent to the prevailing view of unlimited congressional taxing authority in United States v. Kahriger, 345 U.S. 22 (1953).
6. 4 Wheaton 315 (1819).
7. *Ibid.*

8. *Ibid.*

9. See Collector v. Day, 11 Wall. 113 (1871).

10. South Carolina v. U.S., 199 U.S. 437.

11. For a discussion of this complex problem, see Advisory Commission on Intergovernmental Relations, *State-Local Taxation and Industrial Location*, Report A-30 (Washington, D.C.: The Commission, 1967). In subsequent notes in this chapter this agency will be cited as the ACIR.

12. One of the best and most readable works on this subject is Ira Sharkansky's *Spending in the American States* (Chicago: Rand McNally and Co., 1968).

13. Statistics for the above section are drawn from data in U.S. Bureau of the Census, *Historical Statistics of the United States, 1889-1945* (Washington, D.C.: Government Printing Office, 1949).

14. ACIR, *Sources of Increased State Tax Collections: Economic Growth Vs. Political Choice*, Report M-41 (Washington, D.C.: The Commission, 1968), p. 8.

15. Ecker-Racz, p. 32.

16. Much of the data for the discussion of intergovernmental aid is taken from the Office of Management and Budget's *Special Analyses: Budget of the United States Government, Fiscal Year 1977*, especially "Special Analysis O: Federal Aid to State and Local Governments." (Washington, D.C.: Government Printing Office, 1976).

17. ACIR, *Changing Public Attitudes on Governments and Taxes: 1975.* Report S-4 (Washington: The Commission, July, 1975), p. 1. Note that a January, 1967 survey by Gallup showed dramatically different results. The posed question was: "Which do you think spends the taxpayer's dollars more wisely—the State government or the Federal government?" Forty-nine percent said the state, 18 percent the federal government, 17 percent replied "neither" and 16 percent had no opinion. The difference between the two polls could be explained by the variation in the questions, the different response choices, the sample, or the five intervening years. The last named appears less likely considering national government events during that period. Note that one-third of the respondents did not know if, or believe that, either level of government spends the taxpayer's dollar wisely. See *Gallup Opinion Index*, Report 19, January, 1967, p. 6.

18. See, for example, Gallup polls of March, 1967; March, 1969; and February, 1973.

19. ACIR, *Public Opinion and Taxes* (Washington: The Commission, 1972), p. 10.

20. William Watts and Lloyd A. Free, *State of the Nation* (New York: Universe Books, 1973), p. 294.

21. Floyd J. Fowler, Jr., *Citizen Attitudes Toward Local Government, Services and Taxes* (Cambridge, Mass.: Ballinger Publishing Co., 1974), p. 82.

22. *Ibid.*, p. 58.

23. ACIR, *Fiscal Balance in the American Federal System*, Vol. 2, *Metropolitan Fiscal Disparities*, Report A-31 (Washington, D.C.: Government Printing Office, 1967); and ACIR, *City Financial Emergencies: The Intergovernmental Dimension*, Report A-42 (Washington D.C.: Government Printing Office, 1973).

24. 5 Cal. 3d 584 (1971). See also the very important Rodriguez v. San Antonio Independent School District, 93 S. Ct. 1278; 36 L Ed. 2, 16 (1973).

25. *Serrano v. Priest.*

26. U.S. D. C. (Minn. Third District) Federal No. 3-71 Civ. 23a (1971).

27. Ecker-Racz, p. 166.

28. *Congressional Record,* October 11, 1965, p. 25618. Nationally-known economist Walter W. Heller supports this estimate. See Heller's *New Dimensions of Political Economy* (Cambridge: Harvard University Press, 1966), p. 140.

29. *Federal-State-Local Relations: Federal Grants-in-Aid,* House Report No. 2533, House Committee on Government Operations, 85th Congress, 2nd Session, p. 7.

30. An excellent summary of some views about the grant-in-aid program is contained in Deil S. Wright's *Federal Grants-in-Aid: Perspectives and Alternatives* (Washington, D.C.: American Enterprise Institute, 1968), especially, pp. 35-111.

31. For an interesting account of one city's dealings with the grant process, see Jeffrey L. Pressman, *Federal Programs and City Politics: The Dynamics of the Aid Process in Oakland* (Berkeley: University of California Press, 1975); and Jeffrey L. Pressman and Aaron B. Wildavsky, *Implementation: How Great Expectations in Washington Are Dashed in Oakland; Or, Why It's Amazing that Federal Programs Work at All, This Being a Saga of the Economic Development Administration as Told by Two Sympathetic Observers Who Seek to Build Morals on a Foundation of Ruined Hopes* (Berkeley: University of California Press, 1973).

32. James Strouse and Philippe Jones, "Federal Aid: The Forgotten Variable in State Policy Research," *Journal of Politics,* Vol. 36 (February, 1974), pp. 200-207. See, also, Edward M. Gramlich, "Alternative Federal Policies for Stimulating State and Local Expenditures: A Comparison of Their Effects," *National Tax Journal,* Vol. 21 (1968), pp. 119-129; Russell Harrison, "Federal Categorical Grants and the Stimulation of State-Local Expenditures," *Publius,* Vol. 5, No. 4 (Fall, 1975), pp. 123-136; and Sharkansky's *Spending in the American States.*

33. Quoted in U.S. Congress, Joint Economic Committee, *Revenue Sharing and Its Alternative: What Future for Fiscal Federalism*, Hearings before the Subcommittee on Fiscal Policy of the Joint Economic Committee, 90th Congress, 1st Session, 1967, p. 34

34. Wright, pp. 48-49.

35. *Federalism* (3rd ed.; New York: Oxford University Press, 1953), p. 6.

36. *The New Federalism* (New York: Oxford University Press, 1972), pp. 48-49.

37. P. L. 90-577.

38. Two excellent, non-technical discussions of present grant problems and reform proposals are the American Enterprise Institute's *Grants-in-Aid Reform Proposals* (Washington, D.C.: The Institute, 1970); and the Tax Foundation's, *Federal Grants: The Need for Reform* (N.Y.: The Foundation, 1973).

39. See Wright, pp. 35ff.

40. See R. J. May, *Federalism and Fiscal Adjustment* (London: Oxford University Press, 1969).

41. H.R. 748. See also his 1967 proposal, H.R. 5450.

42. In order of mention: *Washington Post*, March 11, 1971, p. A-21; *State Legislatures Progress Reporter*, Vol. 5, No. 4 (September-October, 1970), p. 1; and *Washington Post*, editorial, August, 1, 1972, p. A-18.

43. In order of mention: *Washington Post*, March 2, 1973, p. A-2; *Washington Post*, August 10, 1972, p. A-2; and *Washington Post*, July 22, 1972, p. A-2.

44. See, for example, F. Thomas Juster, editor, *The Economic and Political Impact of General Revenue Sharing* (Washington, D.C.: Government Printing Office, 1976), especially chapters 7 and 8.

45. Quoted in Mavis Mann Reeves and Parris N. Glendening, *Controversies of State and Local Political Systems* (Boston: Allyn and Bacon, 1972), p. 475. For a discussion of many of these adverse conclusions about revenue sharing, including pre-adoption arguments such as the separation of the spending and taxing powers, see Edward C. Banfield, "Revenue Sharing in Theory and Practice," *The Public Interest*, No. 23 (Spring, 1971), pp. 33-45.

46. Juster, p. 7.

47. Quoted in National Association of Counties, *County News*, March 1, 1976, p. 7.

48. David A. Caputo and Richard L. Cole, "Initial Decisions in General Revenue Sharing," *Municipal Year Book, 1974*, p. 99. Thirteen percent were "uncertain."

49. *Ibid.*, p. 101.

50. Juster, p. 7.

51. ACIR, *Changing Public Attitudes on Governments and Taxes*, 1975,

52. Department of the Treasury, Comptroller General of the United

States, *Revenue Sharing: Its Use By and Impact on Local Governments. A Report to Congress* (Washington, D.C.: 1974), p. 20.

53. Department of the Treasury, Comptroller General of the United States, *Revenue Sharing: Its Use By and Impact on State Governments. A Report to Congress* (Washington, D.C.: 1973), p. 21.

54. Department of the Treasury, *Revenue Sharing: Its Use By and Impact on Local Governments*, p. 21.

55. Juster, p. 5.

56. Office of Management and Budget, *Special Analyses*, p. 216.

57. Richard Lehne, "Benefits in State-National Relations," *Publius*, Vol. II, No. 2 (Fall, 1972), pp. 75-93. This section draws heavily from Lehne.

58. Morley Segal and A. Lee Fritschler, "Emerging Patterns of Intergovernmental Relations," *The Municipal Year Book, 1970* (Washington, D.C.: International City Management Association, 1970), pp. 13-38.

59. *Ibid.*; see also F. Ted Herbert and Richard D. Bingham, "The City Manager's Knowledge of Grants-in-Aid: Some Personal and Environmental Influences," *Urban Affairs Quarterly*, Vol. 8 (March, 1972), pp. 303-306.

6

Interstate Relations: Interactions Among Equals

Relationships among the states demonstrate all the diversity that contributed to making this country both vigorous and complex. These relations are quite a different matter than those between the national government and the states or between a state and its local units. In the first place, interactions are among equals on a horizontal rather than on the hierarchical basis that exists in the other instances. Second, some very sticky, fundamental matters are involved, such as State A diverting the water or polluting the streams of State B, or State C limiting the fishing rights, and thus the livelihood, of residents of State D. In the past it has meant that persons who thought they were lawfully married for the second time discovered that their out-of-state divorces were not legal and that therefore they were bigamists.

Women have found that their share of the family property differs as they move from state to state. Commerce and other interstate intercourse have been impeded. Multiple traffic regulations have slowed movement of goods and increased highway hazards. Persons old enough to buy alcoholic beverages in one state have been denied that privilege in a neighboring jurisdiction. Until the enactment of the Twenty-sixth Amendment in 1971 lowering the voting age to eighteen, a citizen might vote at that age in Georgia or Kentucky, but be unable to vote for one more year if he moved to Alaska, two more if it were to Hawaii, or three more if he went to one of the other states. The tremendous variety among the states produces both creative and confusing situations requiring change and adjustment throughout the systems.

The diversity of fifty political entities stands in refreshing contrast to the uniformity that could prevail were the American system to operate on a unitary basis. There are opportunities for experiment on a state rather than on a nationwide scale; and, in fact, past commentators have referred to this type of uncentralized system as a "laboratory for democracy." Citizens are offered choices as to the kind of place where they would like to live. Differing standards can be established in matters dividing society such as the sale of alcoholic beverages, legalized abortions, obscenity, or the quality of public services.

Interactions among the states are increasing. This reflects the growth of intergovernmental relations among all units resulting from accelerated public spending, proliferation of services, and technological advances that have shrunk the continent. An interesting aspect of this expanding intergovernmental intercourse is the growing acceptance of regional organizations on a multistate, substate, or metropolitanwide basis. Such regional interaction progresses unevenly, with starts and stops; nevertheless it is now a major aspect of the American governmental system. Not only have major regional organizations such as the Appalachian Regional Commission, the Ozarks Regional Commission, and the Upper Great Lakes Commission been established, but the national government also has regionalized its administrative apparatus to the extent that "the cities of New York, Atlanta, Chicago, Dallas, Kansas City, Denver, and San Francisco have acquired informal status as regional capitals because they contain the offices of numerous Washington agencies."[1]

Another important development is the increase in cooperation among the states as they move positively to solve the problems confronting them. We know of no empirical research on the number and handling of interstate disputes other than court cases, but there appears to be less friction among the states than in the past. Contributory factors seem to be the decline in boundary disputes, the necessity of cooperation to solve interstate problems, and the recent national encouragement of intergovernmental cooperation in various ways. The threat posed by national dominance also serves to solidify the achieving of interstate cohesion.

FRICTION AMONG THE STATES

Dissonance existed among the colonies and under the

Articles of Confederation; in fact, ten serious boundary disputes raged at the time of the Philadelphia Convention. Despite the general growth of interstate cooperation since then, all interstate relations are not harmonious. It is not always possible to avoid friction with one's neighbors, especially if his activities affect the welfare of one's family. States continue to disagree, sometimes loudly.

MATTERS IN DISPUTE

Many arguments have been over boundary lines and riparian rights, an outgrowth of conflicting charter grants and interpretations. The Mason-Dixon line grew out of a dispute between Maryland and Pennsylvania; and boundary conflicts have raged between Colorado and New Mexico, Delaware and New Jersey, and Indiana and Kentucky, to name a few. Since rivers form many interstate boundaries, they are the bones of contention in many controversies. Disputes have arisen as to which state owns the rivers and can regulate their navigation and fishing rights, how the water will be allocated, and how pollution will be controlled. The allocation of water is particularly important in the western states where water is scarce, but arguments over the diversion of streams have not been limited to this section of the country. New Jersey and New York went to court over New York's diversion of the Delaware River, and Minnesota and North Dakota were also involved in a contest over the straightening of rivers and the flooding of land. Fishing and the use of boats cause much interstate irritation. Virginia and Maryland engaged in an "oyster war" for more than two hundred years, contesting the right to harvest oysters in the Chesapeake Bay, and many states have been involved in controversies over the licensing and regulation of boating.

In the commercial field, states compete for the location of industries by reducing business taxes, and they are rivals as charterers of corporations. The Depression of the 1930s encouraged economic competition among the states and the erection of trade barriers to protect home industries. States used their police, taxing, and licensing powers to impose rigid rules of inspection, regulate the sale of selected products (for example, sausage), and restrict the importation of certain agricultural products. (They obstensibly limited importation for protection from disease but actually did so to prevent sales in competition with the state's own products.) In addition, they regulated trucks as to length, width, weight, number of lights, and so forth. They further imposed chain store taxes, discriminatory taxes on nonresidential commercial vehicles, special license fees for out-of-state corporations, vendors license fees on nonresident sellers, and discriminatory premium taxes on foreign insurance companies. Other states retaliated in kind, bringing forth impediments to commerce, overlapping taxes, and increased intergovernmental friction. Interpretation of the power of Congress "to regulate commerce with foreign nations, and among the several states," means that the states cannot levy these types of taxes and fees to the point of interfering with interstate commerce. The special levies, however, are often designed to give a slight competitive advantage to a state's own commerce.

Environmental pollution surged to the fore as a source of interstate controversy at the middle of the present century as states sought to clear the air and rivers of waste. Whenever the source of pollution was over the boundary in another state, the difficulties of solving the problems were increased, particularly when the polluter was a governmental jurisdiction.

Irritation surfaces in the apportionment of responsibility for the solution of urban-suburban problems—such as those of transportation, housing, and waste disposal—in interstate metropolitan areas. The overflow of troubles from a large city located on one state boundary to the small city bordering the large center but situated on the other side of the boundary also creates friction. Some difficulties of Whiting or East Chicago in Indiana, for example, are interstate in nature because of the proximity of these cities to Chicago.

SETTLEMENT OF DISPUTES

Many minor disputes are settled by negotiation among the respective state officials. These individuals often are acquainted with their counterparts in the other jurisdictions because they are members of interstate professional or public interest group organizations, or because other activities have thrown them together. A governor can pick up the telephone and talk to the governor of a neighboring state, or a state highway engineer to his counterpart across the river. Sometimes national agencies stimulate the interface of state officials.

Disagreements involving more complicated matters, such as the conservation and use of water resources, may be resolved by

formal agreement involving interstate compacts or other contracts. (They will be discussed later in this chapter.) In the past,
Congress occasionally has been able to placate both parties as in
the boundary dispute between Ohio and Michigan. When Ohio
was admitted to the Union in 1803, its exact northern boundary
was not determined because of conflicting language in two acts
of Congress. Michigan, which was still a territory, objected to the
boundary described by the Act of 1802; she claimed her territory
existed by authority of the Northwest Ordinance of 1787 to a line
drawn east from the southern tip of Lake Michigan. Responding
to pressure from the Ohio legislature, Congress authorized a
survey of the disputed territory, but Michigan refused to agree to
its findings. Congress eventually satisfied both parties in 1836 by
granting to Ohio the disputed territory and compensating
Michigan with the upper peninsula, located north of Lake
Michigan, an area about nine times the size of the land that was
lost.[2]

If matters reach an impasse, states occasionally go to court.
When one state sues another, it is a civil suit originally brought
in the United States Supreme Court. According to one student of
the judiciary, the Court treats cases between states as matters of
arbitration rather than as questions of law and encourages states
to settle the dispute themselves if possible. It attempts to avoid
having to force states to comply.[3] Under the Articles of
Confederation, Congress was made the arbiter of disputes between
states and actually settled at least six during the Confederation
period. The most important was a conflict between Pennsylvania
and Connecticut over what is now western Pennsylvania.[4] The
Constitution transferred the role of arbiter to the Supreme Court,
giving it original jurisdiction over all cases "to which a state shall
be a party." This original jurisdiction was made exclusive by the
Judiciary Act of 1789.

Despite the controversies under way at the time of the
establishment of the Court, only three suits between states were
brought before 1849. During the next ninety years at least
twenty-nine such suits developed. All the early suits involved
boundary disputes; in fact, during the first sixty years of the
Court they constituted the only cases between states coming
before it. More modern litigation involves water rights, pollution,
debts, enforcement of contracts, and efforts by two states to
prevent a third from enforcing a law to restrict the interstate flow
of natural gas in the event of a shortage.[5]

The Court construes liberally its own power to settle

controversies between states, indicating that the particular subject of the controversy is irrelevant; because the parties are states they have a constitutional right to come into the courts of the Union. Nevertheless, the Court sometimes looks at the subject and declines original jurisdiction. It did this in suits brought by states in attempts to enforce their penal laws, holding that its original jurisdiction extends only to civil suits. The Court also has indicated that its jurisdiction to hear cases between states would be used only when necessary. In the case of *Alabama* v. *Arizona*[6] where Alabama sought to enjoin nineteen other states from regulating or prohibiting the sale of convict-made goods, the Court held that the threatened injury to a state must be imminent and of great magnitude. It further held that the burden on the state bringing the case to establish all its elements is greater than that generally required for private citizens to recover in court. States must appear before the Court when summoned; otherwise the Court will proceed without them as it did when Georgia failed to appear in 1867 in the celebrated case of *Chisholm* v. *Georgia*.[7]

The Court has refused to hear cases brought by one state against another for the recovery of financial losses of its citizens. New Hampshire sued Louisiana in 1883 to collect on bonds issued by Louisiana and held by New Hampshire citizens. The Court declined jurisdiction in the case, ruling that a state may not invoke the original jurisdiction of the Court to enforce the individual rights of citizens.[8] In general, a state may not bring a suit in its own name for the benefit of particular persons. It may sue to protect its own rights or sometimes as a *parens patriae*—as a parent—to protect the welfare of its citizens as a whole. The Supreme Court generally constructs strictly its grant of jurisdiction over these cases which it shares with other national courts.

Compelling Compliance. The Supreme Court has no specified method of compelling compliance with its decisions and interstate suits are typically lengthy affairs. The *Virginia* v. *West Virginia* cases are probably the best example of the time it can take to settle a dispute and the difficulties the Court may have in enforcing its judgment against a reluctant state. When West Virginia separated from Virginia and was admitted to the Union as a separate state, it agreed to pay a fair portion of the public debt that had been incurred by Virginia before 1861. Virginia began negotiations in 1865 for the amount due, but West Virginia was not inclined to pay. In 1906 Virginia brought the first of nine successive cases against West Virginia. In the major cases the Court decided it had jurisdiction and that by 1916 West Virginia owed Virginia $12 million, but West Virginia ignored the demands for payment. Finally, in 1918, Virginia demanded that the Court direct the West Virginia legislature to levy a tax to pay the judgment. The Court was at a loss as to what action to take and set argument for the next term on the steps to be taken to enforce the judgment. At this point, the animosity of the two states having abated somewhat over time, West Virginia provided in 1919 for a bond issue and the debt was finally paid in 1939.[9]

INTERSTATE COOPERATION

Although the relations among the states are sometimes discordant, there is evidence that they increasingly are acting in concert to solve the gigantic problems confronting them. The growth in the number of interstate compacts and contracts, the increase in the number and effectiveness of interstate organizations, and the more frequent conferences and consultations all support the idea of heightened cooperation. State efforts are not always successful because they are likely to be pragmatic attempts to solve particular problems rather than sustained movements to produce intergovernmental harmony. Nevertheless, recent activities have opened new channels of communication and smoothed old ones.

Interstate cooperation is obviously influenced by many factors, some institutional and some human. Constitutional provisions, congressional legislation, executive orders, national grants-in-aid, and the leadership of national administrative agencies stimulate some uniform laws, regulations, and practices. The Constitution makes specific provisions for the rendition of fugitives and for the adoption of interstate compacts, the latter requiring the consent of Congress. National legislation provides for the ratification of compacts, the establishment of regional organizations, intergovernmental personnel exchanges, and interstate functional agencies in fields such as transportation, to cite only a few cooperative efforts it stimulates.

National statutes, reinforced by executive orders and Office of Management and Budget circulars, require cooperation in such matters as planning for metropolitan areas of an interstate nature. National grants-in-aid sometimes go to interstate regional organizations or contain provisions such as a requirement for an environmental impact statement involving interstate cooperation. National administrative agencies encourage uniformity in rules and regulations. Certainly the Law Enforcement Assistance Administration tries to achieve some sameness in police practices and law enforcement procedures, and the Environmental Protection Agency works toward general standards for environmental pollution control.

Probably even greater propulsion toward cooperation is provided by the staggering problems facing the states, difficulties not coinciding with state boundaries and requiring interstate action to solve. They are aggravated by tremendous population growth and technological developments that allow people greater mobility and increase the pressures on existing facilities. No one state is able to prevent the pollution of the Mississippi, Missouri, or Colorado rivers. Interstate action is required. Problems such as providing for the indigent or upgrading economically depressed areas are often regional or national in scope and require more than one state's successful handling of its share.

States employ various devices for cooperation. The most prominent are informal consultation and agreement, organized conferences, compacts, other contracts, uniform state laws and reciprocal laws, and interstate organizations. States also cooperate through the assignment of personnel to joint projects and through such activities as the interstate cooperation in law enforcement. The latter occurs when police from State A apprehend a criminal fleeing from State B and hold him for rendition, or when arrangements permit police from State A to follow him into State B upon his crossing the line if they are in "hot pursuit." States also devise contingency plans for use of personnel from neighboring jurisdictions in the event of emergencies such as fire or rioting. Sometimes these arrangements are made by compact.

It is most difficult to determine the extent of the informal interstate consultation and agreement that takes place or the matters involved because there are so many channels through which they could occur. Not only do governors visit, telephone, and write to each other, but other state officials also act similarily. There are numerous examples of governors agreeing informally to push a specific program, attend a meeting, or take a hand in a particularly knotty problem affecting another state. Administrators frequently consult, especially on matters affecting the peripheries of their states, such as highway location. Many professional organizations such as the National Association of Accountants, the National Association of Social Workers, and the American Bar Association, as well as public interest groups such as the National or Regional Governors' Conferences, and citizens' groups such as the National Municipal League provide forums for the exchange of ideas. Much time at these meetings is spent in informal conversation and arrangements to deal with problems can be made. The opportunity they create for bringing public officials face to face is probably more valuable than the programs they present, although these, too, can serve to stimulate thinking on mutual problems and facilitate exchange of information.

UNIFORM AND RECIPROCAL LEGISLATION

State concern with the problems created by variations in legislation on a particular subject is shown in efforts to enact uniform legislation and to grant reciprocity to each other. Uniform legislation involves the adoption by each state of substantially similar drafts of statutes on a specific subject, such as securing the attendance of out-of-state witnesses at a trial. Thus, although each legislature enacts a separate statute for its state, there will be a high degree of uniformity among the laws of all states on the subject. Reciprocity is an exchange of privilege. State A may lower its public-college tuition for students from all those states who do the same for students from State A. Or licenses to practice a particular profession, granted by State B, may be recognized in States C and D if State B allows professionals licensed by them similar privileges.

Many organizations promote the adoption of uniform legislation. The most notable of them in view of its singleness of purpose and its long record of activity in the field is the National Conference on Uniform State Laws. Other groups also work toward this end, but most have other major purposes. Over the years the National Municipal League has proposed a series of model state constitutions, model city charters, model county charters, and model acts that have influenced state and local government structures and policies. State constitutional conventions, state legislatures, and the interest groups involved, have used these documents as yardsticks for measuring the desirability of proposed legal provisions. National government agencies such as the Public Health Service and the Environmental Protection Agency, as well as various professional associations, put forward proposals that result in uniform arrangements if adopted. The Advisory Commission on Intergovernmental Relations designs a legislative program concerned with all levels of government, and the Council of State Governments suggests state legislation.

Commissioners on Uniform State Laws. The one agency dedicated solely to putting forward drafts of legislation for possible adoption by the various state legislatures substantially as written is the Conference of Commissioners on Uniform State Laws. The Conference, organized in 1892, consists of a maximum of five commissioners from each state designated by the respective governors. Most commissioners are practicing attorneys and law professors, with a few heads of legislative research and drafting agencies also included. The Conference appoints associate members from legislative research and drafting staffs.

Initiated by the American Bar Association, the Conference works very closely with it. Usually the two organizations hold meetings at the same time and place, and their committees cooperate as projects develop. Drafts of legislation proposed by the Conference are approved by the House of Delegates of the American Bar Association.[10]

Most of the legislation proposed concerns matters outside the normal fields of political contention; much of it deals with commerce. The Uniform Commercial Code illustrates the type of legislation likely to be successful. This code and the Narcotic Drug proposals have been adopted by all states. On the other hand, a full decade lapsed with no proposals for uniform legislation on death tax credits and nonresident individual income tax deductions. Also, after two decades uniform rules of criminal procedure had not been adopted by any state.[11] In matters where states compete, such as in economic development, uniform legislation is difficult to achieve because of the conflicts of interests concerned. Consequently, the number of policy areas in which uniform legislation is acceptable is limited. Legislation is most likely to be adopted when it is highly interstate in character, when it meets a recognized need, and when it is in the area of private law where controversy is less likely to accompany social change.

The success of the Conference in pushing uniform legislation rests principally on the support that the drafts receive from groups equipped to pressure for legislation in the states. The Conference has no difficulty getting the drafts introduced, but it does not function as an organized pressure group for their adoption. The state bar associations are particularly important in this respect. When the organized legal profession is united behind a proposal, the chances of Conference drafts receiving a favorable legislative reception are enhanced. Legislation on which those involved—such as the industry itself—disagree, such as on uniform regulation of interstate motor carriers, stands little chance of adoption.[12]

The method of drafting and adopting uniform legislation is illustrated by the history of the Uniform Commercial Code, which almost completely rewrote the entire field of sales contracts and personal and commercial credit. Work on this code began in 1940. An initial draft was published ten years later, and its final promulgation occurred in 1958. Committees from the Conference worked closely with the American Law Institute and the American Bar Association. Proposed drafts were introduced into several state legislatures for their comment, and legislative research agencies assessed their effect on existing statutes. Much discussion and criticism in both the legislatures and the banking and credit associations resulted in the drafters seeking to clarify existing law, and to fill in gaps such as that pertaining to the protection of consumers in credit contracts. New drafts were written. The New York Legislature authorized an interim committee study and its report was studied before final drafting. Discussions of its 1950 draft filled two issues of *Law and Contemporary Problems,* a journal published by Duke University Law School. In 1958, the final draft was approved by the House of Delegates of the American Bar Association. The American Banking Association supported the code before various legislatures.

In this case the Conference of Commissioners on Uniform State Laws served as negotiator between the state legislatures and the various professional groups concerned with technicalities of the law. In particular, it attempted to alleviate concerns expressed by the Council of State Governments and its affiliates, especially the Association of State Attorneys General. Its adjustment of the various interests concerned, as well as its attempts to work out the highly technical problems before the legislation was introduced, doubtlessly contributed to adoption of this uniform legislation in all fifty states. Negotiation of interest group conflicts outside the legislative chambers is a component of much legislation adopted in the United States.[13]

INTERSTATE COMPACTS

Additional evidence of the increasingly strong inclination of the states to cooperate with other states can be found in the growing number of interstate compacts; however, these instruments still play a minor role in solving interstate problems. Compacts are formal agreements between states somewhat in the nature of treaties on the international scale. The Constitution requires that they have the approval of the Congress. This is usually but not always the procedure, either before or after the agreement. There are instances of completed compacts that do not have congressional consent, such as the Southern Regional Educational Compact, but the line between the ones that require such consent and those that do not is imprecise. Generally, those transferring political control or power or adversely affecting a constitutional grant of authority require congressional approval; others do not.

Congress approved compacts rather routinely until the 1930s when they began receiving closer scrutiny. Consent to the Oil and Gas Compact was limited to four years and has required periodic resubmission ever since. In 1942 President Franklin Roosevelt vetoed a bill consenting to an interstate compact among Colorado, Kansas, and Nebraska on the use of the waters of the Republican River. He did so because the compact appeared to restrict national control of a navigable stream and limit national interest in the development of water resources. The compact was subsequently redrafted and approved. Recent acts of consent for many compacts reserve the right of Congress to alter, amend, or repeal them. Some statutes of consent provide that Congress or any of its standing committees may require submission of information by the compact agency which Congress demands.[14] Whether these provisions are enforceable or not has not been determined by the courts.

These congressional requirements grew out of a controversy between the House Committee on the Judiciary and the Port Authority of New York and New Jersey in which the Committee subpoenaed Austin J. Tobin, executive director of the Authority, to appear and bring with him records about the Authority's internal management. The Authority, supported by its parent states of New Jersey and New York, refused to submit documents on the ground that it was an agency of the two state governments and thereby immune from investigation of its internal affairs by a congressional committee. After losing the case in the United States District Court, Tobin won an appeal to the Court of Appeals. Since the case was carried no further, *In re Tobin* is the prevailing opinion.[15] It should be noted that the opinion was on the ground that the Committee exceeded its grant of authority from the House of Representatives. The Court did not decide whether or not Congress could investigate compact agencies, although statements in the opinion indicated that there might be limits beyond which Congress could not go.

A compact is usually initiated by the states involved and then submitted to the Congress after approval by the state legislatures concerned. Once in operation it has the same effect as a treaty between two nations. It is binding on all citizens of the signatory states, both as to public and private rights. Compacts, properly drawn and entered into, are within the protection of the contract clause of the Constitution and the Supreme Court has original jurisdiction over their enforcement. Congress also has authority to compel compliance. States cannot escape their financial or other obligations under them.

Figure 6-1 shows that until 1920 relatively few compacts were approved. There were thirty-six between 1783 and 1920. Since that date, the pace of agreement has accelerated with 65 being adopted between 1921 and 1955. During the decade of the 1960s alone, 47 compacts were approved; this is more than were put into effect through 1930. By the date of the country's Bicentennial a total of 177 had been ratified.[16] Nevertheless, their impact on the operation of the federal system has been slight.

Before 1920 compacts were bistate agreements, but since that time they have frequently included more than two states and occasionally Canadian provinces. A significant development is the national-interstate compact in which the national government is a signatory party and a participant and is not limited merely to approving or disapproving the agreement.

A national-interstate compact is enacted as a statute in each participating jurisdiction and applies to the states with the same effect as an interstate compact. When the national government enters, it, too, must enact a statute joining in the endeavor. This statute differs from the acts of consent for interstate compacts because it is regarded as a national statute while the consent legislation is not.[17] Consequently, it is binding on national agencies as well as on state governments. This gives it a potential for inspiring a much closer coordination of national and state law and administration than other legal devices.

FIGURE 6-1

GROWTH OF
INTERSTATE COMPACTS
1783-1976

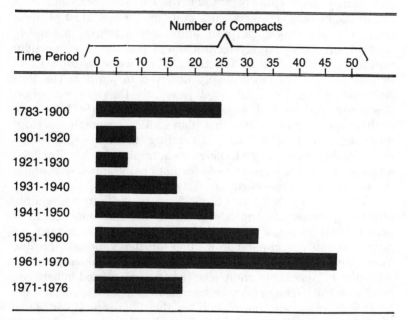

Council of State Governments, **Interstate Compacts, 1783-1970** (A Compilation) (Lexington, Ky.: 1971), p. 3; 1971-76 data from the Council of State Governments.

Congress can modify or negate the compact by taking contrary action at a later date.[18]

Weldon V. Barton classifies compacts into four categories: regulatory; metropolitan area; river basin development; and state service.[19] The first category includes those concerned with regulatory functions in an advisory or operational capacity, such as the Interstate Oil Compact or the Ohio River Valley Sanitation Compact. Both these compacts created commissions with important powers to regulate matters affecting oil or water. Thirty-three states are signatories to the Interstate Oil Compact which was "created almost as a desperate alternative to federal control, which the oil industry and the oil states both dreaded."[20]

Metropolitan area compacts afford a legal basis for the states involved to cooperate and establish permanent interstate agencies to plan and administer urban programs. Examples include the Delaware River Joint Toll Bridge Compact between New Jersey and Pennsylvania and the Palisades Interstate Park Commission between New York and New Jersey. Most of these compacts are single purpose and their activities are fairly routine, involving largely technical and managerial rather than political decision-making functions. Three agencies established in this fashion are more deeply involved in politics. The Port Authority of New York and New Jersey, the Delaware River Port Authority, and the Bi-State Development Agency (St. Louis) are multipurpose commissions that plan unified economic development and undertake varied operating functions. All enjoy considerable autonomy, largely as a result of their financial arrangements. They are eligible for national grants-in-aid under the Urban Mass Transportation Act of 1964.

The river basin compacts range in scope from one simply allocating water among states to a national-state compact establishing an agency with formal authority in water resource policy roughly comparable to that of the nationally-created Tennessee Valley Authority. There has been a recent surge in the adoption of river basin compacts; twenty were agreed to between 1927 and 1961. The national government is a participant in some of the more recent ones such as the Delaware River Basin Compact where it is represented on the Commission. Most of these compacts, like those in the regulatory category, were established to avoid action by the national government to solve the development problems of the river basins.

State service compacts exist in numerous functional areas such as crime control and prevention, education, welfare, and health. They attempt to reduce duplication of services and provide better services through interstate cooperation. Under the Interstate Compact for the Supervision of Parolees and Probationers, adopted by all states and the Virgin Islands and Puerto Rico, thousands of persons on parole or probation have been permitted to go to a state other than the one in which they were convicted. Their probation or parole is supervised in that state by its probation and parole officers in the same manner as they would oversee their own parolees or probationers. The compact provides a uniform legal procedure for meeting the needs of these people and replaces the rules of rendition that could make interstate cooperation difficult.

Interstate service compacts frequently serve as models for subsequent adoption of similar arrangements among other states. The Southern Regional Educational Compact of 1948, providing for cooperation in the field of higher education, was a model for the Western Regional Education Compact of 1951 and the New England Higher Education Compact of four years later. The Western Interstate Corrections Compact of 1958 was followed the next year by the New England Interstate Corrections Compact. Often service compacts are drafted with a view to nationwide adherence by all states. This was true of the Compact for Education (EDUCOM) and those on mental health, placement of children, and juveniles.

Because the individuals who could profit most from these compacts are generally politically powerless they are not very effective in promoting action under the compacts. The state officials who administer them consequently determine their effectiveness. States are often reluctant to commit their funds for interstate use so that often no compact agency is established to promote actual usage of the service compact. Where these agencies do exist the paucity of financing has hampered their effectiveness in planning and mobilizing support for interstate action.

Compacts are useful in many ways. They are important devices for settling disputes between states, although they sometimes elevate to the state level disputes between private claimants, such as in the instance of water basin development. It should be understood that many compacts, especially in the river basin category, result from activities of private economic groups with special interests in the resources involved—that is, farmers, private power producers, manufacturers, and processers. They use the compact device to block stronger national action or control because most of them feel more competent to deal with the states than with the national government. The use of interstate compacts to maintain state control of economic matters is not necessarily detrimental to the national interest; but it could delay coordinated national action in dealing with problems of nationwide concern. The Oil Compact, for example, may slow down action to arrive at a national energy policy. Weldon Barton writes, "Acceptance of a compact as a 'compromise' between national action and inaction may provide a tool to groups subject to regulation to play the states against each other in order to retain control in their own hands."[21]

Substantial evidence exists that the states use compacts to

protect their power in the federal system, and such use is applauded by the strong supporters of the states. Compacts may also serve to disrupt direct national-local relations, as in the instance of the Compact for Education, and to alleviate the pressure for transfer of authority over some social problems to the national government. They are useful in coordinating efforts to solve problems and to reduce duplication. They help to bridge the gap created by jurisdictional lines which makes areawide solutions to areawide problems more difficult.

In a penetrating analysis of interstate compacts in which Illinois is a participant, Marian E. Ridgeway cautions that the recent proliferation of compacts has taken place without adequate attention. While admitting that compacts are essential to any nonnational interstate undertaking of a binding nature and are advantageous in some instances, she points out that as a consequence of this lack of attention there is insufficient identification of their deficiencies and a failure to realize they are largely unproven. They may be attempted in improper spheres. Sometimes drafting is inadequate and frequently the proposals do not receive enough study during enactment. Once in effect, they are not systematically reviewed nor are they sufficiently evaluated by impartial observers. Possibly more important is Ridgeway's assessment that once operating, with compact commissions and "non-profit" corporations, these instrumentalities tend to be independent of public and state control. This produces a lack of responsiveness to the general public and to the states. Furthermore, compacts are highly responsive to special interests. With time, there is diminishing control by the states and increasing control by the professional bureaucracies staffing them.[22] Ridgeway writes:

> What has most clearly emerged from the research is a conviction that increasing involvement of states in interstate compacts heralds the beginning of a new shape for American federalism: a complex system being made even more complex, less clearly compartmentalized, more difficult to control by law and popular action because less easily seen and less easily organized for the placing of responsibility and authority. In this new stage of federalism's evolution, the people of the United States appear to play a diminished role. Authority, planning, negotiation, decision-making, administration move into the realm of governors, special economic development interests, combinations of mayors and other locally elected officials, revenue bond purchasers, appointed technicians and specialists, and private planning consultants. In Robert Salisbury's terms, it is a "new convergence of power." State legislatures and the Congress

assume the task and role once held in the state government by the voters; the giving or withholding of consent. The one remaining role for the people is taxpaying.[23]

The question of equal representation on the basis of population is also raised in the solutions of problems by compact because each state usually has one vote in the compact agency, thus underrepresenting the more populous states. Despite these misgivings, increased use of compacts is likely to continue.

In addition to the more formal compacts, other contracts between states are used to further mutual purposes. They have had a long history in education, for example. In southern states they were utilized in the past to provide higher education for blacks, particularly in specialized fields. Instead of admitting black students to the state university or law school, or establishing such schools for blacks, some states contracted with other states to accept eligible black students into their schools. The state where the student was a resident paid the state portion of the cost. This kind of arrangement is no longer legal when used to deny equal opportunity to all citizens of a state. It may still be used, however, to provide specialized training provided no discrimination is involved. State A, for example, may contract with State B to accept all its students who have completed its two-year medical program, and make a payment to the accommodating state in addition to the tuition paid by the student. This procedure is more likely to be used for education in programs not commonly offered, such as veterinary medicine. A wide variety of other services also may be provided by contract.

INTERSTATE ORGANIZATIONS

Many other interstate organizations operate with the express purpose of furthering cooperation among the states. They range from formal organizations in which the state formally participates as a political entity (for example, the Council of State Governments) to groups involving state and local officials (such as the National Sheriff's Association). Some are bistate, others are national or regional in scope. They vary widely in organization, membership, and function. A few of the most prominent will be discussed below.

The Council of State Governments. Prominent among interstate organizations is the Council of State Governments, founded in 1925 as the American Legislators' Association and given a new name with broadened activities eight years later. It is a leading proponent of the states' position in intergovernmental relations as well as a medium for interstate cooperation. The Council is a joint agency supported by the governments of all the states and under their control. Its purposes are set out in its articles of organization:

> The purpose of the Council shall be to strengthen state government and preserve its role in the American federal system by forceful expression of the views of the States; assisting the States in improving their legislative, administrative and judicial practices; promoting state-local and interstate cooperation; facilitating state-federal relations; and serving as a broad instrument for bringing together all elements of state government.

Government of the Council is vested in a governing board of more than 100 members, representing the states, affiliated organizations, regional conferences of the Council, various areas of state government, and regional organizations. It meets annually to establish organization policy and allocate funds. Nine organizations are affiliated with the Council and numerous others cooperate with it. Affiliates are the National Governors' Conference, the National Conference of State Legislatures, the Conference of Chief Justices, the National Association of Attorneys General, the National Conference of Lieutenant Governors, the National Association of State Budget Officers, the National Association of State Purchasing Officials, the National Conference of Court Administrative Officers, and the Council of State Planning Agencies.

Commissions on Interstate Cooperation. States participate in the Council of State Governments through Commissions on Interstate Cooperation or similar official bodies in each state. Organized in the manner of joint committees of the legislature with members from both the house and the senate, about four-fifths of the commissions also have representatives of the executive branch, including the Governor. In some states the legislative council or the legislative research agency functions as the commission.

Little in-depth research has been done on the commissions. What there is reveals substantial variations in functions and accomplishments. The most successful ones, at least in the past, have had sufficient funds to employ executive secretaries or research staffs, a factor seemingly contributing to their effectiveness.[24] These commissions have made significant contributions to the enactment of uniform and reciprocal legislation, rules, and procedures. They have formulated and promoted interstate compacts and have facilitated the adoption of national-state and regional programs. Some have conducted substantial research and disseminated information. In some states, to the contrary, the commissions have been scarcely used. One factor depressing their importance in certain states has been the legislative council, which has assumed the leadership in developing legislative programs.[25] It may be that the work of the Council of State Governments, the National Conference of State Legislatures, or other interstate or state organizations puts the commissions in the shade. In any event, their substantial potential for influencing intergovernmental relations appears to remain largely untapped.

National Governors' Conference. Governors of the fifty states, American Samoa, Guam, Puerto Rico, and the Virgin Islands participate in the National Governors' Conference which meets annually in different locales in the United States. Regional Governors' Conferences also exist. Organized in 1908, the National Conference seeks to serve as a medium for exchange of ideas, foster interstate cooperation, improve national-state and interstate relations, and work for greater efficiency in state administration. The National Conference undoubtedly provides a useful forum for the exchange of ideas and enables governors to meet face to face, thus establishing a base for future cooperation. But it has been criticized because its output has often seemed meager in comparison to the time, effort, and money going into meetings as well as for its heavy emphasis on social activities. In the past, its impact has been negligible except as a forum for prospective presidential candidates. Recent meetings have seen more time devoted to work than earlier ones, although the entertainment is still lavish. Perhaps it is unrealistic to expect a substantial work output from an organization of this sort, composed of busy executives with heavy responsibilities to their constituents at home. Its role in improving communications among governors is not negligible. Recent years have seen it assuming more responsibility for putting forward the position of the states in the federal system. The opening of a Washington office gives the governors increased presence in the nation's capital.

Views of the Conference are stated in the resolutions adopted at the annual meetings. Products of the work of standing committees, the resolutions are reviewed by the executive committee and then accepted or rejected by the annual meeting. For its 1973-74 policy positions, the Conference approved or continued positions on ninety-seven matters covering the broad areas of crime reduction; executive management and fiscal affairs; human resources, natural resources and environmental management; rural and urban development; transportation, commerce, and technology, and some miscellaneous matters including approval of presidential voting rights for citizens of Guam and the Virgin Islands.[26]

INTERSTATE REGIONALISM AND FEDERALISM

Regional organizations are not part of the constitutionally defined federal system. As in the case of local units of government, the United States Constitution does not explicitly refer to regional organizations as such, although in providing for interstate compacts, it defines the process through which they may be organized. The colonists experimented with regional arrangements more than 300 years ago when the New England Confederation was created to furnish a common defense against the Narragansett Indians and to provide for the peaceful settlement of common problems such as boundary disputes. Since that early beginning, use of regional organizations has been relatively infrequent.

ECONOMIC, CULTURAL, AND POLITICAL REGIONALISM

Although regional structures have until recent years played a minor role in American history, regionalism understood in economic, cultural, and political terms has been very important.[27] Approached from this vantage point, regionalism is viewed as a spatial concept in which certain areas of the country are grouped together because of homogeneous characteristics clearly distinguishing them from neighboring areas. Thus, when one speaks of the South, of New England, of the Midwest, or of the West certain images immediately come to mind that make the particular region distinctive from the rest of the country.

Regions are often perceived in economic terms. While the Northeast has a highly diversified and industrial economy, other sections of the country have specialized and agricultural or mineral-based economies. More importantly, regions have definite economic development and income patterns that are important factors in the establishment of regional configurations in taxing, spending, and intergovernmental fiscal relations. For example, in 1970 less than 7 percent of New England families had incomes below $3,000, while 15 percent of the South's families fell into that impoverished category. Further, while only 37 percent of southern families had incomes greater than $10,000, almost 55 percent of those in New England were in the higher category. These disparities have been among the factors that have led to the creation of special economic and social development regional organizations, such as the Appalachian Regional Commission or the Ozarks Regional Commission.

Economic aspects of regionalism also show up in taxing and spending patterns. Ira Sharkansky, a leading researcher on the topic, observed regional patterns in per-capita amounts spent for government services, distributions of expenditures by functions, and sources of revenue.[28] Major differences among regions are lessening, but sameness within regions is increasing as well. Consistent regional patterns appear in reliance on national grants-in-aid, distribution of functions to either the states or the localities, and state-local intergovernmental financial assistance. State-local centralization, which also has regional characteristics, is an important determinant of taxing and expenditure responsibilities.

Non-economic, historical factors also affect current regional fiscal trends. As Sharkansky notes,

> the political attitudes and values of original settlers or large groups of subsequent migrants may have been critical. Locally oriented administration and the heavy use of local revenue sources is evident in New England and in several other regions (Great Lakes, Upper Middle West, and Plains) that received many settlers either directly from New England or from intermediate regions settled by New Englanders.[29]

Likewise, the strong debt restrictions in the constitutions of Great Lakes states probably resulted from earlier excessive spending for public improvement projects in that area. Also, reaction to the laissez-faire extremes of early lumber and mineral barons may have produced what Sharkansky calls "the generous public services and high level of state and local government expenditures" in the Mountain region.[30] Regardless of the relative weight of economic variables and non-economic historical factors, what is evident from Sharkansky's research is "the power of regional norms to persist over time and to influence current styles in state politics and public services."[31]

Regionalism also has important cultural or social aspects. In general, the average American thinks of a region in terms of specific perceptions about its collective social behavior. Many such perceptions of regional cultures may be nothing more than a stereotype held over from past years. Irrespective of the accuracy of the image, its existence gives a cultural identity to a region. The intergovernmental impact of regional cultural differences is evident daily. The conservative, states' rights, anti-centralization philosophies of many southerners, the individualism and strong local orientation of New Englanders, the cooperative Progressivism of midwesterners, and the maverick tradition of westerners all give parameters and biases for intergovernmental behavior. As the Advisory Commission on Intergovernmental Relations correctly notes, "the importance of cultural regionalism cannot be underestimated."[32]

The extremes of cultural regionalism can lead to attempts to dissolve a federal union. The major effort at dissolution failed in the United States after a bitter fratricidal conflict. Regional cultural differences have been the source of secession in many other federal systems.[33] Canada, for example, has had a constant struggle to maintain the cultural regionalism of its French-speaking population and yet avoid the extremes of secession. In the United States today, the awareness of cultural similarities often leads to regional cooperative actions and organizations and only rarely to interregional conflicts as in the early case of the isolation and hostility of the South over the position of blacks in American society.

The political aspects of regionalism come about largely from a region's economic and cultural uniqueness. Most observers of American politics can readily point to sectional political patterns. They include variations in participation levels, consistent one party dominance, and regional political philosophies. They also consist of on-going attitudes toward the system (e.g., federalism or centralization) and toward specific issues (e.g., abortion or national aid to education), and perceptions of public trust or political alienation. The U.S. Senate Subcommittee survey utilized at various places in this book gives repeated evidence of regional attitudinal differences. In terms of philosophy, for example, only 22 percent of the respondents from the East agreed with the statement "the best government is the government that governs least," whereas 44 percent of those from the Midwest agreed. The South (28 percent agreeing) and the West (35 percent agreeing) fell between these two extremes.[34]

Regional patterns are evident for almost every aspect of American politics and, more specifically, intergovernmental relations. Concerning public trust toward levels of government, for example, the survey asked "Do you feel you have more, less or same confidence in the Federal [National] government compared to five years ago?" A total of 62 percent of the western respondents had "less confidence," while only 50 percent of the traditionally more hostile South had lost confidence. The other regions were less than but close to the western responses (Midwest 59 percent and East 60 percent).[35] There was significantly less loss of confidence toward the states and localities among all regions of the country.[36]

Diffusion of innovations among the states is the last political aspect of regionalism to be considered here. Jack L. Walker has analyzed how innovations such as new taxes, regulation of professionals, fair housing legislation, and home rule for cities, are spread, or diffused, among the states.[37] Walker notes that there are "innovative" states which have consistently pioneered the adoption of these types of changes. Over the years New York, Massachusetts, and California have been the most innovative states in the Union, while Wyoming, Nevada, and Mississippi have been the least receptive to innovation. More importantly for this discussion, the research shows that there are regional leaders, states such as New York, Massachusetts, Florida, and New Mexico, which can be seen as "regional pace setters" with followers, usually within their own region of the country, that "tend to adopt programs only after the pioneers have led the way."[38] Certain states provide leadership for more than one region. New York, as a result of its prominence, size, and geographic location, serves as a model for the New England, Mid-Atlantic, and Great Lakes regions.

In part, the regional patterns of innovation adoptions are caused by common needs, resources, and historical and cultural experiences of neighboring states. Also, it is important to note what Sharkansky calls a "copy your neighbor" syndrome.[39] When talking about or analyzing a state's problems and progress, the tendency is to compare the state with its immediate neighbors. Thus, a candidate for governor of Georgia is much more likely to compare that state's educational system with that of Florida or South Carolina than he is to look to California or New York for analogies. In Sharkansky's terms, this "legitimates one's own programs to those of nearby governments."[40]

Regional associations and meetings also encourage this type of diffusion patterns. A meeting of the Southern Governors' Conference is sure to stimulate discussion of new revenue-raising techniques or administrative changes such as the creation of a state department of local affairs. Professional civil servants show evidence of constant patterns of regional intergovernmental communications. For example, budget officers of major agencies in the states of Florida, Georgia, Kentucky, and Mississippi were asked: "Have you or any of your colleagues contacted officials in other states in an attempt to learn how they deal with a particular situation that you have encountered in your work?" Of those answering affirmatively, 87 percent listed states in the region[41] and 35 percent listed states bordering directly on the respondents' states. This is not unexpected, since as one study notes:

> The legitimacy of regional comparisons tends to feed upon past habit. Because officials have consulted with their counterparts in nearby governments, they have learned who can be trusted for credible information, candor, and good judgment. Unless an official is committed to an intensive program of research before making his own policy decisions, he may be satisfied after making a few calls to individuals with whom he has dealt amicably in the past.[42]

Economic, cultural, and political regionalism is slowly declining in importance. The onslaught of the national television and radio networks, the increasing mobility of American families, and the impact of the national government's equalization programs have an homogenizing effect on the United States' population. Over the decades we are becoming more alike as we lessen our emphasis on regional history and traditions, lose our dialects, and achieve incomes and life styles closer to the national average. Just as the importance of this type of regionalism began to decline during the 1950s and 1960s, the importance of regional organizations began to increase. The Advisory Commission on Intergovernmental Relations writes that "indeed the awareness of the cultural similarities of a region often are the basis for cooperative action in the political process."[43]

REGIONAL ORGANIZATIONS

Although the national government has used regional administrative organizations since 1788, the states have relied only sparingly on multistate organizations to solve regional problems. The Port Authority of New York and New Jersey Compact (1921) and the Colorado River Basin Compact (1929) are two of the earliest significant examples of such undertakings.

Multistate regionalism was given a major impetus in 1933 by the congressional creation of the Tennessee Valley Authority, a national agency, generally considered to be the first truly multifunction, multistate regional organization. The National Resources Planning Board gave considerable publicity to the idea of multistate organization during the New Deal, but at the time of its demise in 1943 the Board had not given birth to any regional creations.

From the end of World War II to the mid-1960s there was very little activity for multistate regionalism. The few structures that were set up were unifunctional, generally for economic development such as the Bi-State Development Compact (St. Louis, 1950), and the Delaware Valley Urban Area Compact (1961), or for water resource management, such as the Delaware River Basin Compact in 1961.

The 1960s saw a major change in the federal system with the emergence of many national-multistate organizations. Beginning in 1961 with the creation of the Delaware River Basin Commission, a rapid succession of these new structures emerged. In 1965 the Appalachian Regional Commission (ARC) was created. As part of the trade-off for the creation of the ARC, the Congress, under Title V of the Public Works and Economic Development Act of 1965, also authorized the Department of Commerce to establish national-multistate regional development commissions. Five regional development commissions were created by 1967—Ozarks, Four Corners, New England, Upper Great Lakes, and Coastal Plains. Further, Title II of the Water Resources Planning Act of 1965 authorized the establishment of similarly-structured river basin planning commissions. Six river basin commissions were created under Title II by 1971—Pacific Northwest, Great Lakes, Souris-Red-Rainy, New England, Ohio, and Susquehanna.

With these actions, thirteen new instrumentalities of federalism—six for economic development and seven for water resources management—were created. All but nineteen states became partners in one or more commissions, with two dozen states belonging to more than one. Pennsylvania, for example, belongs to five commissions, while New York is a member of six. Other proposed commissions, if favorably acted upon by Congress and the states, should bring practically all the states into at least one of these national-multistate bodies.

Why were these new intergovernmental organizations created? An assistant director of the Advisory Commission on

Intergovernmental Relations summarized the feelings that stimulated the new approach in the following terms:

> The shift in the sixties then was in response to a new and different cluster of problems, the most significant of which was the spill-over character of certain pressing policy issues. Common to all of these recent regional efforts was the view that the traditional interstate compact approach involving only the participating States was inadequate for certain program purposes and that the Federal-single State relationship did not cover adequately the interstate ramifications of these functional concerns. Put more positively, the Federal-multistate partnership concept emerged as a popular formula for resolving some of the administrative, political and fiscal difficulties that had emerged—at least in certain regions—in the economic development and water resources planning and management fields.[44]

Some centralists see these national-multistate bodies as a means of circumventing the limitations of traditional interstate compacts and furthering national policy. At the same time for their more state-oriented defenders, they are sometimes viewed as a statutory "means . . . of achieving additional impact on Federal policy and administrative decisions in their respective program areas."[45] Most observers agree that the strong points of these multistate bodies are: (1) they are means of securing additional national money, beyond the normal grant-in-aid programs; (2) they are likely to strengthen the hands of state governors in relations with the national government and other forces within the states; and (3) they aid in the solution of some difficult multistate problems.

For all these positive points, the national-multistate commissions are still untried new experiments in federalism with many unanswered questions. Are geographically fragmented problems to be united spatially, only to be divided functionally? Once removed from the electorate, how are these agencies to be held accountable? Are the commissions to become new power centers, eventually being relatively autonomous of both the states and the national government? The answers to these questions will not be apparent for at least another decade. By that time the commissions will surely be institutionalized as part of the federal system.

The Appalachian Regional Commission. A brief examination of the Appalachian Regional Commission will give some insight into the operation of the national-multistate commissions. Created by the 1965 Appalachian Regional Development Act, the Commission was to be, as characterized by the Advisory

Commission on Intergovernmental Relations, "an experiment in intergovernmental relations."[46] Its purpose is to provide for comprehensive multistate economic development in the depressed Appalachian area by achieving both national and state goals. The original stimulus for the Commission came from the affected states and local areas.

The ARC covers 397 counties in thirteen states,[47] with a total population of over eighteen million people. Twelve of the states had a net out-migration from their Appalachian portions during the 1960-1970 period. The area has continuing high unemployment, lower personal and family income, populations with low education levels and few job skills, and generally lacks adequate public facilities. These patterns have continued for decade after decade, even during periods of high affluence and economic expansion in the rest of the country. This situation provides the *raison d'etre* for the ARC and the Title V regional development commissions.

The governing body of the ARC consists of the national co-chairperson and the thirteen state representatives. The national co-chairperson is appointed by the President and has a veto over the Commission's activities, which he has never used. While taking an active part in ARC policy deliberations, he also serves as a liaison with the President, executive departments, and appropriate committees of Congress.

The states are represented by the governors or their representatives. The degree of personal involvement and decision-making by governors has generally reflected the portion of the state covered by the Commission. The states have established a permanent liaison officer called the States' Regional Representative. That officer, along with the Commission's executive director and the national co-chairperson, compose the ARC's Executive Committee which oversees the day-to-day activities.

Funding comes from various national grant-in-aid programs, direct national appropriations, and state and local matching contributions. Approximately 45 percent of the Commission's budget is derived from state and local matching funds. The states have made most of their contributions in the field of highway construction, while the local units have made greater efforts for non-highway functions. Road construction costs account for approximately 60 percent of the ARC's annual expenditures. Recent amendments to the 1965 Act have repeatedly expanded the Commission's functional powers in such areas as child nutrition and health, child development, nonprofit housing, education, pollution control, and mine-area restoration.

INDIVIDUALS AND INTERSTATE COOPERATION

Since the beginning of the Republic, America has been a mobile nation. As individuals and commerce move back and forth across state borders, provision must be made for their protection and regulation. The "full faith and credit" and the "privileges and immunities" clauses as well as provisions for rendition, all first stated in the Articles of Confederation and carried over practically unchanged to the Constitution, are the means through which the states cooperate to regulate and protect the individual.

FULL FAITH AND CREDIT

The Constitution provides that "Full faith and credit shall be given in each state to the public acts, records and judicial proceedings of every other state." The clear intention of this provision is to protect the individual as he moves from state to state. A man born in New York, married in Florida, and graduated from college in Wisconsin must be sure that his records are duly recognized as he settles in California. Similarly, this clause protects against a person moving to a different state to evade such responsibilities as debts.

The Constitution further sets forth that the "Congress may by general laws prescribe the manner in which such acts, records, and proceedings shall be proved, and the effect thereof." Congress has enacted such legislation, but it is still up to the states to grant the "faith and credit." For the most part, states willingly abide by the interpretation that the laws, records, and legal proceedings of one state, proven and authenticated, have the same effect in the courts of another state as they are presumed to have in their own. The willingness notwithstanding, "full faith and credit" often becomes complex and drawn out because of legal problems known as "conflict of laws." Suppose, as an illustration, a will is written in Georgia for a resident of that state who then moves to Tennessee and dies. It is the responsibility of the state of Tennessee to probate the will according to the laws of Georgia, not those of Tennessee. Similarly, a civil judgment against a resident of New York who moves to California to avoid payment is enforced by the latter state's judicial branch. These provisions pertain, of course, only to civil proceedings. Interstate criminal questions are handled under the rendition provisions of the Constitution.

PRIVILEGES AND IMMUNITIES

Individuals are further protected in the interstate system by the "privileges and immunities" clauses. Article IV provides that "The citizens of each state shall be entitled to all privileges and immunities of citizens in the several states." In addition, the Fourteenth Amendment mandates that "No state shall make or enforce any law which shall abridge the privileges and immunities of citizens of the United States." Thus, certain "privileges and immunities" are protected because a person is a citizen of both the United States and of a state.

The problem is the lack of clarity, even to constitutional lawyers, as to the meaning of these clauses. In general, the concept of privileges and immunities means that no state may discriminate against the citizens of another state in favor of its own. A state, for instance, must allow a citizen of another state the right to purchase property and must tax that property at the same rate as taxes on indigenously-held property. It must further afford the nonresident full police protection and use of the courts, and guarantee his right to move in and out of the state.

The states need not grant immediately all political privileges to newcomers. For example, a citizen of Arizona must meet all the constitutional and statutory requirements of California before being able to vote there. Further, resources or institutions of a state may be reserved for the exclusive use of its residents or a state may charge higher rates for their use by nonresidents. Thus, there may be higher fees for nonresidents' use of state parks and, as is generally the case, a state may require additional out-of-state tuition at its colleges. A person does not automatically bring his privileges and immunities from his home state. A doctor, therefore, has to meet his new state's professional standards before he is permitted to practice there. Lastly, these provisions do not extend to business corporations even though they are treated as individuals in almost every other question of law. A state thus may impose higher license fees for "foreign" corporations.

RENDITION

The Constitution provides that "a person charged in any

state with treason, felony, or other crime, who shall flee from justice, and be found in another state, shall, on demand of the executive authority of the state from which he fled, be delivered up, to be removed to the state having jurisdiction of the crime." This provision assures that since a state crime can be punished only in the state where committed, a person cannot evade his just punishment by fleeing to another state.

Rendition[48] is a relatively simple process. The governor of the home state simply presents evidence of indictment, criminal charges, or conviction, and requests the return of the fugitive for trial or imprisonment. The fugitive may ask the courts of the host state to determine the legality of the rendition papers, but he cannot seek to be found innocent or guilty of the actual crime. A returned prisoner may be tried for crimes in addition to those for which rendition was originally requested.

Although the Constitution says that the person *shall* be "delivered up," the courts have ruled that a governor may not be compelled to do so. On rare occasions states refuse to "deliver up." Reasons for refusing range from the observation that the fugitive has become a model citizen of the host state to questions of the justness of the law or expectations of an unfair trial for the accused. Expectations of unfairness occur most often when questions of race or so-called "political crimes" are involved. Even though the governors have the option, practically all requests for rendition are honored because no state wishes to become a sanctuary for the criminals of another. Furthermore, a rendition-denying governor of today may be the rendition-requesting executive of tomorrow. Because the rendition process is somewhat cumbersome in its formality and occasionally uncertain in its outcome, Congress has made it a national offense to flee across state boundaries to avoid prosecution or imprisonment.

NOTES

1. Ira Sharkansky, *The Routine of Politics* (New York: Van Nostrand Reinhold Company, 1970), p. 89.
2. Albert H. Rose, *Ohio Government: State and Local*, 3rd ed. (Dayton: University of Dayton Press, 1966), p. 14.
3. Samuel Krislov, *The Supreme Court and the Political Process* (New York: Macmillan Publishing Co., 1965), p. 145.

4. Alfred H. Kelly and Winfred A. Harbison, *The American Constitution: Its Origin and Development* (New York: W. W. Norton and Co., 1948), p. 103.

5. Charles Warren, "The Supreme Court and Disputes between the States," *Bulletin of the College of William and Mary*, Vol. 34, No. 5, pp. 7-11, 13-14 (1940). For a more extensive treatment see the same author's, *The Supreme Court and the Sovereign State* (Princeton, N.J.: Princeton University Press, 1924). See also *The Constitution of the United States Of America: Analysis and Interpretation*, prepared by the Legislative Reference Service of the Library of Congress, Edward S. Corwin, editor (Washington, D.C.: Government Printing Office, 1953), pp. 591-599. This discussion relies heavily on the last-named publication.

6. 291 U.S. 286 (1934).

7. 4 Wall. 475 (1867).

8. New Hampshire v. Louisiana, 108 U.S. 76 (1883).

9. Robert E. Cushman and Robert F. Cushman, *Cases in Constitutional Law*, 3rd ed. (New York: Appleton-Century-Crofts Educational Division, Meredith Corporation, 1968), pp. 276-277.

10. Phillip Monypenny, "Interstate Relations—Some Emergent Trends," *Annals of the American Academy of Political and Social Science*, Vol. 359 (May, 1965), pp. 54, 56.

11. Francis D. Jones, "Uniform State Laws," *Book of the States*, 1972-73 (Lexington, Ky.: Council of State Governments, 1972), p. 99.

12. Monypenny, pp. 56, 58.

13. *Ibid.*, pp. 56-57.

14. Advisory Commission on Intergovernmental Relations, *Multistate Regionalism* (Washington, D.C.: Government Printing Office, 1972), pp. 157-158. This agency is subsequently cited as ACIR.

15. 306 Fd2 270 (1962), Certiorari denied 371 U.S. 902 (1962).

16. Weldon V. Barton, *Interstate Compacts in the Political Process* (Chapel Hill: University of North Carolina Press, 1967), p. 3; Council of State Governments, *Interstate Compacts, 1783-1970* (A Compilation). (Lexington, Ky: 1971), *passim*; 1976 data from Council of State Governments.

17. Delaware River Joint Toll Bridge Commission v. Colburn, 310 U.S. 419 (1940); Hinderlider v. LaPlata River and Cherry Creek Ditch Company, 304 U.S. 92 (1938).

18. ACIR, p. 156.

19. Barton, Chap. 1. The present discussion of these categories relies on Barton unless otherwise indicated.

20. Richard Leach, "The Interstate Oil Compact: A Study in Success," *Oklahoma Law Review*, Vol. X (August, 1957), p. 284.

21. Barton, p. 57.
22. Marian E. Ridgeway, *Interstate Compacts: A Question of Federalism* (Carbondale: Southern Illinois University Press, 1971), p. 294.
23. *Ibid.*, pp. 308-309.
24. Patricia S. Florestano, *Interstate Cooperation Commissions* (Annapolis: Maryland Commission on Intergovernmental Cooperation, 1974).
25. Frederick L. Zimmermann and Richard H. Leach, "The Commissions on Interstate Cooperation," *State Government*, Vol. 80 (1960), pp. 233-242.
26. *National Governors' Conference Policy Positions, 1973-74* (n.p., n.d.).
27. The literature on this topic is immense. Three important general works are Howard W. Odum and Harry Estell Moore's *American Regionalism: A Cultural-Historical Approach to National Integration* (New York: Henry Holt, 1938); Daniel J. Elazar's *American Federalism: A View From the States* (New York: Thomas Y. Crowell, 1966); and Ira Sharkansky's *Regionalism in American Politics* (Indianapolis: Bobbs-Merrill Co., 1970). The first-mentioned work suggests some important distinctions between the terms "regionalism" and "sectionalism" (pp. 35-51). Sharkansky's book provides an excellent bibliographic essay on the topic (pp. 163-183). In addition to these general works, well-known studies have been produced about specific regions, e.g., V. O. Key's *Southern Politics: In State and Nation* (New York: Alfred A. Knopf, 1949); and Duane Lockard's *New England State Politics* (Princeton: Princeton University Press, 1959).
28. See Ira Sharkansky's *Regionalism*; and *Spending in the American States* (Chicago: Rand McNally and Co., 1968), especially, pp. 93-109.
29. Sharkansky, *Regionalism*, p. 143.
30. *Ibid.*, 144.
31. *Ibid.*
32. ACIR, p. 3.
33. Thomas M. Franck, ed., *Why Federations Fail: An Inquiry Into the Requisites of Successful Federalism* (New York: New York University Press, 1968).
34. U.S. Senate, Committee on Government Operations, Subcommittee on Intergovernmental Relations, *Confidence and Concern: Citizens View American Government*. A Survey of Public Attitudes. (Washington, D.C.: Government Printing Office, 1973), Part II, p. 111.
35. *Ibid.*
36. For local governments, 34 percent of the East, 33 percent of the West, 28 percent of the South, and 26 percent of the Midwest

expressed a loss of confidence. *(Ibid.*, p. 93) The responses for state governments were 34 percent for the East, 27 percent for the West, 23 percent for the Midwest, and 21 percent for the South. *(Ibid.,* p. 99.)

37. Jack L. Walker, "The Diffusion of Innovation Among the American States," *American Political Science Review,* Vol. 63 (September, 1969), pp. 880-899. This summary discussion relies heavily on Walker's research. For a better understanding of the complexity of the innovation/diffusion approach, see Virginia Gray, "Innovation in the States: A Diffusion Study," *American Political Science Review,* Vol. 67 (December, 1973), pp. 1174-1185; and Jack L. Walker, "Comment: Problems in Research on Diffusion of Policy Innovations," *ibid.,* pp. 1186-1191.

38. Walker, "Diffusion of Innovations Among the American States," p. 893.

39. Sharkansky, *The Routines of Politics,* pp. 86-105.

40. *Ibid.,* p. 86.

41. The eleven states of the confederacy, plus the Border States of Delaware, Maryland, Kentucky, West Virginia, and Oklahoma. See *ibid.,* p. 89.

42. *Ibid.,* p. 88.

43. *Multistate Regionalism,* p. 3. Much of the following discussion of regional organizations is based on this excellent study.

44. David B. Walker, "Interstate Regional Instrumentalities: A New Piece in An Old Puzzle?" *Journal of the American Institute of Planners,* Vol. 38 (November, 1972), p. 359.

45. *Ibid.,* p. 361.

46. *Multistate Regionalism,* p. 13. This report contains an excellent description of the ARC's first half dozen years' existence (pp. 13-52). Much of the following summary is taken from this source. The report also has a good review of the aforementioned Title V regional economic development commissions (pp. 53-92), and the Delaware River Basin Commission and the Title II water resource management commissions (pp. 94-134). For a comprehensive discussion of regional organizations, see also Martha Derthick with the assistance of Gary Bombardier, *Between State and Nation: Regional Organizations in the United States* (Washington, D.C.: The Brookings Institution, 1974).

47. Alabama, Georgia, Kentucky, Maryland, Mississippi, New York, North Carolina, Ohio, Pennsylvania, South Carolina, Tennessee, Virginia, and West Virginia.

48. The term *rendition* is used instead of *extradition* because the latter also refers to a similar process between independent countries, while the former term refers only to an interstate process.

7

State-Local Relations:
Strong Interdependence

In his attempts to cut through the maze of governmental units to get his children to school, our friend Henry Wooton, first mentioned at the opening of chapter 1, may have to take a route different than that to be followed by a resident of another state. No state's local governments are identical to those of any other state, and variations also are present in the allocation of functions among local governmental units. In some states a citizen such as Wooton would look to the state highway department for repair of the road. A resident of another state might have the gravel to fill the holes supplied by a local road district.

The diversity of local government institutions in the United States attests to the pragmatism of intergovernmental relations. Each state, with its own tradition, culture, and needs, establishes local units and assigns their functions in response to the demands of its own citizens—citizens who have environments different in many ways from the state next door. Geography, economics, history, demography, political and social culture, and many other characteristics distinguish one state's citizens from those of another, although, as we discussed in chapter 6, there are regional patterns. Consequently the solutions these citizens fashion for their problems will not necessarily be the same as those designed by their neighbors. Neither will the relationships among their institutions be exactly like those elsewhere. One would not expect Delaware's relations with its cities to be the same as those of Texas with its municipalities, and they are not. Neither are they identical to those of neighboring New York, New Jersey, or Pennsylvania.

Despite this diversity throughout the country, state and local officials experience all the satisfactions and frustrations in dealing with each other that officials involved in other intergovernmental interactions do. At the same time, their relations are marked by certain attributes that do not affect the relations of other officials to the same extent. State and local officials have a high degree of political interdependence involving strong influence on each other and together they influence other governmental jurisdictions—particularly the national government. Their constitutional and legal systems bind them closer and often establish formal requirements of intergovernmental interactions. Shared needs enhance their relations and possibly contribute to more stable relations than exist in other intergovernmental relations. Common traditions, cultures, and economic systems strengthen their interdependence. These may mute cries for change and mitigate the friction involved in certain adjustments. A sense of pride in their own state sometimes provides grease for the friction points.

Because of their strong interdependence, states and localities attempt to exert strong influences on each other. Toward this end, they have numerous instruments of persuasion and coercion. The state possesses an arsenal of legal powers for use with its local units, including the power to create and abolish them and to determine their powers. These are supplemented by administrative controls ranging from very mild techniques, such as the requirement of reports, to extremely coercive devices, such as the issuance of orders. In addition, the state influences through fiscal controls as well as through the important financial assistance it gives localities. Politically, the state is potent also as the governor decides on the location of roads or other public improvements or as economic development is furthered. It should be kept in mind that the governor is the leader of his political party in the state and may use this power as a tool to deal with local officials and party leaders.

Localities are not helpless in the face of this legal goliath. They can effectively counter state influence through their delegations in the state legislature, through political party organizations and state associations (such as the state league of municipalities), and through their votes in elections for state officers. Local governments have further influence by lobbying directly, resorting to court action or threatening it, stimulating public opinion in their behalf, and calling for local home rule. National financial assistance, especially revenue sharing, has strengthened local hands. A closer look at the various aspects of the relationship should bring the state-local picture into focus.

POLITICAL RELATIONSHIPS

The most pervasive and the most nebulous relations between states and their local units are political. Political interdependence is high, although the localities probably have the edge in strength. Citizens in cities, towns, and counties are also residents and voters in the state and can exert influence through the ballot box. By support or nonsupport for the state elected officials, a locality may vent its displeasure or approval. Votes of large urban areas can be especially effective in this respect and candidates for statewide office hasten to seek support of city voters and officials. Ballot boxes also may determine issues, as constitutional amendments and other proposals are subject to referenda. In some states citizens resort to the initiative to propose legislation the state legislature has ignored or rejected, use the referendum to force a popular vote on already passed legislation, and accept or reject bond issues for state programs and projects. Occasionally, recall elections may be used to remove from office state officials unpopular on the local level. With the exception of the vote on constitutional amendments and bond issues, these devices are available in only certain states. Where they do exist they offer last-resort opportunities for local counter-offensives against the state.

The political balance may also be tipped toward localities by local control of political party organization. County executive or central committees are usually the most powerful segments of the party organization. These organs, as well as other parts of the party apparatus—especially the state committee, state convention, and finance committee—may be used to influence the nomination, financing, and electoral support of candidates for state office, favorable or unfavorable to the local position, as well as to mold public opinion.

Richard Lugar, then mayor of Indianapolis, in speaking of the use of the political party in the successful effort to merge Indianapolis and surrounding Marion County in 1970, said,

> Each one of us as an office holder or a participant in civic life can find a very high degree of intergovernmental cooperation within one of the two major parties and attempt to influence the dialogue at the congressional level or at the state and local level through

that party and offer at least a way of proceeding. At least we have found that to be effective in terms of the Indianapolis situation vis-a-vis the rest of the state of Indiana, because we had to have that support in order to make reforms.[1]

Characteristics of the political party system may be determinative, or at least influential, in state-local relations. The amount of interparty competition within a state; the degree of cohesion in a given party, particularly in the dominant party; and the extent of openness in the party system may affect the influence of one level of government on the other. When strong party competition is present, a state party organization may be more responsive to local demands than if its uncontested position gave it greater freedom to operate autonomously. Since party competition differs from state to state, with some possessing highly competitive parties and others being essentially one-party states, it may bear importantly on the extent of party influence on intergovernmental relations. Similarly, party cohesion may be a significant factor. A strongly unified party may contribute to cooperative relationships while a highly fractionalized organization may stir up rivalries and disputes. Openness can have a significant impact on relations between a state and its localities. If the state party organization is strongly controlled from one locality, the influence of other areas probably would be reduced. On the other hand, if more than one strong local organization exists, the influence of local units should increase. The ability of citizens to penetrate party councils, whether state or local, and to induce responsiveness to demands may affect state-local relationships on more than one issue.

State legislatures are composed of representatives of the localities who are interested in their own communities as well as in the state as a whole. The locality may seek their support in its cause and probably get their backing because of the dependent relationship. By combination of blocs of local unit representatives—say, from urban counties—or by control of legislative leadership positions, state legislation affecting the locality can be modified. In states where special local legislation is permitted and state interference with local affairs is likely to be higher, tradeoffs among local delegations are the normal procedure. Usually a unified local delegation has no difficulty getting its proposals relative to that locality adopted and will, in turn, vote for other special local measures favored by the representatives of other areas.

Localities may lobby directly with the state or take the less direct route of trying to stimulate public opinion to exert pressure on state officials on their behalf. Each city, for example, may lobby its own representatives or combine with other cities throughout the state in a state municipal association to make demands on all legislators and state elective officials. Counties, towns, and other local units may have similar organizations. Spokesmen for these groups command attention of state officials when they speak with a unified voice for local interests.

Such associations, in addition to performing the usual functions of interest groups, serve as negotiators for their constituent units or candidates. Local opposition, combined under their banners, can sound a death knell for political careers. Furthermore, a few large cities and counties maintain state liaison offices to deal with the state on both political and administrative bases. Also, state advisory commissions on intergovernmental relations have considerable potential for exerting influence.

Local units continue to resort to traditional methods of influencing public opinion, such as adopting resolutions, using communications media, and public speechmaking by officials. Occasionally, a mayor—especially a New York City mayor—proposes that the city secede from the state, a move almost certain to attract press coverage, thus drawing attention to local problems. This device for rallying public opinion is old, dating back at least to 1861 when Mayor Fernando Wood made such a proposal to the Common Council of New York.[2] In their attempts to influence public opinion, localities rely on a prevailing belief in the inherent goodness of local self-government.

Initiatives by the national government, particularly direct grants to cities bypassing the states and revenue sharing, shore up local political powers. Operating with some independence of the state because of an outside base of fiscal resources, the localities are bolder in expressing their frustrations and enumerating their needs. Mayors and other local officials can develop programs and consequently political bases independent of the state.

State governments are not without resources in the political arena. In particular, the governor comes to the bargaining table with a pocketful of favors to dispense or withhold. He can often use them effectively in dealing with local delegations in the legislature, in attracting public support at the polls, or in rallying public opinion to his cause. As his administration makes various decisions—the location of the new highway or bridge, the recipients of the many state jobs at his disposal, the legislation he will propose or support, the location he will push for industrial expansion—the governor can make his political presence felt throughout the state. He is usually the leader of the state party organization and can use the party to influence local campaigns if he wishes. His announced support of a candidate or a slate is often sufficient to make others withdraw. The financial resources at his disposal can be determinative in a primary election. Legislators, as acknowledged political leaders, also can be very influential in local affairs, especially in states permitting special local legislation. As a unit, however, the legislature exerts most of its potency in the legal sphere.

LEGAL RELATIONSHIPS

In the realm of legal relationships, interdependence between states and their local units is particularly strong. This is highly evident with respect to local dependence upon the state. Since the United States Constitution makes no mention of local government, the states are the only subnational units. This is not to say that localities are unimportant in the national view: a multitude of national-local relationships exists. But, constitutionally, local governments are a part of state governments. Many local units pre-dated the Constitution and the states in which they are located and some, in fact, participated in the establishment of the superior governments. Nevertheless, they are generally regarded as deriving their legal existence from the states and as possessing no "inherent right of local self-government."

Unlike the federal relationship between the national government and the states, the state-local arrangement is a unitary one; that is, localities have no powers independent of the state. Cities, counties, towns, townships, school districts, and other units of local government are creatures of the state and under its control. Insofar as local governments collect taxes, provide services, and regulate citizens, they are exercising powers delegated to them by the state.

Unless restricted by the state constitution, the state government is the creator and source of authority for all the local units within its boundaries. Subject to state constitutional limits, the state legislature provides by statute for the creation of local units, specifies their form of government, defines their powers, and has the authority to abolish them. This is true even in states allowing municipal or county home rule. Some states provide in their constitutions for home rule; that is, the power of the municipality or county to select or draft its charter and to exercise broad powers of self-government. Others set out these options in statutes. Even in the constitutional home-rule states the legislatures exercise control over local affairs of statewide importance. Constitutional home rule creates a limited federal arrangement because local powers under this grant are derived from the people of the state and are therefore outside of the determination of the state government.

Local units are not protected from state interference by the national constitutional provisions that no state shall "impair the obligation of contract" or by the due process or protection of the law clauses of the Fourteenth Amendment. In the leading case of *Trenton v. New Jersey*,[3] which has not been overruled, the city legally acquired from the state the property and franchises conferred by the state to a private water company, including the right to take from the Delaware River all the water needed for municipal purposes. New Jersey later began to charge Trenton for the water. The City went to court claiming the impairment by the State of the city's contract, deprivation of property without the due process of law, and denial of the equal protection of the laws. The case eventually came before the United States Supreme Court which unanimously ruled against the City on all three grounds holding it to be merely a department of the state government from which the state may grant or withhold privileges as it sees fit. The United States Constitution gives localities no protection against the state according to this and other cases. If state laws conflict with national laws, however, the state may be prohibited by the supremacy clause of the Constitution from interfering with national grants or licenses to a city to take certain actions to carry out national power. As national activities expand, cities may receive further powers as agents of the national government, sometimes placing them in a conflicting position with the state.[4]

LIMITATIONS ON LEGISLATIVE CONTROL

The general power of the state legislature over the local units in the state is often modified by provisions of the state constitution; the relationships therefore vary from state to state.

There are differences as to degree of legislative control of cities, counties, towns, and other local units within a state, and sometimes among units of one type (such as cities) on a basis of population size. The more common constitutional restrictions include limits on the ability of the legislature to abolish counties or to change their boundaries without their consent, to enact special local legislation applying to one unit of government where a general law would apply, or to abolish certain local offices provided for in the document (i.e., the sheriff, coroner, or surveyor). Constitutional home rule provisions also limit legislative discretion. These and other restraints have important consequences for the ability of the states to solve problems created by population shifts, technological developments, and new citizen demands. Once regarded as desirable for the prevention of legislative interference, some of these provisions are seen now as hampering the ability of the state to solve areawide problems. The prohibition against the abolition of counties, for example, may stand in the way of metropolitan reorganization, the establishment of some other form of regional government, or the combining of small, sparsely populated rural counties. Nevertheless, state legislatures still exercise broad powers of control over most local units.

SPECIAL LOCAL LEGISLATION

Some state legislatures control, to a greater extent than others, the internal operations of local government. This is especially true in states where there are few, if any, state constitutional prohibitions against local legislation applying to one or only a small number of localities. In such states the legislature may enact a law prescribing the salary of a local assessor or the fees to be charged by the justice of the peace in a particular county. Or the legislature may grant the power to levy a certain tax to one city and not to another. In a few states the state legislature enacts annual budgets and tax rates of some communities.

Each legislative session brings local supplicants, hats in hand, to plead for enactment of laws to apply only to that jurisdiction. As a consequence, the state legislative representatives from that area are given substantial influence over the internal operations of the area's local governments. This forces the local government authorities to share control with the legislative delegation or even sometimes to assume a position somewhat subordinate to the legislative delegation, as it determines local tax rates and charter amendments, and functions on a cooperative basis with other local delegations. In some local jurisdictions the role of the legislative delegation has been formalized to the extent that public hearings are held on the special local legislative program to be presented at the next session of the legislature. Such practices raise the question as to whether the delegation is then part of the local as well as of the state government.

A majority of the state constitutions contain restrictions on this type of legislation. These restrictions (1) declare that no special legislation may be enacted where a general law would apply, (2) specifically list matters with which special legislation may not deal (e.g., changing boundaries or amending charters), (3) mandate local request or approval before special legislation may be enacted, or (4) require public laws to be applicable throughout the state. When the constitution provides that no special act may be passed when a general one would be applicable, the legislature cannot legally legislate for one city (or other local unit), if it is possible to handle the matter by a law applying to all cities or all cities in one class. Notwithstanding such prohibitions, many state lawmaking bodies have found it possible to circumvent constitutional intent by classifying cities, usually on a population basis, so that a particular class contains only one city or a small number of cities. Legislation for this class, while written as general legislation, is actually special legislation.

DILLON'S RULE

The grip possessed by states on their localities is strengthened by Dillon's rule, which sets out a strict court construction of grants of authority. Originally applied to municipal corporations, it has been extended to all local governments. The rule states:

> It is a general and undisputed proposition of law that a municipal corporation possesses and can exercise the following powers and no others: First, those granted in *express words;* second, those *necessarily or fairly implied* in or *incident* to the powers expressly granted; third, those *essential* to the declared objects and purposes of the corporation—not simply convenient but indispensable. Any fair reasonable doubt concerning the existence of power is resolved by the courts against the corporation and the power is denied.[5]

Dillon's rule applies in forty-eight states, Alaska and Texas excepted, although New Jersey has directed a liberal interpretation. It operates against change by requiring strict construction of constitutional and statutory provisions relating to local governments. The strictness of the construction depends on the attitudes of judges of the respective state supreme courts. There is an indication of a relaxing trend, especially in the more urban states.

STATE CONSTITUTIONAL
RESTRICTIONS ON LOCALITIES

The general application of Dillon's rule would appear to eliminate the need for restrictions on local exercise of power because under the rule local units have only those powers specifically delegated to them. Nevertheless, state constitutions contain specific limitation on local freedom of choice. They are aimed at defining local powers and specifying the methods governing how power is to be exercised. Provisions relating to form of government, method of electing officials, listing of duties, and tax and debt limits are frequently found. The constraints imposed by these provisions inhibit the ability of local government to respond to changing conditions. Financial restrictions have been particularly inhibitive and have brought forth a wide variety of avoidance techniques. Included are creation of special districts for the performance of certain functions (e.g., sanitary districts for water and sewage disposal), levying of special taxes, and resort to revenue bonds to avoid debt limitations.

The restrictions also have increased the need to seek aid from higher levels of government when necessary taxing authority was not forthcoming. Most of these constitutional limitations were designed to protect the public, but their effect has been to inhibit efforts of localities to meet changing needs. Those preventing or making it difficult to decrease the number of governmental units or increase their size may deter local cooperation or the merger of two or more units. For example, a study by the Advisory Commission on Intergovernmental Relations found that twenty-one state constitutions restrict counties by one or more arrangements. They are (1) freezing the existence of townships or other units smaller than counties; (2) declaring the existence of specific counties; (3) locating county seats; (4) regulating change of county boundaries; and (5) requiring special majorities of the electorate for approval of consolidation or merger.[6]

State statutory restrictions on local units are less important than those of a constitutional nature. They usually repeat the more common constitutional denials. Since local units generally have only granted powers, omission of grants of authority may be more damaging to local initiative than restrictive clauses. Nevertheless, statutory provisions can cause substantial conflict as does the state practice of mandating the terms and conditions of local employment.

BROADER DELEGATIONS OF POWER

Broader delegations of power have long been advocated, but the results have been limited. Constitutional home rule progressed by starts and stops after its initial adoption in Missouri in 1875, with highest interest occurring around 1912, in 1923-24, and during the 1950s. Often it has been eroded by imposition of tax limitation amendments or other restrictive devices. Recent years have seen a renewal of interest in home rule.

The tendency is to look upon the state as the withholder of local power, and much truth is contained in this observation. But it should be noted that, in the past, localities have not rushed to take advantage of home-rule grants. Not a single Wisconsin city or village adopted a charter under home-rule legislation in thirty-five years, and in Maryland only five of the twenty-three counties and Baltimore City (treated as a county under Maryland law) have made use of a 1915 provision permitting county home rule. In similar fashion only six of West Virginia's sixty-eight cities responded to a constitutional home rule grant in the first seventeen years after the adoption of the home rule amendment.[7]

Despite early lethargic responses, some states are making noticeable efforts to unshackle local governments and enable them to deal with metropolitanwide problems,[8] and local response in some states has increased. A recent survey by the International City Management Association showed that 38 percent of cities in excess of 5,000 population have home-rule charters. Larger cities are most likely to use such charters, but adoptions are spread throughout population groupings. The Northeast is the only area with fewer than one-third of its cities with home rule.[9] While fewer states provide for county home rule and only a handful of counties have utilized the power, large counties are moving to change their forms of government by home rule or other methods. The National Association of Counties reports that of the ninety-three counties with more than 400,000 people, sixty-one have adopted new forms of government and most of the others in this group are considering it, except in the eighteen states not permitting change.[10]

A newer approach to strengthening local government is the granting of residual powers. This means that, rather than being limited to powers specifically given to them, local governments would have all powers not denied them. Both the Alaska and Texas constitutions grant residual powers and this approach has been considered in other states. The Alaska Constitution stipulates that a "home rule borough or city may exercise all legislative powers not prohibited by law or by charter."[11] In Texas, the constitution, as interpreted, gives cities but not counties all the powers belonging to the legislature that are not inconsistent with general law. Such provisions bypass Dillon's rule by requiring strict construction of *limitations* on local power.

STATE-MUNICIPAL LEGAL RELATIONS

Cities, towns (New England towns are discussed below), and villages are municipal corporations incorporated by the authority of the state. On the initiative of the incorporators, this is done sometimes by the state legislature, but often by courts or county governing boards. This voluntary creation establishes a local government for the benefit of citizens of a locality rather than for the benefit of the state as a whole. Its general power to enact local legislation distinguishes this local government from most counties and other local units which have some but not all the powers of full municipal corporations. Municipal corporations are legal "persons" in the eyes of the law, possessing a legal being over and above the identity of the citizens who compose them or make up their governments. They can exist in perpetuity, even though all the citizens residing there at time of incorporation die or move away. They are authorized to conduct business in the corporate name, own and dispose of property, contract, and sue and be sued as the "City of ——" rather than as a group of individuals. Municipal corporations have such powers as are set out in their charters, subject to any constitutional or state statutory provisions. The United States has approximately 18,000 municipalities. The number increased by 469 between 1967 and 1972.[12] Much of this increase comes from a steady stream of suburban incorporations, especially in areas surrounding the larger central cities.

Every city has a charter that sets out its boundaries, structure of government, and fundamental powers. These charters are ordinarily state statutes, although the charters for some cities, such as that of the City of Baltimore, are set out in state constitutions, and others may be local provisions adopted under state authority. The charter may be a special one designed for that city alone and enacted by the state legislature. Or it may be a general one set out in the state code of general laws which applies to all cities or to all cities of a class (usually on a population basis). Some state legislatures enact several charters and allow municipalities the option of selecting one of them. Increasingly the states are turning to home rule and permitting the municipalities to draft their own charters and adopt them after submission to popular vote. Most states now have home rule provided for in the state constitution or by act of the legislature. A recent survey by the International City Management Association shows the following breakdown in types of city charters for municipalities with populations in excess of 5,000—home rule, 38 percent; general charter, 23 percent, classification charters, 10 percent; optional charters, 7 percent, and other legal forms, 6 percent.[13] Not all portions of a city's charter necessarily are adopted at the same time or in the same manner. States may alter municipal options for charter change from time to time, and some states permit more than one method of revision.

Cities Versus Legislature. Regardless of their form of government or whether or not they operate under home rule charters, cities are under the direct control of the state legislature. Their status, set out by Judge John F. Dillon in *City of Clinton v. The Cedar Rapid Railroad Company* (1868) is as follows:

> The true view is this: Municipal Corporations owe their origin to, and derive their powers and rights wholly from the legislature. It breathes into them the breath of life, without which they cannot exist. As it creates, so it may destroy. If it may destroy, it may abridge and control. Unless there is some constitutional limitation on the right, the legislature might by a single act, if we can suppose it capable of so great a folly and so great a wrong, sweep from its existence all of the municipal corporations in the State, and the corporations could not prevent it.... They are, so to phrase it, mere tenants at will of the legislature.[14]

Despite strict interpretation of municipal powers, cities have in practice developed considerable strength in relation to the state. Roscoe C. Martin writes:

> The cities are not nearly so supine as Judge Dillon's rule would lead us to believe. Something quite like a federal system has grown up within the states; for while the law calls for state supremacy, practice has produced a considerable measure of municipal autonomy. As a matter of law, the states could of course modify this system in any way they see fit, but in point of fact they find it difficult to abridge any important right enjoyed by the cities. Now and again a state takes punitive action against a city (usually one governed by a political party not in control of the statehouse), but such occurrences are so rare and the storm they provoke so violent as simply to underline the significant change which practice has brought about in Dillon's rule: de jure the state is supreme, de facto the cities enjoy considerable autonomy.[15]

Increasing municipal autonomy may have reduced, but certainly has not eliminated, state influence in city decisions. Very often municipal awareness that the city lacks a particular power removes options depending on that power from the decision-making arena. It passes into the "nondecision making" class, or else the city applies to the state for increased power.

Cities occasionally attempt to use the devices of secession, nullification, and interposition to gain greater freedom from state control. As mentioned earlier, some large cities such as New York have threatened to secede from the parent state, and clusters of "upstate" or "downstate" counties—believing themselves neglected children—at times talk of secession. These pronouncements are principally for propaganda purposes, of course. A more important type of local resistance to state control occurs when localities deliberately enforce state laws for alcohol or drug control far more leniently than elsewhere in the state or than intended by the legislators. Similarly, a municipality may try to nullify a state law, as happened with proposals in Ann Arbor, Michigan, and Berkeley, California, to decriminalize state marijuana laws. The use of these devices by local governments is clearly unconstitutional, only sporatically attempted, and of limited effectiveness.

CONTROL OVER COUNTIES

Counties are the most common, although not the most numerous, units of general local government in the United States.

They exist throughout the nation, except in Connecticut, Rhode Island, and the District of Columbia. The two states have retained county boundaries for election purposes and judicial administration but they do not have organized county governments. A similar situation prevails in three counties in South Dakota, and Alaska has twenty-nine census divisions with no organized local government.[16] No counties exist in limited portions of other states, such as in the independent cities of Virginia. In some large cities, including Baltimore, Boston, Denver, Honolulu, Indianapolis, Jacksonville, Nashville, New Orleans, New York, Philadelphia, and San Francisco, the municipality operates as a composite city-county, either as the result of city-county consolidation or of separation of the city from the county. (This is true, too, of some medium-sized centers such as Baton Rouge.) Despite these exceptions, only about 12 percent of the nation's population is not served by specially organized county governments.[17] Although actually counties, subdivisions in Louisiana are called "parishes" and in Alaska units performing county functions are known as "boroughs."

Counties vary widely in area, size, government organization, functions, and legal powers.[18] Important responsibilities are vested in them in the South, Midwest, and West, but where they exist in New England they are relatively weak. Governments in rural counties have a very limited range of functions, while the big urban counties of the large metropolitan areas have taken on the complexion of cities in the services they perform. Indeed, much of the literature on local government refers to the "urban county" as if it were a distinctive type of quasi-city, quasi-county form of government. Because of the population decline in many rural counties and the population increase in metropolitan areas, both types of counties have to adjust to changing needs and demands.

County governments are involuntary creations existing for the benefit of the state and not for the particular benefit of the citizens within the counties. The typical county administers state laws and does very little ordinance-making on its own. Consequently it is considered a quasi-municipal corporation, not a full municipal corporation. The county can exercise only powers delegated to it by state laws and the constitution. These documents set out the organization of the county government and define its powers. (Most counties are not incorporated and normally do not have charters.) To accommodate to recent urbanization trends, counties are increasingly being recognized as units of local self-government with powers of independent action. For example, a 1968 amendment to the Pennsylvania Constitution declares all counties to be municipal corporations. Traditional county functions concerning public safety, corrections, education, libraries, health, welfare, and highway transportation have been expanded to include such activities as air and water pollution control, mass transit, parks and recreation, housing, and zoning. These services are provided to meet citizen demands, not because they are required by state law.

As noted earlier, some states provide for county home rule to enable counties to adopt charters and to operate more independently. When this is done, the status of the counties is then changed so that they can be designated, for all practical purposes, as full municipal corporations because they have charters and are authorized to enact local legislation for the explicit benefit of their own citizens. Constitutional home rule modifies the traditional unitary relationship of the state and the counties and establishes a limited federal arrangement.

Home-rule counties make up a very small percentage of the more than 3,000 counties in the United States. There are only seventy-four charter counties.[19] The *Baker v. Carr* and subsequent reapportionment decisions of the 1960s provided impetus to the adoption of home-rule charters by reducing the impact of the lightly-populated counties in both houses of the state legislatures. These counties, as a consequence, have become increasingly concerned about relying on urban-dominated legislatures to enact legislation affecting their internal affairs. This is the reverse of the earlier situation when urban counties sought to extract themselves from the yoke of rurally-dominated legislatures.

LEGAL RELATIONS WITH TOWNS AND TOWNSHIPS

The terms "town" and "township" are often confusing because they describe different entities in different places. In most of the nation small urban places are known as towns. They may or may not be incorporated as municipalities and have established governments. In some states they are a class of municipal corporations. New York and Wisconsin designate as towns units that would be known as townships if they were located elsewhere. In the six New England states, towns differ from both of those just presented. There they include both urban and rural areas. Like counties, they generally blanket the state, one town being immediately adjacent to the next with no intervening distance, except where cities or villages have replaced them or in a few "unorganized areas" where no local government exists at all. Towns are the principal units of government in New England. They are particularly well known for the use of the town meeting, which may be composed of all eligible citizens or may be representative in form, and is the town's chief policyforming body. Towns are classed as municipalities in New England, but their status seems to be more nearly that of quasi-municipal corporations than full municipal corporations.[20] Their subordination to the state is complete, as exemplified by an action of the Legislature of Connecticut which, despite local opposition, declared that a bridge should be constructed and maintained at the expense of the specially-benefited towns.[21]

Almost half the states have townships, but only one of this group, Indiana, uses townships for its entire area and population. In some states—for example, New Jersey, Pennsylvania, and Wisconsin—operating townships include all territories outside municipalities. About three-fifths of the townships in the nation have populations of less than 1,000.[22] Township governments exist mainly in Northeastern and North Central states, but they may be basic units of rural government in other parts of the Midwest, in the Middle Atlantic states, and in a few other places. Because of their involuntary creation and their existence for the benefit of the state in general, townships are viewed as quasi-municipal corporations.

Townships differ greatly in functions and governmental organization. They seem generally to be losing power and purpose except on the fringes of large urban areas. There, they are increasing in power and may become full municipal corporations, relatively indistinguishable from cities. Regardless of size, structure, and function, they are in the same relation to the state as other units of local government; that is, they are dependent upon the state for their authority to perform functions and offer services, subject to any restrictions that the state may impose. They may have a limited (not general) authority to enact ordinances. The state confers specific power to adopt regulations pertaining to roads and bridges or to the construction of buildings, for example, but does not grant authority to legislate generally on local affairs.

OTHER SUBSTATE JURISDICTIONS

The state deals with many other substate governmental jurisdictions in its everyday operations. Most of them are special districts created by the state, one or more of its units of general local government, or the private initiative of a group of citizens (the last named action often subject to approval of some local authority such as a circuit or district court), to perform one or several functions. Some states use them more freely than others. Independent school districts comprise the most numerous—more than 15,000—and the most important type of special districts. However, there are almost 24,000 nonschool special district governments in the United States.[23] The latter include fire protection, sanitary, soil conservation, airport, water, and recreation districts, among others. Special districts may have their own taxing and bonding power, or they may be financed by fees for services. They are independent units of government, enjoying considerable autonomy from other local governments.

Special districts may be solely within a county, multicounty, or include parts of counties and municipalities. Some are interstate. They may blanket a state as school districts often do or they may be confined to one area. Utilization of nonschool special districts has increased greatly in recent years. Many new districts were structured to cope with areawide problems in governmentally fragmented metropolitan areas, while others were established to provide urban services in unincorporated areas. Created to deal with special problems, they reflect little uniformity in boundary or function. Some are very large and important such as the Chicago Sanitary District; others may be concerned with the operation of a single cemetery or library.

In addition to state- and locally-created special district governments just discussed, more than 3,000 districts that are not regarded as independent governments have been established to qualify for national governmental aid. At least half of them cover more than one county. They include metropolitan-area councils of government, state planning and development districts, substate clearing houses responsible for A-95 review functions,[24] law enforcement and criminal justice planning regions, single county and multicounty community action agencies, and substate comprehensive area manpower planning systems. Others are regional comprehensive health planning agencies, air quality regions, local development districts, resource conservation development districts, and economic development districts.[25] Also, statewide substate district systems have been established by forty states.[26] A recent report by the Advisory Commission on Intergovernmental Relations states: "What this means is that there is a new kind of areawide agency proliferation that now is part of the mosaic of substate government . . . the pressure for areawide mechanisms for areawide problems will not fade away."[27]

Multifaceted relationships exist between officials of these subordinate (nonindependent) districts and state officials. State options in the creation, design, continuation, and control of such districts are limited by provisions of congressional statutes setting up requirements for grants-in-aid in some instances and by local and interest group pressures in others. There is a continuing effort to achieve identical boundaries between state-established and nationally-sponsored subordinate districts and agencies, and more than one-third are now the same.

The existence of thousands of special district units makes control and coordination of them difficult and undermines general purpose governments. It complicates and makes almost unfathomable the maze of intergovernmental relations, and makes it difficult to know who speaks for the community; nevertheless, they are politically expedient devices in many instances. As far as intergovernmental implications are concerned, the state, through them, is allowed an input into matters that otherwise would be entirely local. Furthermore, sometimes local citizens can unite through a special district to solve a problem or offer a service which otherwise might involve the cooperation of several units of local government. As Daniel J. Elazar points out, special districts may even increase the independence of state and local interests in their relations with the national government by concentrating energy at key points and then letting the districts negotiate with the national agencies. He writes:

> In terms more familiar to the game of poker, the existence of special government institutions is a means of paying the ante that gives interests a right to sit in on the game, a license to negotiate and bargain with other governments and the interests they represent. Once the ante is paid, the possibilities of coming out ahead are substantially equalized for all players, thus allowing local governments to serve local interests and not just administer national programs.[28]

COURT ENFORCEMENT OF LEGAL RELATIONSHIPS

Constitutional restrictions and requirements, as well as those set out in statutes and by administrative rules and regulations, may be enforced against local officials through the state courts. Usually such actions are brought by private citizens or organizations such as citizens' associations, "Nader's Raiders," the American Civil Liberties Union, or the National Association for the Advancement of Colored People; but occasionally a state official or agency may initiate the action. Challengers to official action may question the authority by which an officeholder or a governmental entity purported to act or may seek court reviews of administrative actions after administrative processes for remedy are exhausted. They also may seek writs of mandamus to compel the performance of an allegedly nondiscretionary duty or writs of injunction to stop actions or provide relief or damages in certain instances. They further may bring taxpayers suits, or mount defenses against efforts of the local government to assert its rights or to enforce its ordinances and regulations. Often suits against a local government are directed against individual officers rather than against the city, county, or town, so as to avoid the issue of the unit's immunity from suit.[29]

Other forms of judicial action are also used to enforce state control over local officials. Local powers frequently are interpreted in state courts. Local officials are sometimes subject to removal through court action, and the validity of local administrative decisions, as well as state administrative control over localities, may be subject to adjudication.

ADMINISTRATIVE RELATIONS

The interactions of states and localities are most often administrative. Because of their dependence on local administrators for carrying out certain programs, state officials exercise substantial supervision of local activities. This administrative oversight has largely replaced the traditional pattern of direct state legislative supervision of local government. The need for flexibility and continuous supervision was beyond the capacity of legislators who met only a few weeks annually or biennially. Furthermore, as government became more technical, professionals were required to understand its complex details. Consequently, more and more authority for supervision was transferred from state legislatures to state bureaucracies.

The type, area, extent, degree, and effectiveness of state supervision exist in such confusing variation that only the most important can be discussed here. Although some states have established departments of local affairs to coordinate state-local administrative relations, by and large the supervision is on a functional basis. That is, the state department of health supervises local health services, and the state department of assessments oversees local property assessment. Scarcely any field of activity escapes some state supervision, but it tends to be most comprehensive in finance, health, highways, welfare, and education. To some extent supervisory interactions depend upon the distribution of functions among the levels of government. In states where the welfare function has been assumed by the state, for instance, relations in this field may exist only on an intermittent basis. In other states where welfare remains a local activity, state supervision of local welfare departments may be prominent in state-local interactions. At the same time, types of supervision may vary between welfare and health in the same state. In many states, for example, state departments of health have broad authority over local health departments including the power to substitute state administration for local management if there is a state emergency. However, the state is more likely to use its technical staffs to advise local units.

The degree and effectiveness of supervision are subject to variations among states and among agencies, as well as among sizes and types of local units. Small rural units are likely to get less attention than larger governments although occasionally state statutes may exempt larger entities from some control. Shifts in supervision also may occur over time as changes in personnel, financial resources, departmental structure, or the environmental situation, to cite only a few possibilities, come into play.

TECHNIQUES

Most state administrative supervision is low-key, relying mainly on persuasive devices and often providing assistance to the locality. Coercion is sometimes used, but most administrators find less rigid techniques more effective on a day-to-day basis. Heavy reliance on coercion effectively substitutes state for local

FIGURE 7-1

CONTINUUM OF DEVICES FOR STATE ADMINISTRATIVE SUPERVISION OF LOCALITIES

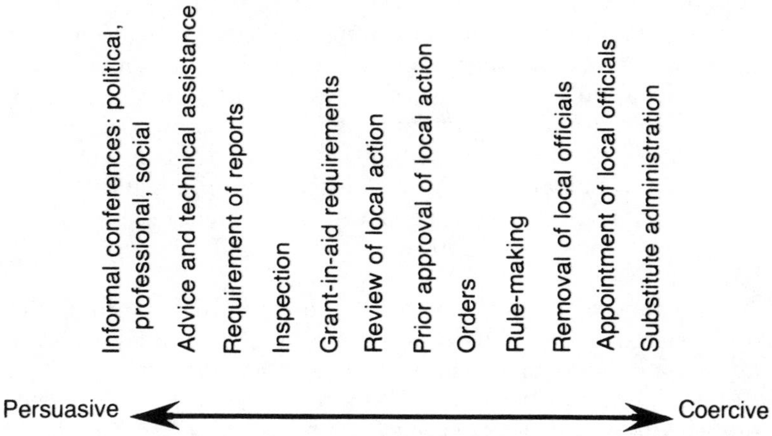

Informal conferences: political, professional, social
Advice and technical assistance
Requirement of reports
Inspection
Grant-in-aid requirements
Review of local action
Prior approval of local action
Orders
Rule-making
Removal of local officials
Appointment of local officials
Substitute administration

Persuasive ←――――――――――――――――→ Coercive

administration. If that is desirable, a transfer of function would afford better results. The administrative techniques range widely, as shown in figure 7-1, which reflects their increasing coerciveness.

State officials often have an opportunity to influence local actions in informal conferences occurring on a professional, political, or social basis. State and local meetings of the American Society for Public Administration, for example, seethe with informal discussions between state and local bureaucrats who use the occasion to confer in a less structured environment. The governor and a county executive may meet at a political party convention or at a groundbreaking ceremony, or they may belong to the same church, lodge, or country club. They may be neighbors or friends who interact often on a social basis. On any of these occasions they may discuss problems of mutual interest. Or they may simply pick up the telephone or write a letter and exchange information. In any case, state officials can use these opportunities to influence local officials. The influence, of course, runs in both directions.

The requirement of reports from the locality to the state, which is one of the mildest forms of supervision, is used extensively. These reports serve a dual purpose—they provide uniform information for the state agency and they focus the efforts of the local official and increase his awareness of what is expected of him. Sometimes the reports are never read and, once this is realized on the local level, they may be hastily prepared or the requirement ignored.

Inspection of local activities frequently occurs, especially in such functions as hospitals or property assessment. The inspections are often the occasion for consultation and advising as well as for establishing contacts that may prove fruitful at a later date. In some but not all instances the inspector has authority to demand changes. Considerable information can be exchanged at inspection time as well as on other occasions such as at conferences, workshops, or professional meetings, and by letter and telephone.

Because of their greater degree of specialization and often professionalism, state bureaucrats are frequently in a position to offer technical assistance. Local administrators, especially in smaller communities, are likely to be generalists or semi-professionals and therefore may not have the skills necessary to deal with some extremely complex problems confronting them. They may look to the officials of state government for aid in establishing pollution standards, designing highways, writing civil service examinations, marketing bonds, and handling many other functions. This assistance may come from bureaucrats in the corresponding department or agency such as a state air pollution expert's aid in establishing local air pollution standards, or from employees of a general agency established to provide assistance. The Maryland Technical Advisory Service at the University of Maryland advises that state's communities on such matters as charter revision and codification of ordinances and undertakes studies on financial administration, personnel, water and sewer rates, and annexation, to name a few.

North Carolina has gone even further and established an Institute of Government at the University of North Carolina at Chapel Hill that not only supplies technical information and research services but also prepares manuals for local officials on the operation of their offices and conducts training schools and workshops for them. Technical assistance of this sort can serve to upgrade the performance of local bureaucrats and can serve a a two-way street in the exchange of information. Other states include these activities in state offices for local affairs established as a part of the general administration machinery of the state and not in a university setting. (These are discussed later in this chapter.)

Some state officials have at their disposal more rigorous controls that can be used if the persuasive devices fail. State statutes may permit state agencies to withhold grants-in-aid to local communities if the conditions concerning them are not met. This action is likely to get results if the sum of money is large enough and the locality is not strongly opposed to the requirement. In addition, state officials may be authorized to review actions taken by local officials (state boards of equalization may review local tax assessments); approve contemplated actions before they are taken (prior approval of a state board of school finance may be required for local school budgets); and issue permits (a state health department permit may be required for liquid waste disposal). They may also license local employees (state departments of education license school teachers and a state housing agency may license local inspectors of modular housing and mobile homes); issue orders (a state water authority may order localities to construct sewage treatment plants); and make rules and regulations (often to set standards in health and safety).

Some states permit the governor or the head of a state agency to remove local officials or employees. In Wisconsin, for example, the governor may remove district attorneys, sheriffs, and other local officials, and in New York all elected sheriffs, county clerks, registers, and, excepting New York City, district attorneys may be removed by the governor.[30] The threat of removal may be sufficient to force a resignation, as happened in the celebrated case of the resignation of New York City Mayor James J. Walker when threatened with removal by Governor Franklin D. Roosevelt. Some states go even further and permit governors to appoint local officials on a regular basis. In Maryland, for example, the governor appoints the boards of education for most counties. In Alabama the governor may appoint a special force of inspectors to assist him in locally enforcing state law. Heads of state agencies also may occasionally appoint local administrators, especially in the field of health.

Substitute administration, in which state performance of some local function is temporarily instituted, is the ultimate in state control; it is used only in crisis situations. It is most widely authorized in public health emergencies, with most states providing for state takeover of local health services if local officials do not perform satisfactorily. Actual use of the authority is rare. Many states permit the assumption of control of local finances by state agencies when local units default on bonds. State law enforcement officials may sometimes supersede local officials. The national guard may be ordered by the governor to take over in emergencies such as fires, floods, riots, or other situations where local officials are incapable of acting.

STATE OFFICES FOR LOCAL AFFAIRS

State offices for local affairs, while not new, have proliferated recently and broadened in scope. These are agencies organized for the direct provision of state technical services to localities and for dissemination of information about the availability of services from other agencies. They serve as clearinghouses for information on state and national matters affecting localities and bring the problems faced by local government to the attention of the governor.

The first such office was the Pennsylvania Bureau of Municipal Affairs in the Department of Internal Affairs, created in 1919. Its functions were limited primarily to supervising municipal finance and compiling financial statistics.[31] In a short time a few other states created similar agencies. Not until the late 1950s, however, did states begin to shift emphasis from controlling local governments to providing services for them. The state offices for local affairs established since then are usually non-interfering and constitute state recognition of responsibility for dealing with local—and particularly urban—problems.

State agencies for local affairs exist in most states. Impetus for their general creation came from a report by the Council of State Governments to the National Governors' Conference in 1956, which recommended that each state establish an agency to determine the needs of urban and non-urban areas. The Governors' Conference, and later the United States Conference of Mayors, the National League of Cities, and the National Association of Housing and Redevelopment Officials endorsed the idea.[32] The national Demonstration Cities and Metropolitan Development Act of 1966 gave added emphasis to the establishment of such state agencies by authorizing grants-in-aid "to assist States to make available information and data on urban needs and assistance programs and activities, and to provide technical assistance, to small communities with respect to the solution of urban problems."[33]

State agencies for local affairs may be established as part of the governor's office, as a separate department, or as a division of an existing department. Several agencies have established regional offices within their states to make their services more accessible.

Functions of the agencies vary considerably. Joseph F. Zimmerman groups them into eight categories: (1) advice and information; (2) research and publication; (3) planning and area development; (4) preparation of policy recommendations affecting local governments for the governor; (5) promotion of interlocal cooperation; (6) conducting training programs for local officials; (7) coordination of state services and federal grants; and (8) control functions. Few agencies exercise control functions; those that do regulate financial activities by prescribing forms, revising budgets, approving bond issues, and the like.

Recently new functions have been added to the duties of the state offices for local affairs in several states, which give them characteristics of strong, independent operating departments. Pennsylvania, New Jersey, Missouri, Ohio, Connecticut, and Washington are examples.[34] These newer functions include responsibility for administering the national "701" planning assistance program, nationally-assisted housing and urban renewal programs, the anti-poverty program, and others. National grants-in-aid are often channeled through these offices. The Connecticut office, for example, is connected with at least fourteen national grant-in-aid programs.

State agencies for local affairs appear to be important to local units chiefly as coordinators of national programs. This is most evident from the perspective of officials of the smaller cities who look to them for assistance on these matters and for technical assistance, program evaluation, and financial aid. Larger cities, on the other hand, have their own channels of communication with the national government; moreover, they do not rely on these agencies for technical and financial assistance. They regard agency assistance as more valuable in the coordination of state programs. However, only 129 officials of 838 respondents to a survey conducted by the International City Management Association of chief administrative officers in cities of over 10,000 cited state agencies as making significant contributions to local problem solving. This attitude may have resulted from the fact that most state agencies for local affairs were in their infancy at the time of the survey (1969).[35] Responses also indicated that large cities with populations of over 50,000 initiated more contacts with the state agencies, communicating with them about once a week, while smaller cities began less interaction. The state agencies, however, originated contacts with the smaller communities about 25 percent more often than with the larger local jurisdictions.

Perspectives on State Assistance. Most city chief administrative officers who responded to the survey revealed that their states did not provide significant assistance to them.[36] Officials of only 295 cities of the 804 responding to the question cited the states as contributing significantly to local problem solving. Population size seemed to be a factor as cities under 50,000 found the state of greater assistance than did the larger places. Regional variations were important also, with executive officers of northeastern cities regarding their states as more helpful than those in other regions. The lowest rate of favorable responses came from the South.

LOCAL ASSISTANCE TO THE STATES

Not all the assistance provided in state-local relations comes from the states. Local governments are frequently in a position to help their states in a number of ways. Their officials often act as state agents in administering state programs because of legal requirements of state statutes—for instance, the county assessing property for state as well as for city and county taxation and local police enforcing national, state, and local law. Local governments often aid in informal ways, too. The expertise of a local civil servant may provide technical assistance in a state program, or the facilities of the local school system may be used by state highway officials for a meeting to discuss a new transportation program. The city designated as the state capital or a locality that has within its boundaries large state institutions such as a state college or a state university may find itself providing many kinds of services for the state, ranging from parking to the protection of property. There may be little or no recompense for such efforts, except the prestige and commercial advantages of having a state institution located within its boundaries, because state property is exempt from local taxation.

STATE-LOCAL RELATIONS IN FISCAL MATTERS

In financial matters more than in any other realm of

state-local affairs the state's attention is likely to be focused on its local units. In this field more assistance, supervision, regulation, and conflict are likely to occur. States and localities share the burden of financing most of the nation's domestic programs and fiscal interactions are prominent in most matters of mutual concern. Their fiscal fates are intertwined.

In the early years little theorizing took place about state-local fiscal relations, according to the late W. Brooke Graves, a leading authority on the development of intergovernmental relations. The tendency was to act on the basis of certain fundamental assumptions: (1) government itself was a necessary evil and the less we had of it the better; (2) governments should do as little as possible; and (3) taxes should be held to an absolute minimum because money spent by the government did not benefit the community's economic life as did private expenditures. In Graves' words:

> Some changes in these attitudes became noticeable around the turn of the [twentieth] Century as government began to expand and assume a more positive role, but by this time, the constitutional and statutory framework, not to mention the psychological climate of the community, had become so fixed and rigid that progress was always difficult and often impossible. Local units found themselves confined in a constitutional and statutory strait-jacket. Limitations applied to the kinds of taxes and the subjects taxed, as well as to the tax rates. Strict limitations were imposed upon the power to contract indebtedness, and no debt could be authorized without approval in a popular referendum, although this is now known to have little or no deterrent effect on the incurring of public debt. These restrictions continued through the end of World War II.[37]

Operating under Dillon's rule, localities could levy only those taxes authorized by state statute and thus specific restrictions were generally unnecessary to bind them. Furthermore, some states adopted tax limitations, often by constitutional amendment, which imposed a severe financial strain on localities. Taxation in excess of these limits required approval by referendum. When coupled with debt limits and state requirements that localities finance certain functions, little discretion over finance remained with local officials. A constitutional amendment in West Virginia in the 1930s limiting property taxes threw the state into a financial crisis. Reductions of up to two-thirds in property tax revenues (almost the only source of local funds) produced early school closings, dismissal of public employees, and curtailment of vital services. One municipality did not have enough money to operate its water system and another could not pay its police officers. The obvious remedy, an increase in property assessments, was politically infeasible. The assessors were elected by the voters, and it would have been political suicide to increase assessments in the midst of the declining land values of the depression years.

Many restrictions have been substantially loosened recently, most notably with respect to revenue sources. In addition, local units have found ways to skirt some restrictions; the increased use of revenue bonds to finance local projects is an illustration. National grants-in-aid and revenue sharing, which make available substantial amounts of money for local use, also got localities to some extent from under the state's fiscal thumb. In fact, some experts, such as David B. Walker of the Advisory Commission on Intergovernmental Relations (ACIR) express the opinion that revenue sharing established a tripartite fiscal and administrative system. The extent of this development remains to be seen as the program develops further. Nevertheless, many constitutional and statutory restrictions on local finance still apply, especially in public indebtedness.

STATE ADMINISTRATIVE SUPERVISION
OVER LOCAL FINANCE

States exercise substantial administrative supervision over the fiscal activities of their local governments. These run the gamut of the previously-discussed administrative controls. They include, for example, state certification of assessors; supervision of the assessment of property for taxation and of tax collections; and approval by a state unit of local agency budgets, tax levies (imposition of taxes), and the incurring of debt. Also included are control of the debt procedures such as the marketing and repayment of bonds; supervision of accounting, auditing, and financial reporting practices; and selection of depositories for public funds. Some states require the purchase of certain items for local use such as school buses to be made through state agencies.

State fiscal supervision leads to both cooperation and conflict between the state and local levels of government. Technical assistance in many areas of finance, training programs for local officials and employees, and other fields result from state-local cooperation. Despite these benefits, local personnel resent the strictures and red tape involved in following state direction. A recent survey of local officials found that 55 percent of the local administrators regarded "intergovernmental red tape" as a major impediment to doing a good job.[38] Nevertheless, the continuous interface provided by state supervision opens major paths for state-local communications.

STATE FINANCIAL AID

Shackled with constitutional and statutory provisions, local governments began to receive increasing amounts of outside money, principally from the state, to help them provide locally-administered services. State aid grew until by 1969 the amount the state contributed more than exceeded one-half the amount raised locally (54 percent) and by 1975 was estimated to equal 60.3 percent of the locally-raised funds.[39] More than one-half of the state aid goes for education. In the two decades ending in 1970, state financial assistance to localities multiplied sevenfold, although it must be remembered that this figure has not been adjusted for inflation and other factors. Throughout this twenty-year period, state aid made up a fairly consistent portion of state general expenditures, between 33.4 percent and 37.3 percent.[40] State grants-in-aid include national funds channeled through the states as well as money appropriated by the state legislature. States serve as distributing agencies for most national grants that "pass through" their hands to localities, but the states usually exercise little discretion in the distribution of these grants which make up only a small portion of total intergovernmental assistance to localities. In the case of shared taxes, the state serves as tax collector and returns the money to the localities.

Local governments are becoming increasingly dependent on outside financial resources.[41] One of every two dollars spent by local units in 1970 came from intergovernmental payments. Of course, wide variation is present among the states in the purpose as well as the per-capita amount of state aid to localities. To some extent these variations reflect the difference in allocation of state and local fiscal responsibilities. Some states provide a service directly while other state transfer funds to localities to administer the function. For example, education, which generally is a major area of state aid to localities, is not as-sisted at all in Hawaii where it is a state function. Similarly, several states, such as Alabama and Montana, which handle public assistance on a state level, give no financial aid to

TABLE 7-1

STATE PAYMENTS TO LOCAL GOVERNMENTS BY FUNCTION,
SELECTED FISCAL YEARS 1902-1973
(In Millions)

Year	Total	Education	High-ways	Public Welfare	Other Specified	Other Un-specified
1902 ...	$ 52	$ 45	$ 2	—	—	$ 5
1913 ...	91	82	4	—	—	5
1922 ...	312	202	70	$ 4	$ 1	35
1927 ...	596	292	197	6	3	98
1932 ...	801	398	229	28	6	140
1934 ...	1,318	434	247	211	281	145
1936 ...	1,417	573	285	245	151	163
1938 ...	1,516	656	317	346	17	180
1940 ...	1,654	700	332	420	21	181
1942 ...	1,780	790	344	390	32	224
1944 ...	1,842	861	298	368	41	274
1946 ...	2,092	953	339	376	67	357
1948 ...	3,283	1,554	507	648	146	428
1950 ...	4,217	2,054	610	792	279	482
1952 ...	5,044	2,523	728	976	268	549
1954 ...	5,679	2,930	871	1,004	274	600
1956 ...	6,538	3,541	984	1,069	313	631
1957 ...	7,439	4,212	1,083	1,136	340	668
1958 ...	8,089	4,598	1,167	1,247	390	687
1959 ...	8,689	4,957	1,207	1,409	391	725
1960 ...	9,443	5,461	1,247	1,483	446	806
1961 ...	10,114	5,963	1,266	1,602	462	821
1962 ...	10,906	6,474	1,327	1,777	489	839
1963 ...	11,885	6,993	1,416	1,919	545	1,012
1964 ...	12,968	7,664	1,524	2,108	619	1,053
1965 ...	14,174	8,351	1,630	2,436	654	1,102
1966 ...	16,928	10,177	1,725	2,882	783	1,361
1967 ...	19,056	11,845	1,861	2,897	868	1,585
1968 ...	21,950	13,321	2,029	3,527	1,079	1,993
1969 ...	24,779	14,858	2,109	4,402	1,275	2,135
1970 ...	28,892	17,085	2,439	5,003	1,408	2,958
1971 ...	32,640	19,292	2,507	5,760	1,823	3,258
1972 ...	36,759	21,195	2,633	6,944	2,235	3,752
1973 ...	40,822	23,316	2,953	7,532	2,741	4,280

SOURCE: Tax Foundation, Inc., **Facts and Figures on Government Finance** (18th edition; New York: The Foundation, 1975), p. 173.

localities for welfare. Table 7-1 illustrates the purposes and trends in amounts of state aid to local governments. Again, the figures do not reflect constant (non-inflationary) dollars.

Approximately 60 percent of the money received from outside sources goes for education, but public welfare, general local government support, and highways account for significant amounts. As a consequence of the dominance of state aid for education, school districts receive the bulk of the state funds, followed by counties, cities, and other local units.

A recent ACIR study of state aid to local governments recognizes the lack of a "system" for state financial aid which is a "patchwork of disjointed, uncoordinated state-local fiscal arrangements, each created with little concern as to how it might affect others or whether it would promote long-term overall state goals and objectives." It urges states to set up coordinating machinery, to develop performance standards, and to establish yardsticks for determining local government viability. States should also consider fiscal capacity and tax effort in devising grant formulas.[42]

STATE ADVISORY COMMISSIONS ON INTERGOVERNMENTAL RELATIONS

A few states formally recognized the need for intergovernmental relations in the formation of public policy by creating state advisory commissions on intergovernmental relations. They have functions similar to those of the Advisory Commission on Intergovernmental Relations on the national level. Arizona, Kansas, and Texas are among the leaders in this field; their commissions consisting of representatives of both state and local governments study and advise on matters involving more than one level of government. In other states existing agencies assumed some of the same functions. These agencies provide a many-faceted view of government activities and problems and may serve as very useful political devices for the governors by taking on the responsibility for recommending decisions that might otherwise be infeasible politically. By bridging the gap between states and localities, they can stimulate wider acceptance of intergovernmental proposals. At the same time, their effectiveness depends principally on the support they receive from the governor's office.

ADJUSTING RELATIONSHIPS

This chapter has pointed out the highly interdependent nature of state-local relations. Because of the common cultural, political, and economic attributes they share, states and the local units within their borders have closer relationships than the relations among the states, between the states and the national government, or between local units. While they do undergo constant adjustment, these state-local relations are marked by greater stability than most other sets of governmental interactions. Because of the many governments concerned, the multitude of legal provisions and administrative arrangements under which they operate, and the wide range of programs involved, ample opportunity exists for extensive sharing, assistance, friction, and conflict.

The growing tendency for the national government to become involved in local affairs increases the stress on state-local relations in a manner somewhat like the affluent visiting grandparent does on the relations between parent and child. National financial assistance to localities enhances the political potency of the local units as opposed to the states, just as the indulgent grandparent makes parental discipline more difficult. Executive orders and other national administrative actions require interface on such matters as housing, planning, and environmental protection. National court rulings sometimes put cities at odds with the state. And nationwide problems, such as energy shortages, mandate state action that affects local units.

As state and local governmental systems move to accommodate to a changing national role as well as other changes in society, adjustments are made in the existing arrangements. States have begun to fight harder to retain their dominance in state-local relations—through lobbying and political pressure and by upgrading their own administrative and representative machinery. At the same time, they are responding to local pressure to loosen the bonds on local action, permitting these units to restructure their governments and exercise more discretion in local affairs. They are providing additional opportunities for interlocal and state-local cooperation. Localities are increasingly taking advantage of the loosened strings and flexing their political muscle to improve their status, particularly through their interest groups and representatives. Each adjustment causes tremors in the federal system, creating tensions and heightening the need for other changes. Every action, no matter how small, produces a reaction.

NOTES

1. *The New Federalism: Possibilities and Problems in Restructuring American Government*, A Conference of the Woodrow Wilson International Center for Scholars (Washington, D.C.: 1973), p. 33.
2. W. Brooke Graves, *American Intergovernmental Relations* (New York: Charles Scribner's Sons, 1964), p. 710.
3. 262 U.S. 182 (1923).
4. See William Anderson, *Intergovernmental Relations in Review* (Minneapolis: University of Minnesota Press, 1960), pp. 88-90.
5. John F. Dillon, *Commentaries on the Law of Municipal Corporations*, 5th ed. (Boston: Little, Brown and Co., 1911), Vol. 1, Sec. 237. Italics in original.
6. Advisory Commission on Intergovernmental Relations, *State Constitutional and Statutory Restrictions Upon the Structural, Functional, and Personnel Powers of Local Government*, Report A-12 (Washington, D.C.: Government Printing Office, 1962), p. 38. In subsequent notes this agency will be cited as ACIR. All its reports are published in Washington by the Government Printing Office.
7. *Ibid.*, pp. 35-36; Jean E. Spencer, *Contemporary Local Government in Maryland* (College Park: University of Maryland, Bureau of Governmental Research, 1965), p. 26; Mavis A. Mann, *The Structure of City Government in West Virginia* (Morgantown: West Virginia University, Bureau of Government Research, 1953), p. 3.
8. ACIR, *State Aid to Local Governments* (1969), p. 100.
9. Alan Klevit and ICMA Staff, "City Councils and Their Functions in Local Government," *Municipal Year Book, 1972* (Washington: International City Management Association, 1972), p. 15.
10. *County News*, October 26, 1973 (Washington: National Association of Counties), p. 4.
11. *Constitution of Alaska*, Art. 1, Section 11. A borough is classed as a county.
12. Bureau of the Census, *1972 Census of Governments: Governmental Organization*, Vol. 1, p. 2.
13. Klevit and ICMA Staff, p. 15. (1971 survey)
14. 24 Iowa 455, 462, 463 (1868).
15. Roscoe C. Martin, *The Cities and the Federal System* (New York: Atherton Press, 1965), p. 32.
16. ACIR, *Profile of County Government* (1972), p. 10.

17. *1972 Census of Governments*, p. 1.
18. Victor Jones, Jean Gansel, and George F. Howe, "County Government Organization and Services," *Municipal Year Book, 1972*, pp. 211-239.
19. National Association of Counties figure. This is an increase of twelve over late 1973.
20. "Towns in New England states, and townships or towns in states that have adopted the general township organization system, partake of the nature of municipal corporations, being referred to sometimes as 'quasi corporations' or 'quasi-municipal corporations' possessing to a certain extent corporate capacity, and sometimes with the general control of matters of local concern ... Being merely quasi corporations or quasi-municipal corporations, towns or townships are not endowed with the full and plenary powers usually conferred by charter or general law on municipal corporations proper, and the mere conferment of additional and special powers on a town does not convert it into an actual municipal corporation." *Corpus Juris Secundum* 4. For an analysis of town meetings in one state, see Joseph F. Zimmerman, *The Massachusetts Town Meeting: A Tenacious Institution* (Albany: Graduate School of Public Affairs, State University of New York at Albany, 1967).
21. State v. Williams, 35 A 24, 68 Conn. 131.
22. *1972 Census of Governments*, pp. 2-3.
23. *Ibid.*, p. 1. There are also 1,457 other "dependent" school systems regarded as agencies of other governments.
24. For an explanation of this process see Executive Office of the President, Office of Management and Budget, "OMB Circular No. A-95 (Revised) What It Is—How It Works" (Washington: n.d.).
25. ACIR, *Profile*, p. 3.
26. ACIR, *Striking a Better Balance* (1973), p. 26.
27. ACIR, *Regional Decision Making: New Strategies for Substate Districts*, Vol. I of *Substate Regionalism and the Federal System* (Washington: 1973), p. 222. In an effort to curb special district proliferation (as well as hasty municipal incorporations), several states have created local boundary commissions.
28. Daniel J. Elazar, "Fiscal Questions and Political Answers in Intergovernmental Finance," *Public Administration Review*, Vol. XXXII, No. 5 (September/October, 1972), p. 477.
29. David J. McCarthy, Jr., *Local Government Law in a Nutshell* (St. Paul, Minn.: West Publishing Co., 1975), p. 282.
30. *Constitution of the State of Wisconsin*, Art. VI, Sec. 4; *Constitution of the State of New York*, Art. III, Sec. 13.
31. Joseph F. Zimmerman, "State Agencies for Local Affairs: The Institutionalization of State Assistance to Local Governments."

Mimeographed. (Albany: State University of New York at Albany, Graduate School of Public Affairs, Local Government Center, 1968). Much of the information in this section is drawn from this source.

32. John N. Kolesar, "The States and Urban Planning and Development," in *The States and the Urban Crisis*, edited by Alan K. Campbell (Englewood Cliffs, N.J.: Prentice-Hall, Inc. for the American Assembly, 1970), p. 116.

33. Public Law 89-754, sec. 901.

34. *Unshackling Local Government*, Revised edition. Twenty-fourth Report of the Committee on Government Operations, 90th Congress, Second Session. House Report No. 1270 (Washington: Government Printing Office, 1968), p. 37.

35. A. Lee Fritschler, B. Douglas Harman, and Morley Segal, "Federal-State-Local Relationships," *Urban Data Service*, December, 1969. (Washington: International City Management Association, 1969).

36. *Ibid.* Caution must be exercised in extending the findings of this survey to attitudes of all local officials because only chief administrative officers in cities over 10,000 were surveyed and the response rate was relatively low (40 percent).

37. Graves, p. 724.

38. Senate Committee on Government Operations, Subcommittee on Intergovernmental Relations, *Confidence and Concern: Citizens View American Government, A Survey of Public Attitudes*. Committee Print (Washington: Government Printing Office, 1973), Vol. 1, p. 121. Survey conducted by Louis Harris and Associates.

39. ACIR, *Significant Features of Fiscal Federalism* (1976), p. 57.

40. "State Aid to Local Governments," *Book of the States, 1972-73* (Lexington, Ky.: Council of State Governments, 1972), p. 283.

41. See table 5-5 in chap. 5.

42. ACIR, *State Aid to Local Government, The Report in Brief* (1969), p. 2.

8

National-Local Relations: Dynamic Federalism

National-local relations exemplify the dynamism of American government. Even a casual observer cannot miss their unprecedented growth, the shifting political forces they bring into play, and the rising concern they generate for the traditional place of the states in the federal system. The name of the game is CHANGE as the nation tries to solve the burgeoning problems created by a massive population explosion, urbanization, and tardy state action. The current national-local relationship developed piecemeal as the central government with its vast financial resources responded to the local cries for help. Interest groups, believing they were unable to coax rurally-oriented state legislatures into enacting programs to meet urban needs, converged on Washington for relief. Consequently, national-local intercourse is more frequent and overt than ever before in American history.

These intensified interactions provoked some students of American federalism to treat local governments, especially cities, as third parties in the federal system.[1] Such attitudes are relatively new. Until recently, local governments were ignored in discussions of the operations of federalism and the emphasis was placed on national-state relations with local units treated as arms of the state.

This traditional attitude has as its basis the lack of mention of cities, towns, or counties in the United States Constitution. Their legal authority emanates from the states to which they are subordinate; thus since 1789 the state capitols have served as conduits for contacts between city halls or county courthouses and the national capitol. For the most part, the states still carry out this role. Direct relations exist between national and local governments; but most national-local interactions always have been, and still are, through state channels. This is not to say they will continue to be this way. One of the best examples of pragmatic intergovernmental relations exists in the area of national-local relations where attempts to solve individual problems, with no overall theory of federalism in mind, have resulted in a hodgepodge of arrangements.

PATTERNS OF CHANGE

The position of the states in American intergovernmental relations is central. Any direct relations between the national government and local units that developed before the present century were minor. "Direct federalism," or direct national-local relations with no intervening government, was the exception to the normal pattern of interrelationships. In most instances the national government dealt with the states and not directly with local units. As late as 1932, it was reported that the American delegation to the International Conference of Cities in London represented the only country of more than forty present with no direct administrative relationships between the central or national government and its cities.[2]

According to Roscoe C. Martin, the year 1932 constitutes a sort of "geologic fault line" in American federalism.[3] Since that time the local units have become more vocal partners in its practice. This was the year when Congress first mentioned the word "municipalities" in a national statute authorizing the Reconstruction Finance Corporation to make loans to states and cities in economic distress.[4] In subsequent years of that decade, the New Deal produced a flood of programs, a number of which circumvented the states and went directly to the cities because of the urgent need to distribute relief funds. Many of these programs were administered by agencies established for specific purposes (ad hoc agencies). For example, the Public Works Administration made grants to cities, states, and other governmental bodies for public works projects. The Works Progress Administration, directing a work relief program, supplied labor and administrative costs for the projects, with local units furnishing most of the materials and equipment. The states were bypassed in the construction of most of the city streets, sewers, schools, and other public projects built under these programs.

World War II saw the abandonment of these emergency activities and national-city grants were reduced to a trickle by 1944. The postwar years brought the development of different kinds of grants, mostly channeled through the states. Nevertheless, during the three decades from 1932 to 1963, national payments directly to local governments multiplied more than 94 times from the 1932 total of $10 million (much of which went to the District of Columbia).[5] The trend established in the 1930s continued at an accelerated pace in the postwar years. Grants were made in twenty-nine more areas during the next fifteen years as the national government began financing airports, urban renewal, and later highways, air and water pollution control, and a myriad of other programs. Another surge forward came with the Johnson Administration when national grants-in-aid of all types, particularly those dealing with urban problems, reached an all-time high. Between 1963 and 1966, a total of 219 national grants in 39 functional areas were added. If 1932 can be regarded as the geologic fault line in national-local relations, 1965 could well be considered a seismic avalanche of national grants. A total of 109 new grant-in-aid programs were adopted in that year alone; and their growth continues with more than 70 new ones enacted in 1974.[6] Most of these programs were channeled through the states.

The mounting state and local difficulties and the administrative problems produced by uncoordinated grants-in-aid led to the adoption of national revenue-sharing legislation in 1972. Although not an unmixed blessing, it provided financial resources for localities largely subject to their own control and independent of the states. Early advantages were mitigated by reduction in funds for categorical grants, but enactment of revenue-sharing legislation provided localities with a "foot in the door" for pressuring for increased allocations.

Roscoe C. Martin identifies four major forces that conspired to modify the practice of American federalism from about 1930 onward:

> First was the cash grant-in-aid which superceded the land-grant system after the substantial depletion of the public domain. . . . Second was the depression of the 1930s, which spurred the launching of urgent and massive recovery programs to whose success the cities held the key. Third was the emergence following World War II of a metro-urban society attended by problems without precedent in their magnitude and complexity. Fourth was the demonstrated incapacity of the states to play an effective role in the war on urban problems.[7]

To these should be added three other forces: (5) revenue sharing that increased the autonomy of the localities in regard to their respective states and established the legitimacy of future demands for a share of the national bounty; (6) awareness by local officials that it is easier to look to Washington than to bear the brunt of popular opposition to increased local taxes or, in some instances, to work with the states; and, (7) the increasing sophistication of interest groups, especially urban organizations, in recognizing population—and thus political—shifts and in mobilizing their resources to influence the channeling of funds and the development of programs.

Direct federalism, one of the truly significant developments in American intergovernmental relations, has attracted growing local support and increased state resistance. Many local officials would rather deal with Washington than the state capital. Answers to a 1969 questionnaire, directed to chief administrative officers in cities over 10,000, indicated that 54 percent of those responding regarded the national government as contributing significantly to local problem solving. A total of 38 percent regarded the national government as more helpful than the state government, while only 21 percent found the states more helpful. The relatively low response rate (40 percent) raises a question about the validity of the findings, but apparently a sizable number of local officials would rather deal with Washington.[8] Periodically there are calls for abolition of the states, leaving only national-local relations,[9] and at least one mayor has advocated federal charters for large cities with a grant of power that would allow them to deal directly with the national government.[10] State officials, on the other hand, distrust the growing direct national-city intercourse. They are apt to regard such interaction as a threat to state sovereignty and to the federal system.

A NEW EMPHASIS

The emphasis and administration of national assistance to local government changed as Congress started to treat urban problems as national problems. This was done in response to urban pressure groups which began to organize themselves on a national scale.[11] Traditional interactions of federalism were reversed; the national government increasingly assumed the priority in goal setting for grant programs. Instead of state and local governments determining purposes and priorities, assisted by the central government, national goals were now set with state and local units largely responsible for implementing the national objectives. The programs remain national, executed through state and local governments for administrative convenience.[12] This shift sometimes was accompanied by (1) closer national control over the content of the program, (2) solicitation of proposals by national agencies, (3) increased national financial contributions (sometimes 100 percent), and (4) national supervision to ensure honesty, economy, and more flexibility for the central government in the selection of local agencies with which to deal. The fourth development means that in some programs the national government has the choice of dealing with the established agencies of local government, creating wholly new bodies at the community level with loyalty to national agencies and policies, or even resorting to the use of private organizations as the instrumentalities for the execution of national programs. Selection of the latter two types of organizations brought a storm of protest from existing local government agencies, especially when community action groups were awarded national grants under the Economic Opportunity Act (anti-poverty program). City councils, boards of county commissioners, and other local governing bodies regarded these organizations as threats to their political power. Bitter disputes often erupted.

The coming of revenue sharing in 1972 introduced new freedom for local units into the intergovernmental picture. Relatively unencumbered by the requirements and restrictions ordinarily associated with grants-in-aid, revenue sharing provided guaranteed fiscal assistance to states and localities. The president of the National Association of Counties testified before an Advisory Commission on Intergovernmental Relations hearing that, "This program, as was promised, has allowed local officials and their citizens to consider, set and meet local priorities without the intrusion from above that is present in other federal assistance programs."[13] In addition, revenue sharing placed the responsibility for ordering priorities squarely on the shoulders of local officials—a move not greeted with approbation in every quarter because of its impact on the distribution of political resources locally and its effect on access to the decisionmaking process. Thus, a dichotomy exists in nationally-assisted programs, with those financed by grants-in-aid increasingly oriented to national goals while those supported by revenue-sharing funds reflect local priorities.

THE CURRENT PATTERN

A complex network of national-local relations exists today. The national government deals directly with the people in some activities, such as veterans' benefits, taxation, mail delivery, and old age and survivors' benefits—that could hardly be called intergovernmental. In addition, the national government interacts with cities, towns, counties, townships, special districts, and multijurisdictional agencies such as economic development districts in diverse ways. The most important involve (1) provision of emergency aid; (2) technical assistance and consultation; (3) national inspiration of new local governments; (4) grants-in-aid and revenue sharing; (5) intergovernmental loans; and (6) political intercourse.

These contacts may occur by design as part of a national program, as with grants to local units for the construction of low-income housing. Or they may result from a political action, such as a city obtaining a specific project under a vocational education program because of its influence over the allocation of funds rather than because the national government intended the program to be especially for cities. Or, within a specific geographic area, a Veterans' Administration hospital site is likely to be selected because of the political power of one community as opposed to all the others that would have desired the facility rather than because that site is the most logical location. It is no accident, for example, that so many military installations are located in Georgia; so many, in fact, that someone remarked that another would sink the state. For many years chairpersons of congressional committees dealing with military affairs and military appropriations represented that state and were in a position to steer installations to their home areas.

Considerable contact occurs in everyday operations as various levels of government attempt to solve problems or administer programs. In the selection of a site for a new national court building, the General Services Administration may have to deal with local planning officials as well as with city officials concerned with transportation, sewers, and the like. Most interactions are among those involved in the enactment or implementation[14] of specific programs, such as welfare, health, or highway departments, rather than between the general governments personified by the President on the one hand and the mayor, manager, or county executive on the other. Furthermore, national activities ordinarily unrelated to local government, such as the regulation of the economy or national defense, may have an even greater impact than planned national-local programs. The effects of inflation or recession on local budgets and the consequences of the location of military installations on almost all aspects of adjacent areas are two examples.

EMERGENCY AID

The greatest harmony in national-local relations probably exists in times of emergency, although substantial after-the-event criticism sometimes develops. The perils of earthquakes, floods, or tornadoes generate a degree of cooperation exceeding that existing at normal times. Most emergencies facing governments arise from this kind of natural cataclysmic event. Others are provoked by riots, labor unrest, or civil insurrection such as that arising from attempts to prevent the integration of public schools or the peace demonstrations aimed at ending the Vietnam War.

In the event of a natural disaster, all the resources of the national government are available for emergency relief. The President, upon the request of the governor of a state, may designate a "disaster area," making it eligible for a wide range of assistance. The Office of Emergency Preparedness in the Executive Office of the President is authorized to call upon the resources of all agencies of the national government. National personnel, equipment, and supplies are used to help the people and governments of disaster areas. National funds are allocated for debris clearance, replacement of destroyed roads, bridges, sanitary systems, and other physical facilities, health and sanitation measures, extremely low-interest loans, and meeting other needs. Some national agencies are authorized to act even though a disaster area has not been formally declared by the President. The Corps of Engineers provides help in rescue operations and the restoration of flood control works; the military services aid in transport, maintenance of order, and other activities. Emergency medical care and sanitary services are provided by the Public Health Service, and the Bureau of Public Roads works to restore roads and bridges, to mention a few kinds of available aid.

Emergency assistance in the event of riot or other civil insurrection usually comes through the state. A mayor may call upon the governor to send in the National Guard, which is a state organization until called into the national service. If this does not suffice, the governor may ask the President for national troops and the President may send them entirely at his discretion. He may also send national forces, even over state protest, to protect national property or enforce national laws.

Localities often help the national government deal with emergencies. Local police may back up national agents in enforcing national laws on counterfeiting, kidnapping, or smuggling, or help guard national facilities in both emergency and ordinary situations. Local fire departments may rush to protect national property as those of nearby Maryland and Virginia did during the 1968 riots in Washington, D.C. Most emergency assistance comes from the national government, but some does go the other way.

ADVICE AND TECHNICAL ASSISTANCE

Fortunately, most intergovernmental relations do not involve emergency situations. The national government deals with localities on an every-day basis in the routine handling of public affairs. Almost every national agency consults with or gives technical assistance to local officials at one time or another. Washington may consult with city or town officials in the location of a post office, with a county about the agricultural extension service, with a local police chief or sheriff through the facilities of the Federal Bureau of Investigation, with local welfare officers because of a mutual concern over public assistance. Conversely the exchange of information may come at the behest of the local government. A county may call upon the United States Department of Agriculture for advice on rural development, conservation, or meat inspection, or upon the Public Health Service for assistance in combatting the spread of a contagious disease. A town may ask the United States Civil Service Commission for assistance in recruiting and training public personnel or in managing a merit system. The Catalogue of Federal Domestic Assistance lists over 1,000 assistance programs administered by more than sixty national departments or agencies. Most of them include provisions for technical advice and assistance, and hundreds of them are available to local governments.

The professional and technical advice and assistance that are passed back and forth through professional channels set up a relationship which infuses life into program administration. No policy has meaning until an individual brings it to life. This interrelationship among professionals is the life thread of program effectiveness. Professional workers of all jurisdictions are more likely to identify with the program than with the level of government; this results in a continuous flow of information from one level to another. Local educators and professionals of the United States Office of Education, for example, exchange information as they seek to improve the education system. Local officials may seek advice on the technical aspects of curriculum development. At the invitation of a congressional committee concerned with education or on their own initiatives, local educational professionals may appear before the committee to give testimony concerning educational problems. Or these committees or their staffs may visit local communities to gather information for new or improved national programs. All along the line ideas and information are exchanged until the program that emerges is hallmarked by many smiths. Professional interaction increased even more recently when the Intergovernmental Personnel Act, permitting the exchange of personnel between levels of government, went into operation.

This professional identification with program rather than with national, state, or local level of government is in direct contrast to the attitude of policymaking officials who are more interested in a record of accomplishment. For his part, the mayor may be more concerned that it is a *city* project than that it is designed in the best possible manner.

The vertical contact among national, state, and local professionals may be greater than the interdepartmental relationships among agencies with the city, town, or county. Administrators in the local welfare system may have more contact with their state and national counterparts than with administrators in the local police, park, health, or housing agencies. Encouraged by categorical grants-in-aid, each made for one purpose, this may result in a "functional feudalism" which glorifies relations down narrow vertical lines to the detriment of general local government, thwarting its efforts to exert overall control of agencies under its jurisdiction.[15] That is, the mayor may find it difficult to direct and coordinate activities of health and welfare (and other) departments when the professionals in these agencies exhibit more loyalty to health and welfare programs than to the mayor or to the city.

The two types of interaction—the elected officials control over administrators and the growing professional relationships—are depicted in figure 8-1. Insofar as the interactions shown by

FIGURE 8-1

POLITICAL CONTROL VERSUS PROFESSIONAL INTERACTIONS

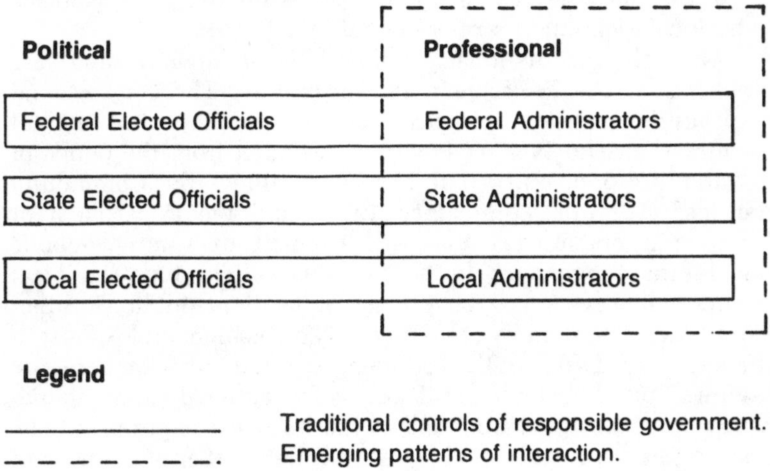

Political	Professional
Federal Elected Officials	Federal Administrators
State Elected Officials	State Administrators
Local Elected Officials	Local Administrators

Legend

_____ Traditional controls of responsible government.

_ _ _ _ _ _ _. Emerging patterns of interaction.

the broken line increase, the traditional controls of elected officials over their respective bureaucracies diminish. This concern pervades intergovernmental relations as reflected throughout this book.

NATIONALLY-INSPIRED LOCAL AGENCIES

Another type of national-local interaction involves two types of nationally-inspired local organizations.[16] One category includes those special local organizations outside established local government institutions whose structure and responsibilities are set out by national law. They are created by the states to meet certain requirements for participation in national programs. Primary responsibility for their proliferation rests with the Department of Agriculture which was especially active in promoting them during the New Deal days of the 1930s. While enthusiasm for them has lessened since that time, they still blanket the country. There are nearly 3,000 soil conservation districts (many of them independent governments) in all states, Puerto Rico, and the Virgin Islands. There is also a host of other local agencies that are not separate governments. Included are Agricultural Stabilization and Conservation Service committees, Extension Service sponsoring groups, Grazing Service advisory boards, farm-loan advisory boards, and other agricultural organizations. The customary way of organizing these agencies is by local election of farmer committees.

Not all the nationally-inspired local organizations are creatures of the Department of Agriculture. The controversial community action agencies, which mobilize and funnel resources for the War on Poverty, emanated from the Office of Economic Opportunity (but have been under the Community Services Administration since 1974), and the Department of Commerce encourages the establishment of rural economic development agencies. In both of the latter programs, local agencies involved may be private rather than public. Further, Circular A-95 issued by the Office of Management and Budget in the Executive Office of the President required areawide planning reviews for almost all applications for national grants-in-aid. Many communities responded to these review requirements by creating new governmental agencies. The number of councils of government, for example, increased from 18 in 1965 to 81 in 1968. More than forty new economic development districts were created during the same three-year period in response to other national legislation. The total for both is now more than 650, with 494 performing review functions.[17]

Critics of nationally-inspired local governments and agencies point up their effect on established general local governments. Speaking of the Department of Agriculture, the late Morton Grodzins said:

> The Department has contributed to the low state of rural (especially county) government. First ASC offices in every rural county compete with the county government in attracting leaders, skilled personnel, electorate attention, and in other ways. In many areas, county operations are dwarfed by ASC programs, as measured by dollar expenditures or impact on the resident, or both. This competition has without doubt been deleterious to county government. More important, by not working collaboratively with local governments (or states) the Department of Agriculture has deprived these governments of significant advantages.Grant programs in other fields have been used to raise standards of personnel, organization, and performance. They have increased the scope of activity of states and cities, and they have added to the stature of those institutions.[18]

The second category of nationally-inspired local organizations includes those promoted by national statutes that are more immediately under the supervision of the states or regularly-constituted local governments. The former selective service system, the civil defense organizations, and the city demonstration agencies (Model Cities Program) are examples.

NATIONAL GRANTS-IN-AID AND REVENUE SHARING

National financial assistance to localities is one of the foremost forces bringing about national-local collaboration as well as creating intergovernmental tensions. Most of this assistance is in the form of grants-in-aid, usually either formula-based or project categoricals channeled to the states and then distributed to local units. The national government also makes a number of grants directly to localities, and funds for urban areas sometimes fall into this classification. Beginning with the Partnership for Health Act of 1966, block grants were added in health, law enforcement and crime prevention, social services, employment and training, and community development and housing. General revenue sharing was adopted in 1972, creating a tripartite system of national financial assistance to localities. Nevertheless, almost 600 categorical grants are still available.

Changes in the form, emphasis, and distribution of national fiscal assistance have implications for the balance in the federal system. The shift away from complete reliance on categorical grants has meant more discretion for local units in program development and greater independence from state control. Block grants and revenue sharing are accompanied by fewer conditions and restrictions; thus, localities have more spending options under these programs than with categorical grants. Visibility in the federal system is increased as localities receive money independently of the state and as they lobby for formulas more favorable to their interests. Furthermore, less face-to-face contact should be necessary in situations where fewer conditions are imposed since less negotiation is necessary.

The shift in emphasis from national aid for local programs to promotion of national priorities has increased the role of localities as expediters of national aims. In spending certain funds, local governments are agents for the implementation of priorities set by the national government. Distribution of some grants directly to local units and provision for local entitlement on a formula basis in revenue-sharing funds has lessened local reliance on the state for financial aid and authorization as well as strengthening the hands of local governments as competitors of the states in the national political arena.

Direct national-local grants disturbed the balance of the federal system and promoted confrontations between mayors and governors over the form of grant programs. The mayor (or another local executive) and the governor may find themselves at cross purposes as the local leader endorses national legislation providing grants directly to localities and the governor seeks to channel them through the states. As a consequence of state dissatisfaction with the shift, Congress enacted legislation enabling states to "buy in" to direct grant programs by providing matching funds. Pressure for direct grants developed relatively recently as cities grew in size and the larger ones rivaled states in size of operation. To some extent the struggle reflects the conflict of interests of those who operate in the very large cities with those who are outside. Congress generally would prefer to deal with the states, but city officials can exert considerable pressure and are often supported by some interested national administrators. Nevertheless, the "pass-through" provisions, whereby the states get the money first and then distribute it to local governments, apply in most instances.

Grant money does not come to the locality automatically; each community must seek its share from the limited amount available. To do this the locality often must prepare complicated and detailed plans for the development of a specific project, provide needed government facilities and staff, conduct a vigorous campaign at national and state levels, and establish and maintain standards in the implementation of the program involved.

Much of the interface between localities and the national government occurs in the grant-seeking and program-implementation process. The constant communication, negotiation, checking, and inspection provide significant interactions. Here, too, many tensions are created because the aims of the donor and the recipient in the aid process vary. Jeffrey L. Pressman points out that donors seek to move money, obtain information about the recipient's performance, control the outcome of the project, justify the expenditure of funds to its sponsor, and insure local stability and support. The recipient, on the other hand, seeks to attract money, achieve a steady flow of funds, retain autonomy from donor control, and establish stable and supportive relationships with donor agencies. These conflicting objectives produce tensions among those involved, especially in program implementation. The donor prefers long-term planning, short-term financing, and a number of guidelines as to how the money is to be spent. The recipient favors short-term plans, long-term funding, and relatively few guidelines.[19]

The prodigious growth in number and amount of grants-in-aid occurring since World War II has had effects other than increasing the number of interactions and tensions between national and local officials. Adoption of grant programs in one field may make adoption of other programs considerably less likely. For example, some freeways built under the interstate highway system choked cities and made construction of mass transit systems or the preservation of parkland and open spaces, aided by other national programs, difficult. Furthermore, the absence of any overall system of grants leaves each program to be legislated separately with no clear statement of its relationship to other programs or to any comprehensive national purpose. This makes possible the existence of several grants in the same field for essentially the same purpose. The "market basket" situation thus created enables local applicants to shop around for the program best meeting their needs. Evidence of this already exists in program areas such as parks and open spaces, planning, water supply, and sewage treatment.[20] One government official has reported on a small community that applied to six different agencies for assistance to build a sewage treatment plant. If all six had responded favorably, which at first appeared probable, the town would have made a profit of one and a half million dollars on the project.[21] Block grant legislation, especially the Housing and Community Development Act of 1975, which consolidated categorical grants for urban renewal, neighborhood facilities, open space land, and basic water and sewer facilities, should alleviate this situation.

Grant proliferation also increases the likelihood of difficulties in the implementation of aided programs. Congress may not take sufficient care at the time the programs are legislated to examine the possible administrative problems. Because national officials have the opportunity to formulate ideal programs and because they are free from the political and administrative burdens that the localities must bear, obstacles to implementation may be created inadvertently. The situation may be aggravated when national-city programs are involved. The national policymakers, who have a broad, heterogeneous constituency, are removed from actual implementation of the policy by several strata of administrative organizations and by the distribution of authority in the federal system.[22] Enacting a program, appropriating and allocating funds, and establishing standards are not enough to ensure that the services will actually be delivered to the public. The experience of Oakland, California, with economic development funds for public works projects is informative. Jeffrey L. Pressman and Aaron B. Wildavsky found that despite public-works grant and loan authority to Oakland of more than $23 million designed to create 3,000 jobs, only a fraction of that number had been created five years later. They emphasize that "the technical details of implementation proved to be more difficult and time-consuming than the federal donors, local recipients, or enthusiastic observers had ever dreamed they would be."[23]

LOANS

Loans, as well as grants-in-aid, are made by the national government to local units. While often necessary and valuable, they are not as popular with local governments as grants because they must be repaid. There is no general program of loans whereby a local unit in need of money may borrow from the national government. As a rule, local units borrow as the state and national governments do by selling bonds to the private sector. A few programs exist, nevertheless, where the national government will loan money to localities for specific purposes. Usually the interest rate is quite low in these instances. Among the loans available are those for rebuilding public facilities destroyed by natural disasters; for the acquisition of sites for low-income housing in rural areas; for water and waste-disposal systems; for watershed protection and flood prevention; for access roads, port facilities, railroad sidings and spurs; and for health facilities construction. Excess property may also be loaned for local use. Occasionally the rental of national property to local governments at an extremely low rate amounts to a loan. In a few cases the national government makes grants for subsidizing interest when public agencies (such as colleges and universities or housing authorities) borrow from private sources. National income tax laws that exempt interest from state and local governmental bonds from taxation is also a form of loan subsidy, and one subject to continued criticism. National loans may have major impacts in particular instances; overall their effect in intergovernmental relations is limited.

POLITICAL RELATIONSHIPS

National-local political relations pervade the entire system of American government. They range from the interplay of local interests with congressmen and the national administration through political party action to presidential selection. They may be the most important of national-local interactions.

The representation system in Congress gives local interests leverage in the national government. Because of their dependence upon local support for election, United States representatives (and frequently senators who are elected from the state at large) often respond more readily to local pressures than to national or party desires. This representation of local interests should be distinguished from representation of local governments on the national level. Local governments have no special voice in the selection of members of Congress or the Senate and the representative may not reside within their boundaries. Furthermore, the national legislator and local government officials may have different party affiliations and thus may not be exposed to integrating party influences. This is not to say that local officials have no influence with national senators and representatives. Because local officials are prominent in their communities, because they have a public platform from which to speak and, above all, because they may be important party leaders in the national legislator's party, they will have more access to that individual than most other people. A member of Congress needs the support of local governmental officials and their constituents because both are also constituents of the congressional representative. Furthermore, such a representative is anxious to advance the interests of communities in his district.

Congress members are likely to regard the mayor or county commissioner as better informed on local needs and problems than the governor who usually has fewer information sources in the area. Simply because of the geographic location of the city or county, the representative identifies the local official more closely with his own congressional district. Furthermore, the local official is a constituent of the congress member while the governor may not be. In addition, the member during the course of his service may develop into a de facto party leader in each county in his district as well as a districtwide representative. This accentuates his representation of local viewpoints.

Local governments, as well as private citizens and groups,

call upon members of Congress for assistance in dealing with national departments and agencies. This congressional-administrative interaction, coupled with the "oversight" of administration by congressional committees, provides another access point for local political influence on the national level. Party differences do not deter members of Congress in one state from joining forces to promote local interests.

The lack of centralization in the political-party system enhances local political influence. Because the national Democratic and Republican parties are loose federations of the respective parties in the fifty states and the territories, and because state party committees and convention delegates are usually elected on a local basis, the local influence within the party is strong. County committees may be more powerful than state committees, for example. Local influence may be felt on certain issues, the location of national facilities, the distribution of national patronage, or nomination of candidates, to cite a few instances of impact.

Large urban areas or combinations of smaller ones may be decisive in the outcomes of presidential elections, although it is a mistake to regard the citizens of any one area or type of area as homogeneous in their electoral behavior. The local conduct of presidential elections, if closely contested or if unfairly administered, as was claimed in both 1960 and 1968, may well determine the victor on a national basis.

Collective local influence in the national arena frequently is limited because the basic interests of local units are not the same. Cities and counties disagree on revenue-sharing allotments, for example, and as the nation moves into an era of more block grants and more precise eligibility requirements (note particularly the 1973 manpower legislation and the Community Development Act of 1974) conflict between them is increasing. Large and small cities have diverse viewpoints on programs where city size is a factor. Geographic concerns may further aggravate the situation. Each category of local units has its own organizations through which its interests are pressed. Counties are represented by the National Association of Counties, large cities by the United States Conference of Mayors, and medium- and small-sized cities by the National League of Cities. Other public and private groups representing local interests when they are urban include the National Housing Conference, the Urban Coalition, the National Association of Home Builders, and the National Association of Housing and Redevelopment Officials.

Still other groups join in the fray on particular issues.[24] Recently, coalition building among locally-oriented interests seems to be gaining, and the National League of Cities and the Conference of Mayors merged their staffs although the organizations still operate separately.

Local influence, whether collective or from a single unit, is also diluted because energy must be spread over a wide range of national committees and agencies. There is no one committee in each house of Congress that deals with local affairs, or even urban affairs. In the House of Representatives, for example, localities have to approach the Committee on Banking and Currency in regard to housing; the Committee on Education and Labor concerning education, manpower training, and the anti-poverty program; the Committee on Ways and Means to influence welfare programs; the Committee on Public Works for capital construction projects; and the Appropriations Committee for funds. A similar proliferation faces them in the Senate. Administratively, they deal with a wide variety of executive departments and agencies, most frequently with the Department of Health, Education, and Welfare and the Department of Housing and Urban Development.

Often the national government initiates as well as responds to local interest-group pressures—especially in the realm of urban affairs. Presidents, in particular, are often amenable to pressure from large cities which make up their largest single constituency. Through speeches and other actions they may encourage local interests to arouse public opinion to the extent that the Congress and other institutions of government respond. Members of Congress and their staffs also engineer coalition building for favored projects and programs.

NATURE OF THE RELATIONSHIP

The national-local relationship is fluid, with increasingly important consequences for both levels as well as for the states. The amount of conflict or cooperation it engenders varies according to the specific issue at hand and the individuals involved in the interactions. A substantial amount of cooperation exists along the frontiers of national-local relations, but there is friction at many points too. In fact, the predominant theme may be abrasion rather than harmony. Because national and local officials approach public policy from different directions and with different objectives, tensions result from many interactions, particularly in the implementation of grant-in-aid programs. Here the thrust of the national agencies is toward action to spend the money and provide the services. The local actors are inclined to be more conservative in their actions because they have to bear any unfortunate consequences. They try to avoid changes that might produce criticism. The perceptions those on each level have of the other also produce tension, as officials on one tend to fit actions of participants on the other into the preconceived images they have of how they are likely to act.[25]

Some relationships are beneficial to one level of government, others to both. A few may be competitive, a number one-way coercive. Arranged on a continuum, they might look like figure 8-2.

The United States Coast and Geodetic Survey provides a service to local units that is not reciprocated. It is one-way beneficial. On the other hand, national, state, and local governments participate in the support of the Agricultural

FIGURE 8-2

A CONTINUUM OF NATIONAL-LOCAL RELATIONSHIPS

One-way beneficial	Mutually cooperative	Competitive	One-way coercive
U.S. Coast & Geodetic Survey provides geodetic controls for land surveys and mapping	Agricultural Extension Service gathers and disseminates agricultural information	FBI versus local police or sheriff	Department of Justice enforces Voting Rights Act
U.S. Army quells local disorders	U.S. Public Health Service cooperates with county health department to contain spread of contagious disease	Atomic Energy Commission site approval versus local zoning opposition	HEW enforces school desegregation
U.S. Department of Labor arbitrates dispute between a city and its garbage collectors	U.S. Civil Service Commission and local personnel agency exchange experts under Intergovernmental Personnel Act	U.S. Department of Transportation versus local departments of parks, environment, and zoning over route of interstate highway	Environmental Protection Agency forces local adherence to air quality standards

Extension Service, which maintains farm and home demonstration agents in counties throughout the nation to gather and disseminate agricultural and homemaking information. All three levels of government profit from this arrangement. Although cooperation exists between the Federal Bureau of Investigation and local law enforcement agencies, the relationship is more likely to be competitive. Local officials are reluctant to call in national agents and, when it is done, friction often develops over credit for crime solving. Local governments have little opportunity to take a coercive stance against the national government because they can neither withhold money nor exert force. Nevertheless, they may sometimes bring suit to force the release of appropriated funds for localities. The national government may occasionally force local units to do things they do not want to do, or to refrain from a contemplated activity. The Attorney General's move to force some counties to register black voters by sending in registrars of the national government and by instituting suits against local officials is an example. The action of the Department of Health, Education, and Welfare in withholding grants for public schools until some semblance of racial balance in the schools was achieved is another.

Despite the lack of coercive power, localities have other options. They may decline to participate in national programs and occasionally some have decided against taking part. They may resist national demands to the point where conflict harmful to both levels is threatened. They may arouse public opinion in their favor, and, as mentioned above, they may sue. A recent example of the latter is *National League of Cities v. Usury* (1976). In this case the organization of cities brought a successful suit to have declared unconstitutional a national requirement that states and local units pay minimum wages and set maximum hours for their employees.

CONSEQUENCES OF CHANGING RELATIONS

What have been the consequences of the tremendously accelerated national-local interactions? Certainly every movement in a dynamic system produces adjustment at one or more points, and this is true of the American federal system. Some results are more subtle than others, more difficult to perceive, to classify. Among the easily discernible and major consequences recognizable to this point are: (1) inconsistency, competition, and confusion among programs; (2) increased cooperative federalism and added tensions; (3) diminished state control over localities; (4) governmental restructuring; (5) increased spending and public employment; (6) the undermining of general local government; and (7) shifts of political power.

INCONSISTENCY, COMPETITION, AND CONFUSION

The national government made a massive foray into urban areas and increased its local relationships in rural ones as well. Action came so rapidly and often that inconsistencies and competition, with accompanying confusion, resulted. There is a lack of consistency in arrangements for grant administration. Part of the inconsistency came from efforts to circumvent state administrative departments, such as departments of education, that resisted innovation. Another part resulted from the use of national money for experimentation with new programs rather than for more time-tested traditional programs. In other instances, such as with the anti-poverty program, it was the local "power structure," in the form of the board of county commissioners or city or town officials plus their associates, affiliates, or "bosses" in the community, who needed to be bypassed. While these pragmatic arrangements may have solved some problems from a national viewpoint for a time, they sometimes fractionalized concentrated efforts in a given field on the local level. Almost all the grant-in-aid programs administered by the Department of Health, Education, and Welfare have been channeled through the states. Programs emanating from the Department of Housing and Urban Development, on the other hand, generally bypass the states and go directly to the local communities. The Office of Economic Opportunity's programs were so set up that it was possible to bypass both. Aid to elementary education goes first to the states, aid to nursery schools and kindergartens goes directly to local governments. Two related programs are administered by two separate national agencies and sometimes two separate local agencies.[26] Such situations lead to demands for a restructuring of grants-in-aid and for the substitution of additional block grants, increased revenue sharing, and a tax credit system.

The rush to deal with urban problems in particular produced competing programs among national agencies. Localities often have a choice of programs from which they can select to deal with a particular need. Occasionally efforts to get grants may take a humorous twist as in the confusion over national grants under the Safe Streets Act—a law enforcement program. One community reportedly asked for national money to repave streets riddled with potholes and another requested funds to improve its water supply, contending that firefighters would need a higher water pressure if hoses had to be used against rioters.[27]

All the confusion was not local although the number of programs grew to the point where many small communities could not utilize them effectively. Some members of Congress, anxious to solve a problem raised by constituents, introduced bills to establish programs duplicating those already existing. Both national and local coordinating efforts are inadequate. Lack of coordination in Washington produces conflict there and in the field. This has important consequences for local units because it affects their ability to direct local activities. Attempts to solve the problem are sometimes counterproductive. In fact, the efforts to coordinate had, by 1967, produced more than a dozen types of national-initiated, local *coordinating structures*. James L. Sundquist gives this account:

> . . . in the absence, once again, of an organizational philosophy, no one solution was devised for community-level coordination. Almost as many solutions were conceived as there were federal agencies grappling with the problems of community development. . . . OEO had its community action agencies (CAAs); HUD its city demonstration agencies (CDAs) under the model cities program; Agriculture its resource conservation and development projects, rural renewal projects, rural areas development (RAD) committees, technical action panels (TAPs), and concerted services coordinators; Commerce its economic development districts (EDDs) and overall economic development program (OEDP) committees; Labor its cooperative area manpower planning system (CAMPS) and its concentrated employment program (CEP); the Appalachian Regional Commission, its local development districts (LDDs); and HEW, its comprehensive area health planning agencies. In addition, four agencies, HUD, Labor, HEW, and OEO jointly were organizing neighborhood centers. Finally, in 1968, HUD was given authority to sponsor nonmetropolitan districts in cooperation with Agriculture and Commerce. To complicate the situation further, several states had designed coordinating mechanisms of their own which were related only imperfectly to the patterns being developed by the federal government, and local jurisdictions had formed councils of governments (COGs) and metropolitan and nonmetropolitan planning bodies.[28]

INCREASED COOPERATIVE FEDERALISM
AND ADDED TENSIONS

Two outcomes of the changed relationship between the national and local governments appear to be occurring simultaneously; or, more likely, one may be a direct outgrowth of the other. Cooperative federalism is on the increase, and tensions between the national government and the local units seemingly are growing. The increase in tensions is largely the result of intensified cooperative interactions between the two levels that provide more opportunities for friction and of the increased pressures that rising expectations, aroused by the adoption of national programs, focus on local governments charged with delivering the services. Little research has been directed toward this development, but it is reflected in the pervasive attitude that recent programs aimed at solving basic problems in American society have failed. It is also apparent in remarks and attitudes of officials at both levels.

The general recognition that urban problems are national problems stimulated the growth of cooperative federalism. In addition to efforts to alleviate local financial difficulties through grants and revenue sharing, the national government moved in other ways to demonstrate its concern for local governments. These include: (1) creation of the Advisory Commission on Intergovernmental Relations with local government representation; (2) enactment of the Intergovernmental Cooperation Act of 1968 and the Intergovernmental Personnel Act of 1970, both featuring opportunities and incentives for interlevel assistance; (3) changes and improvements in procedures for consultation of local governments and their organizations prior to adoption of national guidelines, regulations, and procedures for implementing national legislation affecting localities; (4) creation of the Department of Housing and Urban Development and the Domestic Council (a group of high government officials advising the President on domestic matters including intergovernmental relations) and a much more extensive and coordinated decentralization of the national bureaucracy; and (5) adoption of several administrative devices nationally to strengthen the local units and improve national-local communications.

At the same time local units may have become "handmaidens" to higher government as much of their activity reflects demands of state and national programs. They have taken on a major role in carrying out national policies.[29] While this sometimes operates to the detriment of local governments as national priorities are substituted for local ones, it must be noted that national priorities are often seen as references to local demands.

DIMINISHED STATE CONTROL

While cities (and highly urbanized counties and towns) are assuming more important roles in the federal system, state officials are working to strengthen the positions of the states. Built up financially and politically by national funding during the 1960s, urban governments became increasingly independent of state action. Their possible trading of one master for another concerned them less than it did the states, as the latter struggled to maintain some authority over national programs within their borders. There was fear by the states that they might lose their traditional place in the federal system. Such apprehension was expressed by the then executive director of the Advisory Commission on Intergovernmental Relations:

> ... the States are on the verge of losing control over affairs in the great metropolitan areas. If the States lose this control and if they abdicate to Washington in this area, the States will abdicate the bulk of domestic government in this country. If the States do this, as they have been in the process of doing, and if this condition reaches its culmination, the States will become a facade, and will have very little substance to contribute to our federal system. The pattern of federalism will have been very greatly altered.[30]

The situation moderated somewhat with the arrival of the 1970s when states strengthened their constitutional, administrative, legislative, and financial structures and reasserted their positions through pressures at the national level.

GOVERNMENT RESTRUCTURING

On both the national and local levels, increased interactions were accompanied by governmental restructuring. Nationally, the Department of Housing and Urban Development was created in the Cabinet to deal with urban affairs, and the Domestic Council appeared in the Executive Office of the President. National departments have been forced to resort to interdepartmental coordination and to improve their internal functioning. Regional offices of the major agencies were established throughout the country in an effort to decentralize and provide easier local access.

Urban governments changed in form and operation. Community development officers were added to assist in the procurement of national grants-in-aid, and specialized agencies were established for housing, urban renewal, human relations, manpower planning, environmental protection, and for other nationally-inspired programs. In fact, local governments organized to administer national as well as local programs.

In response to the requirements for areawide review of grant requests, many metropolitan areas have seen the emergence of new regional governmental organizations whose primary purposes seem to be comprehensive planning and serving as review agencies. Many of them have professional directors and staffs.

Many structural developments resulted from conditions attached to national financial assistance. For example, localities had to create or designate housing authorities to be eligible for grants for subsidized housing. Others materialized from attempts to ease administrative problems in grant administration (e.g., national regional offices). Some were unintentional. Revenue sharing, for example, gave new vitality to, and possibly prolonged the viability of, many small governmental units such as midwestern townships and New England counties because they were entitled to share under its allocation formula.

Some scholars anticipate that the immediate years ahead will see a shift from functional intervention by the national government to structural intervention. Terming this a "New Structuralism," Richard Nathan notes that evidence is growing in the literature of a view that along with replacement of categorical grants with more general financial assistance the national government should ensure the "proper" structure for state and local governments to enable them to administer the programs. The national government would determine what the "proper" structure would be and use its clout to bring about this preferred arrangement. Nathan points particularly to recommendations of the Advisory Commission on Intergovernmental Relations that a firm requirement be set in all national grant legislation for the operation in all areas of the country of "Umbrella Multi-Jurisdictional Organizations" (UMJOs) with power to approve or disapprove national grants to special districts within their borders and to sign-off all grants to general governments. Should this proposal be adopted, it would require membership of general-purpose local governments in regional organizations that possess authority to review and comment only.[31]

Representative Henry Reuss of Wisconsin has consistently advocated adoption of some of these structural changes as a prerequisite for receipt of revenue-sharing funds. He sets out a "modern governments program," which would incorporate a whole series of reforms, including a reduction in the number of local units and the establishment of decentralized local governments.[32]

INCREASED SPENDING AND EMPLOYMENT

Both the amount of national money finding its way to local units and the proportion of national funds local government spend have increased significantly since World War II. These developments have produced a growing local dependency on national largesse and inflated local budgets. Population growth, expansion of purely local services and revenues, inflation, and rising demands for public services all bear a share of the responsibility for larger local budgets. Nevertheless, grants-in-aid apparently have been important factors in influencing local action in regard to finance. Research on the impact of grants-in-aid is in its infancy and recent studies raise important questions as to how much independent effect grants have on increasing the number of employees.[33] There seems to be substantial evidence that they have stimulated higher employee compensation, fee increases for certain services (such as higher rates for industrial users of water supply and sewage disposal), and a broadening of the purposes of local expenditures. At the other end of the spectrum, national government employment has expanded with the addition of new specialists to administer grant programs.

UNDERMINING LOCAL GOVERNMENT

It sounds incongruous to say that a development that is providing money, offering technical assistance, or possibly elevating cities to partnership in the federal system can be simultaneously undermining local government. Yet this may be true. Often national programs are responsible for the creation of nationally-inspired local public agencies as mentioned earlier, which undermine the authority of existing local units. Such organizations as community action agencies or community development corporations may have commendable social aims,

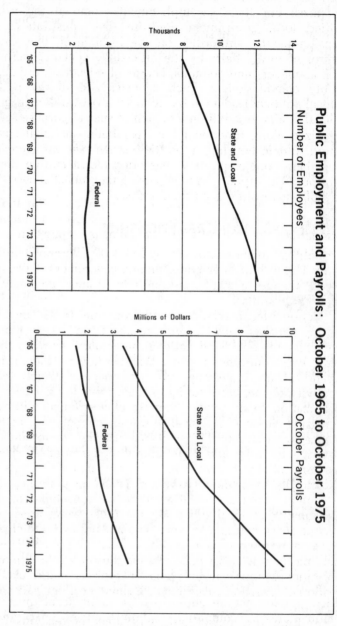

FIGURE 8-3

Public Employment and Payrolls: October 1965 to October 1975

Number of Employees

Thousands

State and Local

Federal

October Payrolls

Millions of Dollars

State and Local

Federal

SOURCE: Bureau of the Census, **Public Employment in 1975** (Washington, D.C.: Government Printing Office, 1976), p. 1.

such as alleviating poverty, and may be effective in many instances; but their accomplishments come at the price of unified local government. Because they constitute separate decision-making authorities on the local level, they mitigate control of local affairs by the officials of general governments such as mayors and councils, boards of selectmen, or boards of county commissioners. Such agencies add to the problems of local political leaders in trying to achieve overall management of local affairs. In addition, creation of special-purpose agencies organized along functional lines paralleling national adminis-tration (public housing authorities, urban renewal agencies) to keep them "out of politics" has often meant cutting them off from political support, thus impairing their effectiveness.[34] This kind of organization is on the increase.

SHIFTING POLITICAL RELATIONSHIPS

Political relationships among levels of government are never static. The web of interactions among government is responsive to any change in status, any shift in balance, and may itself create these shifts.

National-local relations will continue to be dynamic—shifting patterns with changing needs. To the extent that local problems are considered national, intercourse between the two levels will continue to grow. Whether direct federalism will expand at an increasing rate will depend largely on the proclivity of the states to equip themselves to deal with rapid urbanization. In any event, the national government will have an increasing impact on local government policies, activities, finances, and structure. Also it may use the "carrot and stick" approach to bring about alterations in the number, size, and structure of local units. If sufficient national funds were restricted to governmental units of 50,000 or more population, for example, the result could be a gradual consolidation, at least functionally, of local units. On the other hand, allocation of revenue-sharing funds to very small counties, municipalities, towns, and townships is likely to sustain their viability by enabling them to resist pressures for consolidation. Stipulations for regional approval of plans or projects could encourage creation of areawide governments despite local reluctance in this direction.

Shifting local power bases will affect the relationship. The decline of large cities at the same time that more and more people are living in metropolitan areas will mean a shift in local power bases from the big cities to the suburbs. Suburbs no longer look to the central cities as social and economic bases; they are becoming more independent. Nevertheless, as Daniel J. Elazar points out, the large cities with populations in excess of a million are now at the peak of their political power nationally despite their declining population. Their rise to power parallels that of agricultural interests whose strength was most notable a generation after they had begun to decline in numbers.[35]

Local governments, which are becoming more sophisticated in their dealings with the national government, are likely to have increasingly important influence on the design and development of future national programs. Contacts with the national government will be stimulated by local efforts bringing forth even greater national-local cooperation and increased friction. The relationship will continue to be dynamic, changing over time and adjusting to meet new problems and to conform to new power arrangements. This elastic relationship, flexible enough to allow multiple approaches to problem solving, is more likely to withstand the gales of attack than a rigid structure unable to bend with the wind.

NOTES

1. See Roscoe C. Martin, *The Cities and the Federal System* (New York: Atherton Press, 1965).
2. W. Brooke Graves, *American Intergovernmental Relations* (New York: Charles Scribner's Sons, 1964), p. 655.
3. Martin, p. 111.
4. Daniel R. Grant and H. C. Nixon, *State and Local Government in America*, 3rd ed. (Boston: Allyn and Bacon, Inc., 1975), p. 62.
5. Martin, pp. 112-113.
6. 1966 data from Advisory Commission on Intergovernmental Relations, *Fiscal Balance in the Federal System*, Vol. 1. Report A-31 (Washington, D.C.: Government Printing Office, 1967). The Appendix includes the entire list. (In subsequent notes this agency will be cited as ACIR.) For a more recent listing of all national domestic assistance programs, see the current *Catalogue of Federal Domestic Assistance* prepared by the Executive Office of the President, Office of Management and Budget (Washington, D.C.: Government Printing Office). 1974 figures from David B. Walker, "The New System of Intergovernmental Assistance: Some Initial Notes," *Publius: The Journal of Federalism*, Vol. 5, No. 3 (Summer, 1975), p. 131.

7. Martin, p. 111.
8. A. Lee Fritschler, B. Douglas Harman, and Morley Segal, "Federal, State, Local Relationships," Urban Data Service, December, 1969 (Washington, D.C.: International City Management Association, 1969).
9. See Harold J. Laski, "The Obsolescence of Federalism," The New Republic, Vol. 98 (May, 1939), pp. 362-369. More recently Rexford Guy Tugwell proposed a modified version with nationally-dominated administrative units in A Model Constitution for a United Republic of America (Santa Barbara: Center for the Study of Democratic Institutions, 1970).
10. Mayor John Lindsay of New York cited in Gerald Benjamin, "The Process of Change in Federal-Local Relations," Public Administration Review, Vol. XXXII, No. 2 (March/April, 1973), p. 190.
11. See Frederic N. Cleaveland, ed., Congress and Urban Problems: A Casebook on the Legislative Process (Washington, D.C.: The Brookings Institution, 1969).
12. James L. Sundquist, with the collaboration of David W. Davis, Making Federalism Work: A Study of Program Coordination at the Community Level (Washington: © 1969 by the Brookings Institution) p. 4.
13. County News, October 26, 1973 (Washington: National Association of Counties), p. 1.
14. For a discussion of the importance of implementation, see Jeffrey L. Pressman and Aaron B. Wildavsky, Implementation: How Great Expectations in Washington are Dashed in Oakland; or, Why It is Amazing that Federal Programs Work at All, This Being a Saga of the Economic Development Administration as Told by Two Sympathetic Observers Who Seek to Build Morals on a Foundation of Ruined Hopes (Berkeley: University of California Press, 1973); Pressman, Federal Programs and City Politics: The Dynamics of the Aid Process in Oakland (Berkeley: University of California Press, 1975), and Carl E. Van Horn and Donald S. Van Meter, "The Implementation of Intergovernmental Policy," in Public Policy Making in a Federal System, edited by Charles A. Jones and Robert D. Thomas, Vol III. Sage Yearbooks in Politics and Public Policy (Beverly Hills, Calif.: Sage Publications, 1976), pp. 39-59.
15. Sidney L. Gardner, "Model Cities and the Intergovernmental Process: Impact on a Federal Agency—HEW," Model Cities, A Report on Progress, Special Issue of Model Cities Service Center Bulletin, Vol. 2, No. 9, June, 1971, p. 15.
16. Morton Grodzins calls these "federally-engineered local governments." For elaboration see his The American System: A New View of Government in the United States, edited by Daniel J. Elazar (Chicago: Rand McNally and Co., 1966), pp. 191-193.
17. Parris N. Glendening, "The Federal Role in Regional Planning Councils: Trends and Implications." The Review of Regional Studies, Vol. 1, No. 3 (Spring, 1971-72), pp. 93-111. The 1976 data were supplied by the National Association of Regional Councils.

18. As quoted in ACIR, *Intergovernmental Relations in the Poverty Program* (1966), p. 34.
19. Pressman, pp. 107-108.
20. Norman Beckman, "Changing Governmental Roles in Urban Development," in *Shaping an Urban Future: Essays in Memory of Catherine Bauer Wurster*, edited by Bernard J. Frieden and William W. Nash, Jr. (Cambridge: MIT Press, 1969), p. 151.
21. Ralph M. Widner, executive director of the Appalachian Regional Commission, in *Creative Federalism: William A. Jump-I. Thomas McKillop Memorial Lectures in Public Administration, 1966*, edited by Donald E. Nicoll (Washington, D.C.: Graduate School Press, U.S. Department of Agriculture, 1967), p. 93.
22. Martha Derthick, *New Towns In-Town* (Washington, D.C.: The Urban Institute, 1972), p. 94 and Chap. 9.
23. Pressman and Wildavsky, pp. 6, 68-69.
24. For an excellent discussion of urban interest groups, see Suzanne Farkas, *Urban Lobbying: Mayors in the Federal Arena* (New York: New York University Press, 1971).
25. Pressman, Chaps. 4 and 5.
26. James L. Sundquist, *Creative Federalism*, p. 14.
27. *Washington Post*, October 10, 1970.
28. Sundquist, p. 25.
29. Martin, p. 34.
30. William G. Colman in *Creative Federalism*, p. 16.
31. Richard Nathan, "The New Federalism Versus the Emerging New Structuralism," *Publius: The Journal of Federalism*, Vol. 5, No. 3 (Summer, 1975), pp. 111-129.
32. Henry S. Reuss, *Revenue Sharing: Crutch or Catalyist for State and Local Governments* (New York: Praeger Publishers, 1970), especially Chap. V.
33. Richard Lehne, "Employment Effects of Grants-in-Aid Effects," *Publius: The Journal of Federalism*, Vol. 5, No. 3 (Summer, 1975), pp. 101-109; and, Richard D. Bingham, *Public Housing and Urban Renewal: An Analysis of Federal-Local Relations* (New York: Praeger Publishers, 1975), Chap. 5.
34. ACIR, *Impact of Federal Urban Development Programs on Local Government Organization and Planning*, Report A-20, (1964), p. 25.
35. "Fiscal Questions and Political Answers," *Public Administration Review*, Vol. 33 (October, 1972), p. 476.

9

Interlocal Relations: Fragmented Federalism

E. E. Schattschneider writes that the "outcome of all conflict is determined by the *scope* of its contagion. The number of people involved in any conflict determines what happens; every change in the number of participants, every increase or deduction in the number of participants affects the results."[1] This observation is now generally recognized as being a truism. The sheer number of intergovernmental participants and intergovernmental transactions at the local level maximizes the potential for conflict there. The local level is the nexus of the intergovernmental system. Here converge the horizontal and vertical relations resulting from long-established patterns of interactions, both conflicting and cooperative, among the multitude of governments that dots the local landscape. National and state governments are increasingly involved, both because they were invited to interact and because they imposed their presence.

At no other point in the federal system is the harmonious working of the intergovernmental system more needed for survival of the participating governments than at the local level. Municipalities must coordinate with their neighbors to carry out most of the basic functions, such as police protection and planning. Practically any task begun by a city or county will involve interactions with a host of special districts. A county's intention to approve a zoning request for a new subdivision may require prior consultations and agreements with an independent water and sewer district to insure that these services are available to new residents. It may also require a long-range understanding with the independent school board to provide new classrooms or even new school buildings to meet expected enrollment increases. It may even require an agreement with a park and recreation special district to provide adequate open spaces, parks, and recreational programs for the new residents.

Further, all localities must increasingly interact with the state and national governments. With the local government's dependence on the state for its authority, particularly in non-home rule areas, and with an increasing financial reliance on the higher governments, intergovernmental interactions become crucial.

THE INTERLOCAL ENVIRONMENT

Students of the local government system must often be amazed that this system manages to function at all, much less function reasonably well. Local governments have more constituitional-legal limitations placed on them than do either of the other two levels. Yet, in terms of day-to-day basic services for the people, the localities carry far more of the burden than do the higher governments. These service demands produce tremendous and ever-increasing pressures on the most limited, most controlled, least flexible, and least elastic revenue systems in the entire American federal arrangement. The local system has the most fragmented arrangements of authority and decision-making, but faces the biggest challenges in providing areawide services. And lastly, it is obvious that the citizens are often confused about which local government is responsible for what services. The citizens believe they know which responsibilities belong to the national government and which belong to the states, but when it comes to the local level, who is responsible for the missed trash pickup or the corner pothole? The city? The county? The township? A private company? Or, maybe an almost invisible special district, e.g., a tri-county garbage authority? Even with the difficulty of determining responsibility, the frustrated citizen, most often a homeowner, feels the impact of local taxes more than he does those of other levels of government. This results from the heavy reliance on property taxes for all local governments and from the geographical proximity of local units which makes it possible for the citizen more often and more vehemently to express his views to local officials.

With all these contradictions—obvious problems, the temporary breakdowns, the setbacks—the local systems work. All these activities could be performed, without a doubt, in a much more satisfactory manner and yet as confused and disorganized as the local system of governance is, it does meet at least the more fundamental demands placed on them. As Daniel Elazar notes, "if the system appears on the surface to be mildly chaotic, this does not mean that some order does not exist within its bounds."[2] The provider of that order is a reasonably smoothly operating intergovernmental system. On a daily basis pragmatic intergovernmental adjustments lubricate the numerous and obvious "squeak points" that might otherwise cause a burnout or breakdown of the local political system. An examination of the legal and the governmental-political environment will give insight into how the interlocal system works.

THE LEGAL SETTING[3]

While allocating powers to local governments and setting their legal limitations, state lawmakers must be consistently enamored with Cowper's famous dictum "Variety's the very spice of life, That gives it all its flavor." The best word to describe the local legal setting is "variety." There is no consistent pattern of legal arrangements. In some states, counties are the dominant form of local government to the point that they can practically dictate the pace and direction of intergovernmental relations at the local level. In other states, counties may be so weak as to be practically ignored or deliberately excluded from intergovernmental exchanges. Some state legislatures have shown a definite favoritism toward municipalities and have showered them with enough grants of authority, taxing powers, and state financial assistance to give them a dominant position in entering the interlocal arena. In these states, municipalities may often be able to prevent the counties, townships, or other local governments from extending jurisdiction into the city. For example, a large county containing a dozen municipalities may be prohibited from extending county police patrols into the municipal jurisdictions or it must exempt the municipalities from coverage of the countywide master plan. Such arrangements make for neither adequate law enforcement nor adequate planning.

Some states give favored types of local government legal power to create and control territorial growth of other types of localities. A number of states permit the counties to veto proposed new municipal incorporations, and some states even require county approval of municipal annexations. Other states give authority in these matters to their larger municipalities. That is, an existing municipality of a legislatively-defined size may prohibit incorporation within its immediate environs— perhaps up to as much as five miles—and may easily annex surrounding territory, which generally means no referendum is required. The result of these "no incorporation/easy annexation" laws has been to evolve a relatively unfragmented structure in the states with a combination of these laws, such as Georgia, New Mexico, and Texas. Conversely, a highly fragmented local structure is permitted in states that do not have this sort of combination, such as California, Illinois, and Pennsylvania. Different patterns, in part a result of these provisions, are shown in table 9-1, which indicates the average number of local governments within counties for the six mentioned states.

Considering Schattschneider's comment at the beginning of this chapter about the number of participants' impact on conflicts, it is evident that the "no-incorporation" laws, by limiting the number of local government participants, has affected the type and outcome of interlocal interactions. The net effect of the lower number of governments participating is uncertain; it probably varies from area to area and from time to time. It is certain, however, that in situations where local

TABLE 9-1

IMPACT OF "NO INCORPORATION/EASY ANNEXATION" LAWS.

States with no incorporation/ easy annexation laws		States without no incorporation/easy annexation laws	
State	Average number of governments per county	State	Average number of governments per county
Georgia	8	California	66
New Mexico	10	Illinois	63
Texas	14	Pennsylvania	74

SOURCE: Bureau of the Census, **Census of Governments: 1972**, Vol. 1, **Government Organization,** p. 9.

governments must cooperate with one another to solve areawide problems, compete with one another for scarce resources, and jealously guard their powers and prerogatives, the "rules of the game" for local interactions will be considerably different in Georgia with an average of eight local governments per county than in Pennsylvania with an average of seventy-four for each county.

Variations in legal powers of local governments are found within states as well as among states. Most states, for example, give different powers to cities according to their population size. The "no-incorporation" powers are often granted only to the larger cities in a state. Similarly, larger jurisdictions are occasionally given revenue sources denied other local governments, such as a local sales or municipal income tax.

While a great variety exists in the legal environment in which local intergovernmental relations take place, notable regional patterns are present. Counties, for example, are usually stronger than municipalities in the South and the Border states. On the other hand, counties are very weak in New England where strong town and city governments are more important. Connecticut and Rhode Island do not even have organized counties.

THE CHANGING LEGAL SETTING

The legal setting that affects interlocal relations has been substantially modified in recent years by the great increase in new functions performed by local governments. Like the higher levels of government, localities are performing numerous functions that either were not performed at all or were carried out by the private sector until not many years past. The innovative and experimental programs of a decade ago in areas as diverse as pollution abatement, manpower training, drug abuse education, day care, and family counseling, are now commonplace. Further, jurisdictions that traditionally performed very limited functions are now providing a wide range of services, thereby making them practically indistinguishable from municipalities. In many suburban areas the counties now serve functionally as both city and county for their residents. These "urban counties," as they are often called, increasingly serve as rivals to municipalities, blocking the cities' expansion and competing with them for revenues and citizens' loyalties.

These new functions require grants of power and generally

specific state legislative authorization. The states have in recent years readily given such authority, but have at the same time tightly retained control over their creatures. In some instances the states have been able to give new grants of functional power and simultaneously increase their local control. To the extent that this becomes more prevalent, the localities, in effect, will be exercising state powers and administering state programs.

Lastly, the local legal scene has been modified by state actions designed to stimulate interlocal cooperation. Sometimes this has been limited to enabling legislation permitting interlocal cooperative agreements or contract purchase of services from another unit of government, e.g., a small municipality "buying" snow removal services from the county. The cooperative service agreements are not new; Indiana had an authorizing statute as early as 1852. There has been, however, a major growth in this type of interlocal relations in recent years. A survey by Joseph Zimmerman of municipalities participating in intergovernmental service agreements found that the major reasons for this type of activity were to (1) take advantage of economies of scale; (2) provide needed facilities; (3) secure qualified personnel; (4) meet an urgent problem; (5) comply with citizen demand for a service agreement; (6) take the service "out of politics"; and (7) avoid civil service regulations. Further, this survey noted that the propensity to enter into agreements is a function of population size, with the larger units ratifying interlocal service contracts more often than their smaller counterparts. Great variations also existed among regions. In the West, 78 percent of the municipalities had at least one such contract. This was true for only 53 percent of the cities in both the East and the South.[4]

The states have authorized or ordered the creation of cooperative agencies, for example, councils of governments (COGs), to facilitate program coordination, especially in the area of planning. Often this stimulus comes as a result of national planning review requirements (Circular A-95).

States have responded to areawide problems by creating or permitting voters or officials of local areas to establish new multijurisdictional special district governments or agencies, especially for the functions of planning and water and sewage in urban areas, and resource development, fire protection, and economic development in rural areas. These district governments or agencies are generally relatively independent of all existing local governments and are often able to bypass or outright veto their actions.

Finally, in a few places, most notably in the Indianapolis and Minneapolis-St. Paul areas, the state legislatures have stepped in to give a major restructuring of local powers and responsibilities for some or many of the area's local governments.[5] In 1967 the Minneapolis-St. Paul Metropolitan Council was established by state legislative act. The Council has taxing authority, the power to plan and zone and to work in such fields as solid waste, air pollution, and noise abatement. Even with these powers, it is still a council of governments-type arrangement, rather than a "new government." In 1969 the Indiana Legislature enacted a bill that created "Unigov" for the Indianapolis metropolitan area by consolidating the City of Indianapolis and Marion County. This was the largest consolidation in the current century and the first one to occur during this time in the North. More significantly, this is the only recent city-county consolidation to take place without a popular referendum. Such actions by the state legislatures are drastic, of course, but they may be the last resort open to states as the localities so often find themselves unable to function effectively in a politically and governmentally-fragmented system but cannot agree on a new structure for more effective governance.

The public apparently would like to see the power of local governments expanded. In a recent survey, 61 percent of a nationwide sample responded that they wished to see the local governments made "much stronger." Further, 27 percent preferred to see the localities made "only somewhat stronger," but only 8 percent wanted them to be less powerful. The least support for increasing local power came from the suburban respondents (57 percent), while the highest came from the central-city residents (64 percent).[6] The survey data do not show in which way the public feels that local governments should be made stronger. By greater grants of power from the state legislature? By internal administrative reform? Or, by external restructuring, for instance, the creating of an areawide metropolitan government? If past experience is a guide, the public may agree overwhelmingly to make local government stronger, but will surely be bitterly divided over how to do it.

THE GOVERNMENTAL-POLITICAL ENVIRONMENT

As noted earlier in this chapter, the local system of governance is the most fragmented part of the federal system; there are more than 78,000 units of local government. This means for many people the maximizing of democratic ideals about local government, an assurance of many points of access, and perpetuation of neighbor-run, "grass roots" governments. For others, however, the fragmentation is seen as creating a situation in which adequate services cannot be provided because no area-wide authority is present to deal with problems of that scope and human and financial resources are divided among numerous governments. One functional "city" is, then, divided artificially into many political and governmental subunits. This problem and its solutions are to be discussed later in this chapter.

An important element in considering the governmental environment of interlocal relations is the increased number of nonschool district local governments. Although the total number of governments, *including* school districts, declined by almost 77,000 between 1942 and 1972, the total number of local units, *excluding* school districts, increased by almost 16,000 during this same period. Municipalities grew by more than 2,000 during this time. The rate of incorporation of new cities has been increasing recently, with almost 500 new municipalities organized in the 1967-72 period. One-third of these units are suburban, "bedroom-type" entities located outside the larger central cities.

The trend to establish more small and medium-sized municipalities undoubtedly will continue as people flee the central cities. Of course, continuing energy crises and resultant higher gasoline prices and shortages may slow or even reverse this "flight." Indeed, a number of large cities actually gained population during the 1960-70 decade as a result of in-migration and annexation. Even the much maligned New York City had a slight population increase. However, evidence points to more and more people in the future leaving the larger cities for suburban and small-town communities. Gallup finds, for example, that in response to the question "If you could live anywhere that you wanted to, would you prefer a city, suburban area, small town or farm?" only 13 percent named the city, while 32 percent picked the small town, 31 percent the suburbs, and 23 percent the farm.[7] More than two-thirds of the sample wished to live in a suburban area or small town. In many ways this probably represents the idealized view Americans traditionally have about small town life. There is also substantial evidence, however, that this preference is based on strong and perhaps justified reasons for anti-city feelings.

The largest single reason for which people leave the central city is a fear of crime and violence. Gallup reports that "the proportion of women who say they are afraid to go out alone at night in their neighborhoods has grown from an already high 44 percent four years earlier to 58 percent in April, 1972."[8] Further, the same survey notes that 35 percent of the respondents believed crime was higher in their area than for the past year. The largest group of respondents (42 percent) believing crime had increased came from cities of one million or more. Stimulated by these fears and perceptions, only 22 percent of the respondents in 1966 preferred to live in the city. In 1970 that proportion declined to 18 percent, then to 17 percent in the next year, and finally to the reported 13 percent for 1972.[9] Many of those who can afford to leave the larger central cities are doing so. Increasingly, those who remain in such centers are the very wealthy and the very poor.

The emergent pattern is that people are increasingly disenchanted with the city and are moving to the suburbs and to other smaller towns. However, being accustomed to the amenities provided by a municipal corporation, they usually soon seek to secure urban services by creating a municipality, if one does not exist in the area, or by securing similar services from other governments (e.g., urban counties or special districts).

This migration with its accompanying public service demands has led to a great increase in the number of limited-purpose special districts. As efforts are made to overcome the growing local government fragmentation and to provide services in functional areas, such as water or sewage disposal, which are almost impossible to administer on a small government-by-small-government basis, a spur is given for the creation of more and more special districts. During the 1942-72 period the number of special districts grew from about 8,000 to approximately 24,000, with more than 2,600 of that increase occurring in the final five years.

Most observers view this development with alarm. Horizontal fragmentation is being traded for functional fragmentation. Many special districts are nondemocratic because their governing bodies are appointed rather than elected and their activities are generally "hidden" from the public's view. Further, the special districts are generally beyond the control of general-purpose governments because the districts receive their legal authorization from the state, not the city or the county. Consequently the districts' governing boards are often appointed by the governor or chosen by some other method once removed from local elected officials. Furthermore, because they are multijurisdictional, the districts can play off one local government against another. Some of the most acrimonious and protracted inter-governmental conflicts at the local level occur between special districts and general-purpose governments. It is not uncommon, for example, for counties or municipalities to become involved in a five-or six-year struggle with a water and sewer district or with a multicounty planning authority. Often these conflicts are one of the few activities that can bring the cities and counties together in common cause. All the criticisms notwithstanding, the special district form of government consistently had the highest percentage of new creations over all other types of local government in the 1942-72 period.

The complexity of the interlocal system takes its toll on the polity. A U.S. Senate Subcommittee survey asked interviewees to respond to a number of questions about government in the United States. Two questions and responses important for this discussion are shown in table 9-2. The first set of responses shows attitudes toward the entire system, political and govern-mental, and for all three levels of government. The 86 percent agreement rate that government seemed "too complicated" was shared almost evenly by all regions of the nation and by all types

TABLE 9-2

ATTITUDES TOWARD COMPLEXITY OF GOVERNMENT AND LOCAL GOVERNMENT DISORGANIZATION

Question 1: Sometimes politics and government seem so complicated that a person can't really understand what's going on.		**Question 2:** Local government is too disorganized to be effective.
Agree	86%	35%
Disagree	12	54
Not sure	2	11

SOURCE: Adapted from U.S. Senate, Committee on Government Operations, Sub-Committee on Intergovernmental Relations, **Confidence and Concern: Citizens View American Government. A Survey of Public Attitudes** (Washington, D.C.: Government Printing Office, 1973), Vol. II, pp. 267-269.

of communities (central city, suburbs, towns, rural). The second question which specifically focuses on local governments, showed regional and community variations. Thirty-five percent of the interviewees agreed that local government is "too disorganized to be effective." The highest agreement with this statement comes from the East, which is by far the most fragmented region of the nation, with an average of more than sixty local governments per county. The lowest agreement is found in the Midwest (29 percent). Also, nationally 41 percent of the city residents agreed with the statement while about 32 percent of those interviewed from the suburbs, towns, and rural areas concurred.

HOW THE SYSTEM ENDURES

Even with these misgivings about the existing structure of government, it is not likely to be changed in the near future. Pragmatic federalism at the local level induces enough change to keep the system from collapsing. Further, a variety of factors—including traditional political theory about the role of local government, on-going political traditions and patterns of interactions for governments, groups, and individuals, and reasonably workable accommodation devices—converge to give the current interlocal system a surprising amount of durability.

Much of the durability of the local system comes from perceptions of what local government is all about. The political theory of Americans strongly supports the current structure—many small governments run by local, ordinary citizen-legislators. The well-known Jeffersonian concept of "grass roots" government run by the people—miniature republics—has firmly taken hold in the American mind. "Self-government," "rural America," "the government closest to the people," "neighborhood government," and "grass roots democracy," are all terms repeated and defended daily, affirming America's commitment to small local units that can float with considerable autonomy on the turbulent sea of local government.

This belief goes far to perpetuate the current chaotic local governmental system. Never mind that within urban areas governments compete, overlap, duplicate, and often fail to perform. They still are the local governments that one day will stand as the last bulwark in defense of democracy according to the modern-day Jeffersonians. And what is the alternative to the current local government arrangements? A "gargantuan" structure to equal the size of the metropolitan spread cities. The myth of local government being small and close rejects that alternative. Can New York City, Chicago, or Los Angeles really be called a *local* government, it is asked?

Leading scholars such as Paul Ylvisaker,[10] Roscoe C. Martin,[11] and Robert C. Wood[12] have argued that the Jeffersonian model never existed except in a few isolated atypical instances or as a historical construct. These writers generally argue that the Madisonian model of representative government is more in keeping with the American tradition. Wood, for instance, argues that a large areawide government is "more defensible in terms of the values the nation has accepted."[13] The problem is that such logical arguments are confronted by an emotionally held belief. The myth prevails in the face of many such eloquent and logical onslaughts, and it goes far in preserving the current local government system.

The political element overrides the legal setting, the governmental structure, and the parameters of action imposed by strongly-held political theories. The various roles played by individual and collective politics in the intergovernmental relations system has been stressed throughout this book. Also they will serve as the main focus of the next section and therefore need not be commented upon in depth here. It is important, however, at this point to stress that politics is the force that generally stimulates the interlocal system, just as it does in nation-state relations or in interstate actions. Politics causes the dynamic interactions and often the conflicts. And, as if to balance the ledger, it is politics that often overcomes constitutional barriers and ties the system together or facilitates interlocal cooperation.

The mayor of Hyattsville, Maryland, a city of 15,000 with a budget of only $1 million, repeatedly makes successful demands on the county government with its 800,000 population and $225 million budget. His success comes not from his power as the nonpartisan mayor of a relatively small city, but because of his influence with Democratic party leaders and Democratic office holders on the county council and in the state legislative delegation. The success is not based on controlling the party, the county council, or the legislature, but merely on what everyone knows: "Old Charlie can hustle up a vote or two." Likewise, the local assessors of a state meet in a hotel lounge for a few drinks and work out a cooperative method for addressing grievances over municipal assessment procedures. This is done even though the state has not authorized any specific power to undertake interlocal cooperative agreements in this field. Also, the Republican congresswoman seeks national funds to help a local county executive (who also is a Republican) start a program for which the Democratic county council and governor had declined support. Chances are good that the program will help both the congresswoman and the county executive's upcoming reelection efforts.

And so it goes. The fragmented local governmental system moves onward rather dynamically and deliberately because, among other reasons, of a healthy dose of political inputs.

METROPOLITAN REORGANIZATION

The literature of intergovernmental relations has long been concerned with the problem of governmental fragmentation in our urban areas. Simply stated, a general awareness has developed that there are too many units of government in the large urban and metropolitan areas to permit effective governmental operations. Areawide problems are not being solved, in what Robert C. Wood has called the "governmental mosaic of the metropolis."[14] A consensus exists among most students of the metropolis that such fragmentation has produced major problems in policy planning and implementation and a general inability to deal with that social-economic complex referred to as "the urban problem."

Luthur Gulick, speaking of attempts to solve areawide problems such as transportation, pollution, and water supply under the fragmented system, concluded that there is "accumulating evidence of failure everywhere, in spite of many heroic efforts."[15] He continued:

> Once an indivisible problem is divided nothing effective can be done about it . . . Spreading area-wide problems cannot be handled geographic piece by geographic piece. They must be tackled in their entirety, comprehensively, and are difficult even so.[16]

Numerous methods of solving the problems associated with fragmentation have been proposed. They range from temporary and voluntary devices designed to alleviate an immediate difficulty resulting from fragmentation to a total reorganization of the metropolitan governance system by replacing the polycentric arrangement with one metropoliswide authority. Roscoe C. Martin identifies eight *procedural* adaptive devices and eight *structural* adaptive devices. They are:

A. Procedural Adaptation

  1. *Informal cooperation:* an agreement, neither authorized nor prohibited by law, between two or more local units of government to improve services.

  2. *The service contract:* a legal undertaking on the part of one government to supply and on the part of another to receive (and usually to pay for) the service or services named. N.B. The development of the Lakewood Plan.

  3. *Parallel action:* an agreement between two or more governments to pursue a common course of action. The decisions are agreed upon jointly, but their implementation requires individual action by the governments involved.

  4. *The conference approach:* the bringing together, at regular intervals, of representatives of the local governments within a given area for the discussion of common problems, the exchange of information, and the development of agreements on policy questions of mutual interest.

  5. *The compact:* a formal agreement under which two or more governments undertake certain mutual obligations.

  6. *Transfer of functions:* the transfer of one or more functions from one government to another more adequate in jurisdiction and resources—as from a village or city to a county.

  7. *Extraterritorial jurisdiction:* a legal grant by the state which permits the city to go outside its legal limits for certain fields of action.

  8. *Incorporation:* a process by which a given geographic area is transformed into a legal corporation which is recognized by law as an entity having particular functions, rights, duties, and liabilities.

B. Structural Adaptation

  1. *Annexation:* the simple legal device of expanding municipal boundaries to incorporate additional territory.

  2. *City-county separation:* the division or separation of the city from the county. The basic purpose of this device is to divide urban and rural populations so that each may have the kind and level of service it desires and is willing to pay for.

  3. *Functional consolidation:* the consolidating or merging of functions in a particular metropolitan area without necessarily consolidating or abolishing any existing units of government.

  4. *The special district:* a unit of government established to administer one or more designated functions. The new unit does not necessarily need to coincide with previous political boundaries.

  5. *The authority:* a type of public administrative agency with quasi-governmental powers. This type of adaptation is not unlike the special district. The major difference is the normally larger geographic area of the authority and its power to issue revenue bonds.

6. *Geographical consolidation:* the merger or consolidation of two or more units of governments into one government.

7. *Metropolitan government:* a general government with jurisdiction over the whole of a particular metropolitan area.

8. *The regional agency or authority:* a unit of government which represents a regional approach to suprametropolitan problems.[17]

Most adaptations so far have employed combinations of the procedural devices listed in Martin's taxonomy. This is largely a result of the political difficulties accompanying major structural change. Martin's taxonomy can be viewed along two continua, that of effectiveness and that of political feasibility.[18] (See figure 9-1.) What is generally thought to be politically acceptable is often seen as too ineffective, too slow, or too temporary. What is perceived as most effective in dealing with fragmentation is generally simply not acceptable to the voters.

FIGURE 9-1

EFFECTIVENESS/FEASIBILITY CONTINUA

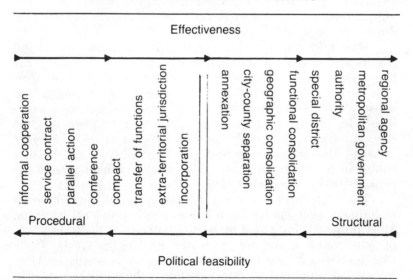

SOURCE: Parris N. Glendening, "The Federal Role in Regional Planning Councils: Trends and Implications," **The Review of Regional Studies,** Vol. 1, No. 3 (Spring, 1971-72), p. 95.

To say that attempted solutions to the problems of metropolitan fragmentation have concentrated on procedural and voluntary adaptations does not mean that efforts to achieve Wood's "one community—one government" have been abandoned.[19] A conservative estimate would suggest that since World War II hundreds of communities have had some organized effort to adopt a form of areawide government, with many of these, of course, being repeat considerations for one area, as in the case of repeated efforts for reorganization in St. Louis. Further, a significant percentage of these attempts has actually reached fruition in the sense of a specific detailed plan of metropolitan governance being submitted to the voters or to the state legislature.

A system of metropoliswide government can be achieved in several ways. Included are large-scale annexation, the creation of a metropolitan-wide general service district, the establishment of a local federal system, or the consolidation of local governments in the metropolis into an areawide government. In particular consolidation has been attempted frequently in recent years. For a variety of legal and political reasons, however, the consolidations are almost always partial, leaving a number of local governments in existence and independent of the new areawide unit. Moreover, in numerous instances the voters have turned down the proposal.

Most efforts at geographic consolidation have utilized the county as the core of the proposed metropolitan government. For many years such a consolidation was viewed as all municipalities and special districts within the county being merged or consolidated with the existing or strengthened county government. In more recent years political realities have dictated that city-county consolidation may mean consolidation only between the largest city and the county, with the smaller suburban municipalities being permitted to remain outside the consolidated government but given the option to join later.

The history of the many proposals for metropolitanwide governance systems has been one of nearly universal rejection. Most proposals are killed by hostile interests or die from a lack of active support and are never presented to the voters. Those that survive and reach the voting booth are generally rejected. Successful adoptions are few. Rejection is the normal outcome of reorganization referenda.

Some far-reaching proposals have been accepted by the voters. Most notable was the successful adoption of a local federal system in the Miami-Dade County area in 1957. The more frequent but still very rare adoptions of city-county consolidation proposals have occurred primarily in the South, with the major consolidations involving Baton Rouge, Nashville, Jacksonville, Columbus (Ga.), Lexington (Ky.), and the previously mentioned Indianapolis change. Thus, the South, which is that part of the country in which the metropolises are least fragmented and in which fragmentation is increasing much more slowly than in other geographical areas is the only section where a noticeable number of areawide structural reorganizations has been taking place.

VARIABLES AFFECTING METROPOLITAN REFERENDA DECISIONS

Not very many years ago it was commonplace to blame rejection of metropolitan reform proposals on the ignorance of the voting public. "If only the people had understood the complexity of the problem and the logic of the proposal," it was often emotionally put forth, "they would have supported it." Today we are beginning to understand better the many variables that come together in a unique combination to spell acceptance or, more predictably, rejection on any particular reorganization proposal. The more important factors—partisanship, race, and indigenous events—deserve consideration.

PARTISANSHIP

Since 1957, when Banfield wrote that "it will be difficult or impossible to integrate local government where the two-party system operates,"[20] partisan division between the normally Republican-dominated suburbs and the normally Democratic-dominated central cities has been seen as a major obstacle to the adoption of an areawide government. Barring the situation of nearly even population division between a central city and its suburban areas, almost certainly one party will run the new government on a continuing basis. Given the importance of viable local parties in the American party structure, the loss of the city hall or the county courthouse could prove disastrous. Banfield warned that "in effect, advocates of consolidation schemes are asking the Democrats to give up their control of the central cities or, at least, to place it in jeopardy."[21] This specter of partisan loss has been raised in many reorganization campaigns. In fact, no proposal has been adopted by voters in areas split by strong partisan antagonisms. The one adoption in a partisanly-divided metropolis (Indianapolis) was imposed by the state legislature.

RACE

Racial cleavages have always played an important part in the politics of metropolitan reorganization. Generally, the variable of race was thought of in terms of white suburbanites who had fled the central city voting against consolidation to insure that they were not reunited with that which they had fled. As Daniel R. Grant observes:

> More often than not, the politics of race has worked against the adoption of proposed metro governments. Lily-white suburbs have tended to vote against having anything to do with "those lower class city-hall types," and proponents of annexation, city-county consolidation, or metropolitan federation were denounced as tax-grabbing thieves who will invade the beautiful suburbs and spread core city blight and ethnic minorities out in the comfortably homogeneous and compatible suburbs. Seldom has the word "race" been mentioned specifically in the campaign advertisements and sloganeering, but this did not prevent its being one of the more important "silent issues" that was discussed only in "safe company."[22]

Recently, much attention has focused on reasons for growing black opposition to reorganization. Many black leaders have taken the position that the deliberate intent of metropolitan reorganization or, at a minimum, the indirect effect of such a proposal is to dilute black voting strength. Studies on referenda in Cleveland, St. Louis, and Nashville point to the importance of black opposition based on this stated fear. There is, of course, a certain irony in racially-based opposition of both blacks and whites.

Some blacks stress that dilution of black voting strength is not a side effect of reorganization; instead it is the reason for it. For instance, LeRoy Johnson, a Georgia state senator, charged that the proposed consolidation of Atlanta and Fulton County was written not as "an effort of extending the tax base of the City but from an effort of curtailing and limiting the Negro voting strength."[23]

Regardless of the intent of city-county consolidation the effect has been to dilute the earlier concentrations of black voting power. Nashville in 1960 had a population that was 38 percent black. The current black population of the consolidated government there is only 19 percent. Jacksonville dropped from 42 percent black before the 1967 consolidation to 23 percent after reorganization. Likewise, black population went from 24 percent in Indianapolis before consolidation to 18 percent after Unigov.

Lastly, some black leaders are accepting the view of writers such as Grant that political control of a dying central city might be meaningless.

> Situations which make it possible for black citizens to elect their own city council are undoubtedly a long overdue contribution to the self-respect and pride of blacks. It is exceedingly difficult to make a value judgment on the relative merits of racial balance in American society and a racial imbalance in communities that permit blacks to elect black officials and whites to elect white officials for separate governments.

> But such value judgments must be made in American society, and this writer suspects that it will be only a Pyrrhic victory if black mayors and black city councils inherit all of the problems and misery of the core cities in our metropolitan areas without the resources of white America to cope with these problems. The National Urban Coalition recently predicted that [within a decade] most American cities would be "black, brown, and bankrupt."[24]

SPECIAL INDIGENOUS EVENTS

Several analysts have concluded that the normal pattern is to reject a reorganization plan unless an unusual special indigenous event is present to alter the natural inclination toward rejection. A major scandal, a total breakdown in one or more public services, or a unique political leader or political event are the stimuli for major governmental change. Thomas M. Scott, for example, argues that radical reorganization, such as city-county consolidation, is possible only when special or unusual political factors cause politicians and citizens to "respond abnormally" in their voting behavior. Scott concludes:

> Radical reorganization plans tend to be approved only in areas with unusual social-economic-political characteristics.... These cases are unique and must be explained as deviations from the normal patterns....

> Practically speaking, this analysis suggests that in the near future radical metropolitan change will continue to win voter approval only under unique circumstances. In the meantime "normal" metropolitan areas (as most are) will forestall crises by dealing with their problems in a piecemeal manner.[25]

A case-by-case review of the successful reorganizations appears to support the argument that a unique situation is needed. A most notable illustration is found in the Jacksonville-Duval County referendum. A group known as the Citizens for Better Government actively compaigned for the new plan by pointing out excessive governmental duplication and ineffi-ciency, one of the nation's highest crime rates, severe water and air pollution problems, extremely high city debts and, most important, repeated cases of graft and corruption. Ten months before the referendum, the grand jury indicted two city commissioners, four council members, the recreation director, and the city auditor. In addition, the tax assessor resigned after a grand jury investigation. Further, fifteen city senior high schools were disaccredited because of inadequate financial support and physical facilities. The disaccreditation came shortly before the August referendum. It was in this unique environment that the consolidation was approved by a margin of 24,725 votes.

OTHER VARIABLES

A review of the many case studies on metropolitan reorganizations suggests many other variables that at one time may play a key role in the success or failure of a proposal. Important issues in at least one campaign include (1) class and class perceptions, (2) alienation and sublimation, (3) apathy, (4) service perceptions, (5) lack of knowledge of the proposal, (6) fear of tax increases, (7) leadership inadequacies, (8) legal requirements, and (9) political philosophies.

THE FUTURE OF
METROPOLITAN REORGANIZATION

What about the future? Will the topic of metropolitan reorganization forever be subtitled "the politics of rejection"? Combining the collective knowledge of the literature on the subject with some possibly enlightened soothsaying, the follow-ing projections can be made about the future of governmental organization of metropolitan areas in the United States.

1. Most problems resulting from fragmentation will be solved by procedural, voluntary, and ad hoc adaptive devices. This rather unimaginative conclusion is a realistic assessment of the political and legal difficulties involved in major structural

change. It also recognizes that for all the rhetoric on the failing of the current arrangement, one must conclude—even if somewhat begrudgingly—that the system *does work!* Wood's similar conclusion, written in 1958, is still valid today.

> Despite our predictions, disaster has not struck; urban government has continued to function, not well perhaps, but at least well enough to forestall catastrophe. Traffic continues to circulate; streets and sewers are built; water is provided; schools keep their doors open; and law and order generally prevail. Nor does this tolerable state of affairs result from an eager citizenry's acceptance of our counsel; we know only too well that our proposals for genuine reform have been largely ignored.[26]

2. There will continue to be some major adoptions of areawide governments in coming years. Many jurisdictions are giving serious considerations to metropolitan reorganization. However, the largest number of these considerations is concentrated in the South and most of the successful adoptions in the near future are likely for reasons expressed herein to be in that region.

3. Many states will be changing the "rules of the game" in order to facilitate metropolitan reorganization. Some states have already abolished requirements for extraordinary or concurrent popular majorities. A few states, e.g., Florida, are encouraging comprehensive review by offering state technical and financial assistance for local government study commissions. Many states, especially in the South, Southwest, and Far West, are trying to minimize future problems by heading off fragmentation with "no-incorporation, easy-annexation" laws. Some of the impact of these changes is shown in the often repeated statistic of approximately six million people affected by annexation during the 1960s. Almost two-thirds of the urban municipalities were involved in some annexation action during that period.

One of the most significant changes in the "rules of the game" is the proposal for ending the requirement for popular referendum approval of a local government change. Some of our largest cities, e.g., Boston, Philadelphia, New Orleans, and New York City, were created by nineteenth century city-county consolidation actions of state legislatures. That approach is likely to be revived in the future. The 1969 Indiana Legislature merged Marion County and Indianapolis. Other state legislatures are considering similar actions. For example, the Alabama Legislature failed to approve by only one vote a consolidation of part of Jefferson County with the City of Birmingham.

One has mixed reactions about reorganization by state legislative action. It does, of course, eliminate many causes of past rejections. However, that approach plays havoc with the strongly-held tradition of popular approval of forms of local government and opens the door to possibly new and dangerous gerrymandering of governmental structures. The Republican-controlled Indiana Legislature was, for example, accused of partisan action to help both the party and the state's newest Republican "star," Richard Lugar, mayor of Indianapolis.

4. If the states and localities are unable to deal adequately with the problems resulting from fragmentation, it is highly probable that the national government will take actions designed to encourage a more rational order to the metropolitan scene. A combination of grant-in-aid funding with metropolitanwide comprehensive planning and review requirements—the famous 204, 701 and A-95 procedures—has already exerted an important influence on local government organization, especially as a stimulus for the growth of some strong councils of governments. Joseph Zimmerman writes that the national government has not been sufficiently aggressive in promoting "a rationalization of the government of metropolitan areas."[27]

Much more direct action on local government organization is the rule, rather than the exception, for other countries.[28] While drastic national governmental action of the type undertaken in countries such as Great Britain, Canada, or Germany is very unlikely for the United States, some type of nationally-approved arrangement, perhaps a compact-based "federal charter," will have to be created for the many multistate metropolises.

NOTES

1. E. E. Schattschneider, *The Semi-Sovereign People* (New York: Holt, Rinehart and Winston, 1960), p. 2.
2. Daniel J. Elazar, "Local Government in Intergovernmental Perspective," in Daniel J. Elazar, R. Bruce Carroll, E. Lester Levine and Douglas St. Angelo, editors, *Cooperation and Conflict: Readings in American Federalism* (Itasca, Ill.: F. E. Peacock Publishers, 1969), p. 417.
3. The legal powers and limitations and the forms of government were discussed earlier, primarily in the state-local chapter (7). This section limits its comments to certain additional legal matters that have more direct bearing on interlocal relations.

4. Joseph F. Zimmerman, "Meeting Service Needs Through Intergovernmental Agreements," *Municipal Year Book, 1973* (Washington, D.C.: International City Management Association, 1973), pp. 79-88.

5. For a discussion of the Indianapolis plan, see, York Willbern, "Unigov: Local Government Reorganization in Indianapolis," in Advisory Commission on Intergovernmental Relations, *Regional Governance: Promise and Performance. Substate Regionalism and the Federal System.* Volume II *Case Studies.* Report A-41 (Washington, D.C.: Government Printing Office, 1973), pp. 45-73. For an analysis of the Minneapolis-St. Paul change, see in the same volume, Ted Kolderie, "Governance in the Twin Cities Area of Minnesota," pp. 111-138. (In subsequent notes the Commission will be cited as ACIR.)

6. U.S. Senate, Committee on Government Operations, Subcommittee on Intergovernmental Relations, *Confidence and Concern: Citizens View American Government. A Survey of Public Attitudes* (Washington, D.C.: Government Printing Office, 1973), Vol. II, p. 121. Survey conducted by Louis Harris and Associates, 1973.

7. *The Gallup Opinion Index*, Report 90, December, 1972, p. 22.

8. *Ibid.*, Report 82, April, 1972, p. 10.

9. *Ibid.*, Report 90, December, 1972, p. 22.

10. "Some Criteria for a 'Proper' Areal Division of Powers," in Arthur Maass, ed., *Area and Power* (Glencoe, Ill.: The Free Press, 1959).

11. *Grass Roots* (2nd ed.; University, Ala. University of Alabama Press, 1964).

12. *Suburbia* (New York: Houghton Mifflin, 1958).

13. *Ibid.*, p. 295.

14. Robert C. Wood, *1400 Governments: The Political Economy of the New York Metropolitan Region* (Garden City, N.Y.: Doubleday and Co., 1964), p. 56.

15. Luther H. Gulick, *The Metropolitan Problem and American Ideas* (New York: Alfred A. Knopf, 1962), p. 23. This view of near complete failure is not universally accepted. See, for example, Robert C. Wood, "Metropolitan Government, 1975: An Extrapolation of Trends," *American Political Science Review*, Vol. 52 (1958), pp. 108-122. Warren emphasizes the positive aspects of public choice in a market situation. See Robert Warren, "A Municipal Services Market Model of Metropolitan Organization," *Journal of the American Institute of Planners*, Vol. 30 (August, 1964), pp. 193-204; and Vincent Ostrom, Charles Tiebout, and Robert Warren, "The Organization of Government in Metropolitan Areas: A Theoretical Inquiry," *American Political Science Review*, Vol. 55 (December, 1961), pp. 831-842. A few authors have argued that the problem is not one of structure, but of a lack of political

will to do the task. See Frances Fox Piven and Richard A. Cloward, "Black Control of the Cities: Heading It Off by Metropolitan Government," *The New Republic* (October 7, 1967), p. 18; and Parris N. Glendening and Mavis Mann Reeves, "The Future of State and Local Government and American Federalism," in Mavis Mann Reeves and Parris N. Glendening, *Controversies of State and Local Political Systems* (Boston: Allyn and Bacon, 1972), pp. 481-483.

16. Gulick, p. 24.

17. Roscoe C. Martin, *Metropolis in Transition: Local Government Adaptation to Changing Urban Needs*, a report prepared for the Housing and Home Finance Agency under the Urban Studies and Housing Research Program (Washington, D.C.: Government Printing Office, 1963). Martin's study is now out of print. For a summary of his 1963 report, see Roscoe C. Martin, "Action in Metropolis— I, *National Civic Review*, Vol. 52 (1963), pp. 302-307; and *ibid.*, Part II, pp. 363-367, 371. For a slightly different taxonomy see ACIR, *Alternate Approaches to Governmental Reorganization in Metropolitan Areas*, Report A-11 (1962).

18. Parris N. Glendening, "The Federal Role in Regional Planning Councils: Trends and Implications," *The Review of Regional Studies*, Vol. 1, No. 3 (Spring, 1971-72), p. 95; and Reeves and Glendening, pp. 479-480. Thomas M. Scott employs a similar approach when he talks of a "continuum of radicalness of metropolitan governmental change." See Thomas M. Scott, "Metropolitan Governmental Reorganization Proposals," *Western Political Quarterly*, Vol. 21 (June, 1968), pp. 254-255.

19. Robert C. Wood, "Metropolitan Government, 1975," p. 111.

20. Edward C. Banfield, "The Politics of Metropolitan Area Organization," *Midwest Journal of Political Science*, Vol. 1 (1957), p. 86.

21. *Ibid.*

22. Daniel R. Grant, "Metropolitan Area Government and the Politics of Racial Balance: Some Public Policy Issues." A paper presented at the Southern Political Science Association Meeting, Gatlinburg, Tennessee, November 12, 1971, pp. 2-3.

23. Quoted in the *New York Times*, November 9, 1969, p. 65.

24. Grant, p. 10. See also Willis D. Hawley, *Blacks and Metropolitan Governance: The Stakes of Reform* (Berkeley: University of California, Institute of Governmental Studies, 1972).

25. Scott, p. 261.

26. Wood, "Metropolitan Government," p. 112. Wood added that "we may not face catastrophe, but this is no reason for countenancing one-hour commuting schedules, for permitting blight, for condoning the repellent sprawl of cheap commercial developments, inadequate parks, congested schools, mediocre administration,

traffic jams, smog, pollution, and the hundred and one irritations which surround us. . . ." (p. 113.)

27. Joseph F. Zimmerman, "Metropolitan Reform in the U.S.: An Overview." *Public Administration Review*, Vol. 30 (September/October, 1970), p. 542.

28. Frank Smallwood, "Reshaping Local Government Abroad: Anglo-Canadian Experiments." *Public Administration Review*, Vol. 30, No. 5 (September/October, 1970), pp. 521-530; and Conrad J. Weiler, Jr., "Metropolitan Federation Reconsidered," *Urban Affairs Quarterly*, Vol. 6 (June, 1971), pp. 411-420.

10

The Future of the Intergovernmental System: Change and Uncertainty

The American federal system has been the object of scrutiny and criticism since its inception. The debate about the nature of the relationship between the colonies and the central authorities before the Constitutional Convention, the compromises on alternative associational arrangements in that Convention, and the exchanges on the subject during the ratification campaigns have all given rise to a continuing discussion about the function and future of federalism in the United States. This discussion has continued unabated for more than 200 years. The temper of the debate has surged or lagged with the topical events of the moment. Some events that focused attention on the operation of the federal system and intensified the discussion about the system's future were the early judicial interpretations of the Constitution which "settled out" many patterns of intergovernmental relations that are still evident, the intense debates over issues such as commerce, tariffs, trade, and slaves before the Civil War, and that War itself. Others were the inability of the states to deal with the emergent giants of industry and finance during the latter part of the last century, the Depression, the civil rights-integration struggle of the 1950s and 1960s, and the problems of the cities and the environment during the 1960s and 1970s.

The direction and enthusiasm for emerging intergovernmental patterns depend naturally on whose ox is being prepared for roasting, to continue the culinary analysis so prevalent in the study of intergovernmental relations. The successes realized from the national judiciary by civil rights leaders surely whet their appetite for greater centralization and national judicial intervention. Similarly the flavor of the times, with increased national governmental activities to insure equal opportunities for all citizens, just as surely dulls the taste buds of many racial separatists for the type of federalism that is emerging.

Evaluations by objective commentators generally give a projection for the system's future that can, at best, be described as "guarded optimism." Two examples from well-known students of intergovernmental relations and federalism will suffice. W. Brooke Graves, whose *American Intergovernmental Relations* has been cited often in this book, concluded his mammoth study with these comments:

> Americans ... face unprecedented problems of national security—possibly even of survival—in a divided world, but they face critical problems at home in the preservation of American federalism, problems which few of them seem to realize. It is quite conceivable that the nation might survive, and its federal system of government be irretrievably lost.
>
> The American federal system has served the people well for nearly 200 years. It has great elements of strength. It has survived crises in the past and will, in all probability, survive others in the future. But there is no assurance that it will always continue to do so unless statesmanlike solutions are found—and found quickly— to meet new problems arising out of an almost completely different set of social and economic conditions under which it must operate now and in the future....
>
> The time may be later than we think.[1]

Richard H. Leach, another well-known authority on federalism, evaluated the future of the American arrangement in an essay replete with statements not giving an optimistic view of the continuation of a viable system. However, his overall theme is that certain relatively mild changes will likely forestall radical restructuring of the federal system, at least for the near future. Leach writes:

> There is ... considerable evidence that the country has already become so nationalized that continuation of a localistic system of government is already an anachronism.... In this view, state and local governments are superfluities, largely irrelevant to an attack on America's pressing problems; the national government alone can launch a successful attack. Not that some sort of local or regional agents of the national government would not be necessary to carry out many facets of that attack. They would be necessary. The point is, however, that they would be agents, even as counties have always been of state governments.[2]

AN ASSESSMENT

These two types of conclusions are increasingly common throughout the literature. We are not quite so pessimistic, however. We think that a viable federal system will be operating in the United States for many years to come. We recognize the problems facing the American system today, but we believe that a burial of the present constitutional structure or the search for another governance arrangement is premature.

In part, our more optimistic view is based on faith in what we have called *pragmatic federalism*. The more the American brand of federalism is studied, the more one becomes impressed with its ability to adjust to meet the specifics of a changing situation or to meet new demands. The system set up more than 200 years ago is not a dogmatic embodiment of any particular philosophy, nor is it an excessively legalistic undertaking. Instead, the heritage is the bare skeleton which must be "fleshed out" by successive generations.

The Founding Fathers were individuals who had substantial disagreements about the most desirable system to adopt, just as another group of fifty-five persons[3] would disagree if a similar convention were held today. Their divergent views were worked out in a series of practical compromises that tried to meet the conflicting needs for a central authority and for decentralized political autonomy. The compromises of 1787 were the beginnings of a system of pragmatic federalism which places responsibilities on each successive generation to make similar practical adjustments in the structures and processes of federalism to keep alive the bargain struck between centralization and decentralization. Past events and emerging trends thus should be recognized for what they generally are—continuing pragmatic adjustments to changing needs.

This does not mean that the federalism system in the United States always works well or that there have not been major failures. One need only think of the Civil War, the inability for almost forty years (1880-1920) to generate any semblance of an effective mechanism to deal with the excesses of emergent industrial capitalism, the continuance of racism by some of the system's subunits, or the severe resource disparities that currently exist among units of government to recognize that the federal arrangement created by Article IV of the Constitution is far from perfect. And yet the important point is that the system does work because it has been able to correct these failures—the

Civil War being the notable exception—as well as to solve the daily problems that arise in a complex and dynamic society. (As will be pointed out later, this, too, becomes a matter of perspective, with some critics arguing that the systemic correction of these problems takes far too long and therefore an entirely new structure is needed.)

THE NATURE OF CHANGE

One of the strengths of the American federal system has been its ability to change. Although rarely formally altered, hundreds of other significant changes have occurred through judicial interpretation, usage, and tradition. The nature of the change process determines the future of any system. Is change in our system an ongoing and incremental process? Or does it occur in system-rending spurts resulting from the buildup of pressures from unmet demands?

Elsewhere we have argued that meaningful and major changes generally occur, sadly, only after a catastrophic and system-shaking event provides a stimulus for action among a generally conservative and complacent populace.[4] The Depression caused a basic rethinking about the nature of the economic system and the role of government. The cultural shock of Selma, Alabama, and related protests and violence led to a new legal and political equality for blacks. And the events following the assassination of President John Kennedy stimulated a long overdue constitutional change (the Twenty-fifth Amendment) for the filling of vacancies in the offices of President and Vice President, provisions utilized just a few years later to elevate Gerald Ford and Nelson Rockefeller to the highest offices.

Must all change be reactive? Are these crisis stimulants necessary prerequisites for meaningful change? Major and comprehensive change will occur only rarely without this type of stimulus, if past history is to be a guide. In substantial part this is because of the strong conservatism of the American public toward its basic institutions. It has been axiomatic throughout our history that "prudence, indeed, will dictate that governments long established should not be changed for light and transient causes; and accordingly all experience has shown, that mankind are more disposed to suffer, while evils are sufferable, than to right themselves by abolishing the forms to which they are accustomed."

The American federal system, of course, need not get itself into situations where such major changes become necessary. A process of continuous incremental change should insure that the basic structures are flexible, accommodating, and contemporary to the point that a major restructuring is unnecessary. Richard Leach sees the continuing pragmatic changes in the system as one of its most encouraging features. He says, "Fortunately, the distinguishing characteristic of American federalism is its capacity for adaptation and change. Indeed, federalism in the United States has been in flux since its adoption and nothing has happened to suggest it has lost that ability."[5]

The combined incremental and separately occurring changes since the end of World War II, when considered in tandem, have produced in many ways a federalism unlike that existing before this period. Many factors have created a new type of federal system unimagined just a short time ago. Some of them are the impact of the enormous growth in grants-in-aid, revenue sharing, and other forms of intergovernmental aid, and the unprecedented national judicial intervention in the areas of state handling of civil rights and criminal procedures and in the area of representation and apportionment. Others are the grand experiments of "Creative Federalism," direct federalism, and "New Federalism," activities in the areas of multistate and substate regionalism, revitalization of the states, and metropolitan reorganization. There was no constitutional convention to redraw the basics of government. There was no single catastrophic event to stimulate public acceptance. Instead, the new system of intergovernmental relations that has emerged was the result of a continuance of accelerated and rampant incrementalism, to use what William Safire calls an "oxymoranic phrase" because "the adjective at first glance appears to fight the noun it modifies."[6] The words are not really incongruous, however. "Accelerated and rampant incrementalism" describes a continuous series of relatively minor or incremental, and generally unrelated, events which have come together to modify substantially America's brand of federalism.

It is not clear what final form of government will emerge from the changes in the post-World War II period. It is probably correct, however, to say that no single final form is being created because the system is constantly in the process of change and evolution. Even if the shape of the emergent government or the crystallization of new patterns of intergovernmental relations are unclear, most observers are certain that the events of recent years have moved the American federal system far along the road marked "centralization."

CENTRALIZATION AND DECENTRALIZATION

The history of American federalism is one of rather steadily increasing centralization. The movement of power to the center government can be traced as a force moving inexorably forward, occasionally slowing, maybe even temporarily hesitating or halting, but almost never retreating. Walter H. Bennett's study on American federalism concludes with what has become a truism of the intergovernmental system:

> The sweep of events in this century and the general character of American industrial society would make it naive to assume that there will be a wholesale reversal of the trend toward governmental centralization. Problems which were once local but have become national in scope are not to be expected suddenly to become local again.[7]

It is possible to identify periods in which centralization surged onward, such as during the Civil War and its immediate aftermath, during the height of the Progressive movement of the early twentieth century with its business and finance regulation—generally meaning national regulation—proposals, during the Depression and its resultant New Deal, during World War II and the post-War international commitments, and during the activists programs of the 1960s in the areas of racial equality and urban development. It is also possible to identify periods when the centralization trend was relatively quiescent, such as that between the end of Reconstruction and the beginning of the Progressive period, or during the administration of Presidents Hoover, Eisenhower, and Nixon. The last two executives had as part of their explicitly stated philosophies and programs the desire to slow or reverse the centralization trend. Nevertheless, it is almost impossible to identify any period in which significant decentralization has taken place.

While the centralization trend has produced misgivings, fears, and opposition from most public leaders, the public, and many students of federalism, there are proponents who cheer on that trend, and who look forward to the final demise of all decentralized centers of power. Herbert Croly, a leading publicist of the Progressive movement, argued that "American government demands more rather than less centralization merely and precisely because of the growing centralization of American activity."[8] Three decades later the influential Harold J. Laski was advancing the centralization argument in this manner:

> My pleas here are for the recognition that the federal form of state is unsuitable to the stage of economic and social development that America has reached. I infer from this postulate two conclusions: first, that the present division of powers, however liberal be the Supreme Court in its technique of interpretation, is inadequate to the needs America confronts; and, second, that any revision of those powers is one which must place in Washington, and Washington only, the power to amend that revision as circumstances change. I infer, in a word, that the epoch of federalism is over....
>
> The view here urged, of course, looks toward a fundamental reconstruction of traditional American institutions. It is not impressed by the view, associated with the great name of Mr. Justice Brandeis, that the "curse of bigness" will descend upon any serious departure from the historic contours of federalism.... What, at least, is certain is this: that a government the powers of which are not commensurate with its problems will not be able to cope with them. Either, therefore, it must obtain those powers, or it must yield to a form of state more able to satisfy the demands that it encounters. That is the supreme issue before the United States today; and the more closely it is scrutinized the more obviously does its resolution seem to be bound up with the obsolescence of the federal system.[9]

The statements of Croly and Laski were written during periods of great systemic difficulty and adjustment. Their views, however, are not merely of historical interest. They state a recurring theme that surfaces whenever federalism faces stress. Harry V. Jaffa, well known for his writings on American political thought, gives a more contemporary (1960) statement of the pro-centralization position. Jaffa's main concern is for greater centralization in the interest of defense and national security, which demonstrates the topicality of the attitudes toward centralization and decentralization. His conclusions, however, are identical to Croly, Laski, and other centralization proponents.

> The case for a stronger national government rests upon one simple proposition: The problems which face the American people, to an extent unprecedented, are national problems and can be dealt with effectively only by the common direction and close coordination of the efforts of all Americans. The only agency which can marshal all the resources of the nation, and order all its efforts to the overriding purposes which all share, is the government of the United States.[10]

Not all the centralists make their case on the basis of broad increases in power to deal with general social and economic problems. Some have a much narrower focus. William H. Riker, for example, noting that the decentralized power arrangement of the federal system has been effectively utilized by racists and segregationists, comes to the sweeping conclusion that "if in the United States one approves of Southern white racists, then one should approve of American federalism."[11]

Not only are the pro-centralization arguments generally rejected by most people who study federalism and by the American public and its leaders, but a certain solace can be had in the system's ability to deal with their focal points of complaint. Brooke Graves, responding to Laski's argument, notes that "to these criticisms, one is justified in answering that under the federal system as it now operates, there is sufficient constitutional power to deal with virtually any problem of national proportions. . . ."[12]

The key to Graves' rejoinder is in the phrase "as it now operates." There undoubtedly were major shortcomings in the system's ability to deal with the problems of the 1920s and 1930s to which Laski was addressing himself. However, the system was able, through pragmatic change and accommodation, to deal adequately with the problems. Likewise, the federal arrangement has been modified enough to provide socio-economic regulations sought by Croly, to alleviate the security and defense concerns expressed by Jaffa, and to overcome the subunits' protection of segregation that Riker feared. To illustrate, what was needed in the last named case was a broader interpretation of protections afforded by the Fourteenth Amendment and a national commitment to get on with the business of desegregation. A national restructuring, including the abandonment of federalism, was not necessary.

ALTERNATE MODELS

Since the beginning of the American Republic, alternate associational arrangements have been suggested. The Constitutional Convention considered several possibilities before agreeing to compromises that gave birth to the current structure. Alexander Hamilton, for example, proposed a highly centralized model in which all sovereignty would reside in the central government and the subunits would be like "corporations for local purposes." Later, John C. Calhoun, looking to the maintenance of state sovereignty, proposed the concepts of concurrent majority and the mutual negative. For the latter, he argues, as had John Taylor of Caroline, that the state and national governments each possessed the power to veto the acts of the other. Such actions would be used only sparingly and, then, only to protect the basic interests and powers of the respective units. The two concepts would have definitely restructured the power distributions within the federal system.

The historical models are periodically resurrected and reexamined during periods of systemic crisis. During the aftermath of the *Brown* v. *Board of Education* decision, many apologists for the South focused on Calhoun's model for federalism. Leach in 1972 refers to Hamilton's model as "one option open to America in the future." He states further that the continuing failure of the states "could rapidly sour the traditional affection Americans feel for them and thus open the door at last to the Hamiltonian model.[3]

Federal systems as utilized in other parts of the world are increasingly serving as models for the examination of alternatives to the American structures and processes. In this age of federalism more than twenty nations are organized on a federal basis. Because large heterogeneous countries most often seek out this associational device, the federal nations cover more than half the land area of the world and include more than one-third of its population.

The comparative models offer illustrations of many different patterns of intergovernmental relations. In addition to recent excellent general studies on comparative federalism, there has been an outpouring of detailed studies on particular aspects of federal systems.[14] Comparative studies of theories of federalism,[15] judicial review in the federal process, and as a device for maintaining the federal balance,[16] fiscal federalism,[17] and causes of failures of federal systems,[18] give a wealth of information on alternate ways of adjusting the federal mechanism. Most foreign models have generated discussions that have been restricted almost exclusively to the academic community. However, evidence exists that they are beginning to be of utility to broader-based policy considerations. During the debates on revenue sharing, for example, alternate methods of federal fiscal adjustment, especially experiences of other nations with revenue-sharing programs, were reviewed by many of the debate's participants.

Lastly, there have been consistent calls for the total

abandonment of the states in favor of creating large regional units of government with more rationally drawn boundaries. This plan is not new. The first issues of both the *Political Science Quarterly (1886)* and the *Annals of the American Academy of Political and Social Science (1890)*, for example, carried articles condemning the states and calling for the establishment of rational regional units of governance.[19] In more recent times the best-known plans for such a total restructuring are those advanced by Rexford Guy Tugwell and Leland D. Baldwin.[20] These proposals generally spring from concerns about (1) the delays and inactions caused by the division of power between the states as currently structured and the national government; (2) inadequate size with regard to both resource potential and service areas; and (3) irrational boundaries which artificially divide natural geographic areas, cities, and other jurisdictions. The proposals envision consolidation of existing states into approximately a dozen regional organizations with very flexible boundaries. (See figure 10-1 for Baldwin's suggested plan.) The regional entities would be far more subject to national review and control than are states under the existing Constitution.

CHANGE AND THE FUTURE OF AMERICAN FEDERALISM: THE STATES AS KEYSTONE

Barring a catastrophic upheaval, these totally restructured models are not likely to be adopted. Nor, in fact, are the strikingly different alternatives of other systems throughout the world being eagerly picked up for experimentation in the United States. Americans are conservative about their forms of government and are reluctant to change them.

A recent survey showed, however, a basic dissatisfaction with what the national government is as compared to what it might be. Respondents were asked two sets of questions about the way the national government really operates versus the way it might work. Responses were consistently 50 percent or higher for what "might be" than for what "is." For those five items recorded here, the average difference between the current situation and a better future is 56 percent (table 10-1). Care must be taken in interpreting these data. They may reflect a reaction to specific events at the time of the survey, e.g., Watergate and the investigation of Vice President Agnew.[21] Also, the questions refer only to the national government and are not a general evaluation or an indictment of the whole system. Lastly, it is

TABLE 10-1

ATTITUDES TOWARD CURRENT AND POSSIBLE FUTURE CHARACTERISTICS OF THE AMERICAN NATIONAL GOVERNMENT

Question: Do you feel we now have a federal government in which . . .? Do you think it is possible to have a federal government in which . . .?

	"Have now"	"Might have"	Difference between "Have now" and "Might have"
Most public officials are dedicated to helping the country rather than being out for themselves.	36%	86%	50%
Corruption and payoffs almost never take place.	13	65	52
The best people are attracted to serve in public life.	17	80	63
The good of the country is placed above special interests.	24	85	61
Public officials really care what happens to the people.	34	88	54
Average difference between "Have Now" and "Might Have" for five questions.			56%

SOURCE: U.S. Senate Committee on Government Operations, Subcommittee on Intergovernmental Relations, **Confidence and Concern: Citizens View American Government. A Survey of Public Attitudes.** (Washington, D.C.: Government Printing Office, December, 1973), Vol. II, pp. 413-427. Survey conducted by Louis Harris and Associates.

probably a natural tendency to have an idealized view of what "might be." Even with these disclaimers, the data suggest a strong undercurrent of dissatisfaction with the current arrangements.

Whether this dissatisfaction is only with the national government, and whether it requires major or incremental changes is not certain. That the system will persist, and should continue to change as pragmatic federalism unfolds over the years is certain. There may even be a time in the far future when a totally new constitution, a la Tugwell or Baldwin is necessary. The resurgence of the states and the constant modernizing of the system by the day-to-day operation of pragmatic federalism make this drastic change unlikely for the near future. The current brand of American federalism and intergovernmental relations will be around for some time. Of this we are confidently and optimistically certain.

This outlook is based largely on what is considered to be the major strength of American federalism—the ability to change through what we have called "rampant incrementalism." True, the rate of change may occasionally appear to be agonizingly slow, especially to an unemployed laborer waiting for governmental alleviation of problems of the Depression or a disfranchised black waiting for the protection of basic guarantees. But over the long run these accommodations have produced a system with a balance between needed centralized powers and desired decentralized powers. Such a system, we believe, should not be lightly set aside.

Effective decentralization cannot be legislated by the central government. To attempt to do so presupposes a central concentration of power. If this is the case, decentralization efforts should be seen more as administrative decentralization and not as a true nonconcentration of political power and sovereignty. Centrally-legislated decentralization is a logical contradiction in terms. It is for this reason that the states alone retain the ability to maintain the federal bargain. Insofar as the states indigenously maintain their sovereignty and the loyalty of their citizens, meaningful decentralization will be possible.

The states have moved far from the position they held that prompted Luther H. Gulick's 1933 assessment of their abilities:

> Is the State the appropriate instrumentality for the discharge of these sovereign functions? The answer is not a matter of conjecture or delicate appraisal. It is a matter of brutal record. The American State is finished. I do not predict that the States will go, but affirm that they have gone.[22]

Is it any wonder that there would have been such evaluations? Brooke Graves, commenting on the performance of the states during the Depression, writes that "first and foremost was the sheer ineptitude which seemed to paralyze the State governments at the time. They almost literally fiddled while Rome burned."[23] He then observes that while the national government was making

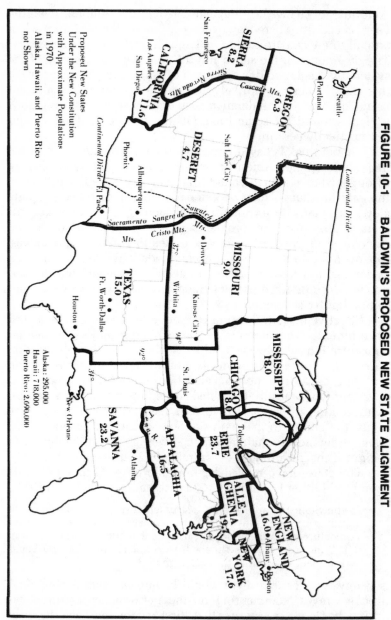

FIGURE 10-1   BALDWIN'S PROPOSED NEW STATE ALIGNMENT

Proposed New States
Under the New Constitution
with Approximate Populations
in 1970
Alaska, Hawaii, and Puerto Rico
not Shown

Alaska: 295,000
Hawaii: 718,000
Puerto Rico: 2,690,000

SOURCE: Leland D. Baldwin, **Reframing the Constitution: An Imperative for Modern America** (Santa Barbara, Calif.: Clio Press, 1972), p.
61.

herculean efforts to deal with the problems of that economic and social disruption, the Pennsylvania Legislature was spending two months of its limited session debating a beer regulation bill, a Sunday fishing measure, and a Sunday baseball bill. Assessments more recent than Gulick's have not been markedly kinder. Witness a well-known American government textbook's claim that "the states are today for those programs involving national financing largely administrative subdivisions of the national government."[24]

These pessimistic views about the states are widely held. We, however, reject them! Although there are some notable exceptions, it seems clear to us that the states have made extraordinary improvements in recent years in their constitutional-legal framework, managerial capabilities, resource collection efforts and potentials, and most importantly, in developing a commitment to meet public expectations. Rather than viewing the states as "weak sisters" or the "fallen arch" of the federal system, we agree with writers such as Ira Sharkansky and Terry Sanford who argue that the states are and will continue to be dynamic and capable partners in the federal arrangement.[25] This is increasingly true. In the long run it will be the states' resilience and viability that will maintain the federal bargain and protect against excessive centralization.

NOTES

1. W. Brooke Graves, *American Intergovernmental Relations* (New York: Charles Scribner's Sons, 1964), p. 911.
2. Richard H. Leach, "The Future of American Federalism," *Politics 1972*, March, 1972, pp. 77-78.
3. Actually, 74 delegates were originally appointed to the Constitutional Convention. For a variety of reasons, 19 of them never appeared and of the 55 participating in the Philadelphia deliberations, only 39 signed the final document.
4. Parris N. Glendening and Mavis Mann Reeves, "The Future of State and Local Government and American Federalism," in Mavis Mann Reeves and Parris N. Glendening, *Controversies of State and Local Political Systems* (Boston: Allyn and Bacon, 1972), pp. 470-485.
5. Leach, pp. 80-81.
6. "Publius" (William Safire), "New Federalist Paper No. 1," *Publius: The Journal of Federalism*, Vol. 2, No. 1 (Spring, 1972), pp. 98-99. "Accelerated and rampant incrementalism" was concocted in that

same linguistic kitchen that gave us phrases such as "loyal opposition" and Safire's own "national localism."

7. Walter Hartwell Bennett, *American Theories of Federalism* University of Ala.: University of Alabama Press, 1964), p. 220.

8. Herbert Croly, *The Promise of American Life* (New York: Macmillan Co., 1912), pp. 274-275. A summary of the ambivalent attitudes of the Progressives toward centralization and federalism is found in Graves, pp. 781-816.

9. "The Obsolescence of Federalism," *The New Republic*, Vol. 98 (May 3, 1939), pp. 367-369. This classical statement is reprinted in Reeves and Glendening, pp. 92-98.

10. "The Case for A Stronger National Government," in Robert A. Goldwin, ed., *A Nation of States: Essays on the American Federal System* (Chicago: Rand McNally, 1963), p. 106.

11. William H. Riker, *Federalism: Origin, Operation, Significance* (Boston: Little, Brown and Co., 1964), p. 155. See also Leach, p. 74.

12. Graves, p. 787.

13. Leach, p. 78.

14. See, for example, Ivo D. Duchacek's *Comparative Federalism: The Territorial Dimension of Politics* (New York: Holt, Rinehart and Winston, Inc., 1970); Carl J. Friedrich, *Trends of Federalism in Theory and Practice* (New York: Frederick A. Praeger, 1968); and Riker, *Federalism*.

15. See, for example, Carl J. Friedrich, *Trends of Federalism in Theory and Practice;* and Sobei Mogi, *The Problem of Federalism: A Study in the History of Political Theory*, 2 vols. (London: George Allen and Unwin, 1931).

16. Richard E. Johnson, *The Effect of Judicial Review on Federal-State Relations in Australia, Canada, and the United States* (Baton Rouge: Louisiana State University Press, 1969).

17. R. J. May, *Federalism and Fiscal Adjustment* (London: Oxford University Press, 1969).

18. Thomas M. Franck, ed., *Why Federations Fail: An Inquiry into the Requisites for Successful Federalism* (New York: New York University Press, 1968).

19. John W. Burgess, "The American Commonwealth," *Political Science Quarterly*, Vol. 1, No. 1 (March, 1886), pp. 9-35; and Simon N. Patton, "Decay of State and Local Government," *The Annals of the American Academy of Political and Social Science*, Vol. 1, No. 1 (July, 1890), pp. 26-42.

20. Rexford Guy Tugwell, *Model for a New Constitution* (Palo Alto, Calif.: James E. Freel and Associates, 1970); and Leland D. Baldwin, *Reframing the Constitution: An Imperative for Modern America* (Santa Barbara, Calif.: Clio Press, 1972).

21. Surprisingly, the corruption question gave the least difference between what is and what is possible. This is largely explained by the low expectations about how well the system might perform in this area.
22. "Reorganization of the State," *Civil Engineering* (August, 1933), p. 420. Quoted in *ibid.*, p. 783.
23. Graves, pp. 805-806.
24. William H. Young, *Ogg and Ray's Introduction to American Government* (12th ed.; New York: Appleton-Century-Crofts, 1962), p. 71
25. Ira Sharkansky, *The Maligned States: Policy Accomplishments, Problems, and Opportunities* (N.Y.: McGraw-Hill Book Co., 1972); and Terry Sanford, *Storm Over the States* (N.Y.: McGraw-Hill Book Co., 1967).

Index